D1536342

Foundation Form Creation with Adobe LiveCycle Designer ES

Cheridan Smith

friendsof

DESIGNER TO DESIGNER™

an Apress® company

Foundation Form Creation with Adobe LiveCycle Designer ES

Copyright © 2008 by Cheridan Smith

All rights reserved. No part of this work may be reproduced or transmitted in any form or by any means, electronic or mechanical, including photocopying, recording, or by any information storage or retrieval system, without the prior written permission of the copyright owner and the publisher.

ISBN-13 (pbk): 978-1-4302-1003-0

ISBN-13 (electronic): 978-1-4302-1004-7

Printed and bound in the United States of America 9 8 7 6 5 4 3 2 1

Trademarked names may appear in this book. Rather than use a trademark symbol with every occurrence of a trademarked name, we use the names only in an editorial fashion and to the benefit of the trademark owner, with no intention of infringement of the trademark.

Distributed to the book trade worldwide by Springer-Verlag New York, Inc., 233 Spring Street, 6th Floor, New York, NY 10013. Phone 1-800-SPRINGER, fax 201-348-4505, e-mail orders-ny@springer-sbm.com, or visit www.springeronline.com.

For information on translations, please contact Apress directly at 2855 Telegraph Avenue, Suite 600, Berkeley, CA 94705. Phone 510-549-5930, fax 510-549-5939, e-mail info@apress.com, or visit www.apress.com.

Apress and friends of ED books may be purchased in bulk for academic, corporate, or promotional use. eBook versions and licenses are also available for most titles. For more information, reference our Special Bulk Sales–eBook Licensing web page at http://www.apress.com/info/bulksales.

The information in this book is distributed on an "as is" basis, without warranty. Although every precaution has been taken in the preparation of this work, neither the author(s) nor Apress shall have any liability to any person or entity with respect to any loss or damage caused or alleged to be caused directly or indirectly by the information contained in this work.

The source code for this book is freely available to readers at www.friendsofed.com in the Downloads section.

Credits

Lead Editor
Clay Andres

Technical Reviewer
Kelly Wardrop

Editorial Board
Clay Andres, Steve Anglin,
Ewan Buckingham, Tony Campbell,
Gary Cornell, Jonathan Gennick,
Matthew Moodie, Joseph Ottinger,
Jeffrey Pepper, Frank Pohlmann,
Ben Renow-Clarke, Dominic Shakeshaft,
Matt Wade, Tom Welsh

Project Manager
Kylie Johnston

Copy Editor
Kim Wimpsett

Associate Production Director
Kari Brooks-Copony

Production Editor
Katie Stence

Compositor
Dina Quan

Proofreader
Patrick Vincent

Indexer
Toma Mulligan

Artist
April Milne

Cover Image Designer
Corné van Dooren

Interior and Cover Designer
Kurt Krames

Manufacturing Director
Tom Debolski

To my wonderful parents, Les and Sandra Smith.
For all that you are and all that you made me.
I love you always.

And for Michael Thomas (Askew).
For the truly amazing person you were and for the glimpses of
the exceptional man you were about to become.
You are always with us.
RIP 1990–2008.

CONTENTS AT A GLANCE

CONTENTS

ABOUT THE AUTHOR

Cheridan Smith has been involved in web development and design since 1997 when she began working on a research team for the Y2K millennium bug. It was then that she learned about the Internet and promptly fell in love with the medium. In her career she has been responsible for websites in the early 2000s such as Weight Watchers Australia and Quicken (`http://quicken.com.au`), and she has worked as the creative services manager of Yahoo! in Australia with clients such as Toyota, 20th Century Fox, and Ford. Currently she is the senior digital interactive project manager for a boutique Australian agency.

ABOUT THE TECHNICAL REVIEWER

 **Kelly Wardrop** has been developing, writing, and teaching web technologies for more than a decade and currently has several books published about the industry. Kelly has taught JavaScript at the University of Miami, she has taught various web development courses for Miami-Dade Community College, and she developed the first online course for Craven Community College in North Carolina. Kelly is a regular freelancer for ICVM Group (www.icvmgroup.com), the president of Visionary Labs, and a consultant for vTribes.com.

ABOUT THE COVER IMAGE DESIGNER

 **Corné van Dooren** designed the front cover image for this book. Having been given a brief by friends of ED to create a new design for the Foundation series, he was inspired to create this new setup combining technology and organic forms.

With a colorful background as an avid cartoonist, Corné discovered the infinite world of multimedia at the age of 17—a journey of discovery that hasn't stopped since. His mantra has always been "The only limit to multimedia is the imagination," a mantra that is keeping him moving forward constantly.

After enjoying success after success over the past years—working for many international clients, as well as being featured in multimedia magazines, testing software, and working on many other friends of ED books—Corné decided it was time to take another step in his career by launching his own company, Project 79, in March 2005.

You can see more of his work and contact him through www.cornevandooren.com or www.project79.com.

If you like his work, be sure to check out his chapter in *New Masters of Photoshop: Volume 2*, also by friends of ED (ISBN: 1590593154).

ACKNOWLEDGMENTS

Until I undertook this project I had no idea of the number of talented people who are behind the production of a book such as this one. I would like to list them in no particular order here, but my deepest thanks and gratitude to you all.

To Kelly Wardrop without whose encouragement, debate, and discussion over the years I would not have had the opportunity to undertake this. Kelly, you are an amazing technical editor and an even better friend. Thanks for your support and your belief in me.

Clay Andres, you are a most patient and gentle editor. Thanks for all your directions and suggestion and for the massive amount of encouragement you have given me throughout this first book of mine. You are an absolute champion. Thank you.

Kylie Johnston, you are an absolute legend! Not only have you shown an unbelievable amount of patience and a Zen-like understanding of the deadline pressures we have been under, you have demonstrated what a huge difference a good project manager makes to a project.

To the fabulous Kim Wimpsett, copy editor extraordinaire, thanks for your patience and expertise in converting my efforts into something that reads fabulously. And thanks also to Katie Stence who took the stained manuscript pages and turned them into something wonderful and "booklike."

And last, but definitely not least, to my wonderful husband David Kerr. For all the dinners cooked and washing done while I have had a laptop glued to my knee writing like a whirling dervish. For all the debate and discussion and for always being around to bounce ideas off and provide reality checks when they were needed. For being the last person at night I see when I go to sleep and the first person I see in the morning. For this and more I thank you, and I love you.

INTRODUCTION

Information. It's the currency of today's busy world. With technology making ever-increasing leaps and bounds, the time things take to be done is now decreasing at a rapid pace. More than ever companies and individuals are finding themselves in the middle of information overload. For many years forms have been the conduit between customers and businesses. You fill out forms every time a company wants information from you, from registering your car at the DMV to filling out an application when applying for a job to filling out payment and credit card details to purchasing goods online.

Adobe LiveCycle Designer ES is an intuitive and easy-to-use point-and-click tool that empowers you to create static, dynamic, and interactive Portable Document Format (PDF) forms. With a logical design interface, you are able to quickly create forms and templates, define the logic behind them, and preview them as they are built, which enables fast and simple trouble-shooting.

LiveCycle Designer forms possess a hierarchical structure that enables them to be converted into Extensible Markup Language (XML). They can also derive their structure from XML schemas and XML documents. They can be saved as PDF or XML Data Package (XPD) documents. In addition, the forms can have JavaScript or FormCalc, which is a simple language that anyone familiar with spreadsheet calculations can easily understand, embedded into them, and they can also communicate with data sources such as OLEDB. When using LiveCycle Designer, you also have the ability to import existing forms built in applications such as Microsoft Word and Microsoft Excel.

Foundation Form Creation with Adobe LiveCycle Designer ES covers all aspects of the form creation process, including the structured thinking that needs to be behind the successful implementation of any form. In this book, you'll create static, interactive, and dynamic forms, as well as see real-life examples of each.

Who This Book Is For

Anyone who is involved in obtaining data from people via forms will benefit greatly from the contents of this book and Adobe LiveCycle Designer ES; however, there are some professionals in particular who will find this book very helpful.

Data architects will find this book useful because they will work with real-life examples to integrate existing data and schemas into forms, as well as define data processes and structures.

Graphic designers will find it easy to translate design methodology into creating forms in Adobe LiveCycle Designer ES. Chapter 2 in particular focuses on the design flow of the form, including the translation of the concept into the layout, the considerations of the hierarchy of information, and the principles of form design.

Web designers and developers will benefit from this book because they will learn how to create forms and documents free from CSS and HTML limitations. They will learn how to further combine the principles of interactivity and design by moving beyond these limitations but still creating powerful and accessible PDF forms.

How This Book Is Structured

Foundation Form Creation with Adobe LiveCycle Designer ES covers all aspects of form design and creation with Adobe LiveCycle Designer ES. It is broken into logical chapters, beginning with a fundamental overview in Chapter 1 and working steadily through each chapter, covering form design methodology and all aspects of form creation and data capture.

- *Chapter 1, "Introducing LiveCycle Designer"*: The first chapter of this book introduces you to the fundamentals of Adobe LiveCycle Designer ES. It introduces you to the stage on which you will build your static, dynamic, and interactive PDF forms and takes you through a overview of what the program can actually do, including a complete summary of the kinds of files you will be working with as you create your forms. It then moves on to give a comprehensive definition of the different kinds of forms LiveCycle Designer can create and which industries will find the program useful. The chapter concludes with an exercise that will demonstrate how to create your first form.

- *Chapter 2, "Understanding Forms and Design"*: This is the chapter where you will learn about the principles of form design. The way your form looks and feels influences the way users will interact with your forms. This chapter offers a comprehensive overview of design considerations that will help make your form a success.

- *Chapter 3, "Understanding the Elements of Form Style: Components, Templates, and Masters"*: Chapter 3 is where you move beyond the basic information and really delve into the working innards of LiveCycle Designer. This is where you will learn about the components that are required to build a form in LiveCycle Designer.

- *Chapter 4, "Learning the Fundamentals of Designing Forms"*: This is the chapter where you begin to really get your hands dirty and learn about creating and opening forms. You will learn all about creating master and body pages and manipulating the fundamental building blocks of your form objects. You will discover how using templates and the Template Manager will help make your form-building process more efficient.

- *Chapter 5, "Understanding Interactive Forms"*: This chapter deals specifically with interactive forms. This is where you will apply your first calculations and scripts to your form, create interactive buttons, and process information that will lead to your users having a richer and more rewarding experience with your interactive form.

- *Chapter 6, "Getting into Advanced Form Design"*: Adobe LiveCycle Designer ES enables you to build intuitive and dynamic forms. In this chapter, you will learn about data display, user input, and sophisticated forms of validation. You will also learn how to localize your forms for different countries and find out how scripting in forms can contribute to creating a successful form.

- *Chapter 7, "Using External Files in Your Form"*: Chapter 7 shows you how using external files and services in your forms can display and validate data and send it to databases. You will create a real-life example using an existing WSDL data connection and move your forms beyond the flat static user experience to a truly rich and compelling experience.

- *Chapter 8, "Performing Advanced Form Scripting"*: This chapter will show you how to move beyond the basic scripting of Chapter 5 and add layers of extra interactivity to your forms using the JavaScript and FormCalc languages. You will learn about Script objects, and using preexisting forms, you will see some real-life scenarios to learn how to use the Script Editor to write your calculations and scripts.

- *Chapter 9, "Completing Your Forms with Data Submission"*: A form's success relies on the quantity and quality of the data that is submitted. This final chapter shows you how to create buttons on your forms that enable the user to submit data.

Layout conventions

To keep this book as clear and easy to follow as possible, the following text conventions are used throughout.

Important words or concepts are normally highlighted on the first appearance in **bold type**.

Code is presented in fixed-width font.

Menu commands are written in the form Menu ➤ Submenu ➤ Submenu.

Where I want to draw your attention to something, I've highlighted it like this:

> *Ahem, don't say I didn't warn you.*

Prerequisites

To follow along with the step-by-step examples in this book, you'll need Adobe LiveCycle Designer ES (8.1) and Adobe Acrobat Reader 7 or later.

Downloading the Code

The source code for this book is available to readers at www.friendsofed.com in the Downloads section of this book's home page. Please feel free to visit the friends of ED website and download all the code there. You can also check for errata and find related titles from friends of ED and Apress.

Contacting the author

You can contact the author at cheridan.smith@gmail.com.

You can do many thing

- Design and crea
- Work with mult
  InfoPath, and M
- Integrate forms
  process of conr
  schemas.
- Handle data sec
- Capture form d
  nesses for such
  Designer ES sup
  when the form
  onscreen but ar
  all times.
- Comply with un
  information be

> An **XML scheme**
> to as an **XML Sc**
> the XML docun
> ment, and it sp
> number. It also
> their data types

Chapter 1

INTRODUC

Forms
fully i
essent

Adobe
forms
What
creati
PDF is
image
reade
Most
the br

Adobe
and c
when
SWF (
as XM
bases

Overview of fo

As technology advance nically through e-mail or
business and sharing in echnology captures data
collecting and distribu d streamlines form pro-
easily create static, inte inks between form fields
programming languages.

Static forms

The term **static** means 1
mitting it through e-m;
able. A **fillable** form ope
fields that you can then
print the form—once p
example of a static forr

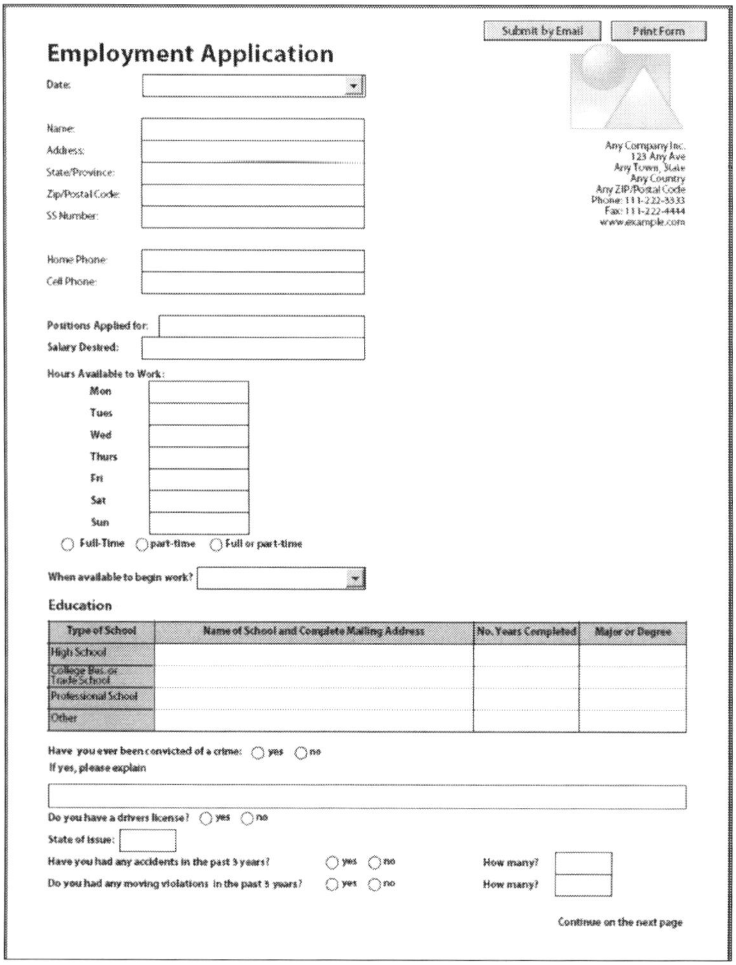

Submit by Email | Print Form

Employment Application

Date:

Name:
Address:
State/Province:
Zip/Postal Code:
SS Number:

Home Phone:
Cell Phone:

Positions Applied for:
Salary Desired:
Hours Available to Work:
Mon
Tues
Wed
Thurs
Fri
Sat
Sun
Full-Time | part-time | Full or part-time

When available to begin work?

Any Company Inc.
123 Any Ave
Any Town, State
Any Country
Any ZIP/Postal Code
Phone: 111-222-3333
Fax: 111-222-4444
www.example.com

Education

Type of School	Name of School and Complete Mailing Address	No. Years Completed	Major or Degree
High School			
College Bus. or Trade School			
Professional School			
Other			

Have you ever been convicted of a crime: yes no
If yes, please explain

Do you have a drivers license? yes no
State of issue:
Have you had any accidents in the past 3 years? yes no How many?
Do you had any moving violations in the past 3 years? yes no How many?

Continue on the next page

Figure 1-2. An example of an interactive form that can be submitted via e-mail

Dynamic forms

Dynamic PDF forms are interactive and use the Acrobat XML Data Package (XDP) technology created in Adobe LiveCycle Designer that dynamically adjusts to data and user events. This means form fields can change based on user input—eliminating excessive form fields and narrowing down the type of information collected as required. In Figure 1-3, you can see a simple form asking for a first name, last name, and favorite flavor. In Figure 1-4, you can see the form updated with new options based on the user's input. This update takes place on the fly as the user inputs information.

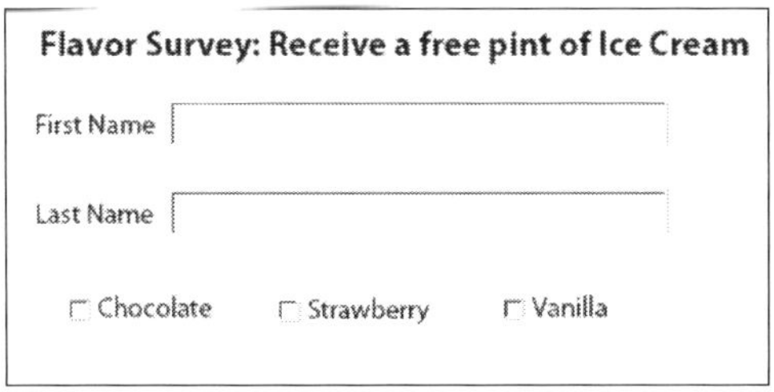

Flavor Survey: Receive a free pint of Ice Cream

First Name

Last Name

☐ Chocolate   ☐ Strawberry   ☐ Vanilla

Figure 1-3. A form prompting for basic information

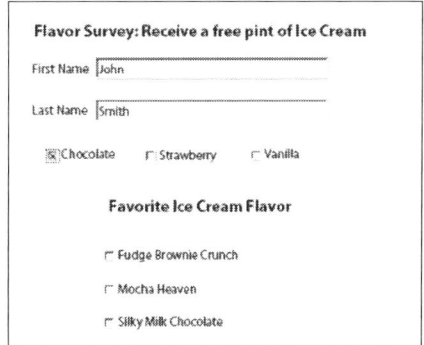

Figure 1-4. The same form from Figure 1-3 updated dynamically after the user selects a flavor option

Industry uses

LiveCycle Designer lends itself well to several professional fields. Form designers, data architects, web professionals, and programmers can all benefit from using Adobe LiveCycle Designer ES. One of the advantages of LiveCycle Designer is its flexibility with a variety of different professional approaches. Different professionals have different needs and goals, and LiveCycle Designer is diverse enough to meet all of those goals.

Graphic designers

A graphic designer's primary job is to design graphics using images, photographs, art, and typography for print or electronic publications. Well-planned and executed graphic design can greatly influence the effectiveness of user interactivity with forms. Images, fonts, and other logically placed elements can be instrumental in how the user engages a form. LiveCycle Designer does not require any programming knowledge and offers a familiar drag-and-drop environment that graphic professionals are used to working in. Graphic professionals can use LiveCycle Designer to lay out their pages much in the same way they use other Adobe products with other types of projects. LiveCycle Designer handles creating the XML schema and document structure, which results in a well-formed XML.

Web designers/developers

The objective of a web designer involves both interaction and design. Web designers are likely to benefit the most from LiveCycle Designer in terms of these goals. Typically, web designers create basic forms using HTML/XHTML for structure and Cascading Style Sheets (CSS) for formatting. Current web standards such as CSS and HTML impose limitations upon the design of a web page because they are limited in typography, layout, positioning, and formatting choices. Adobe LiveCycle Designer ES abolishes these limitations. Web designers can enjoy the freedom of design without forgoing electronic form submission and without conflicting with current web standards or accessibility.

Data architects

Adobe LiveCycle Designer ES gives data architects the ability to enforce various data schemas and structures. Part of a data architect's job is to discover and define an application's precise data structures and processes. Adobe LiveCycle Designer ES enables data architects to quickly and easily specify data validation, formatting, and binding via the Object palette.

Understanding the PDF and XDP formats

The most popular technology that allows interactive and dynamic forms to process via the Web is called XML Forms Architecture (XFA). Adobe LiveCycle Designer ES creates forms using the XFA architecture, which is based on Extensible Markup Language (XML).

To understand how PDFs work in the XFA environment, it's important to understand the PDF and XPD file formats.

> *The XFA specification was first submitted to the World Wide Web Consortium (W3C) in 1999. The XFA is an open standard used to create form-based applications.*

The PDF format

Adobe developed PDF in 1993. With the Internet boom in the early 1990s, there was an unprecedented increase in the dispensation of information, and a need for a standard way of viewing electronic documents was required. PDF was created to meet this requirement.

It is a two-dimensional, fixed document format that can be opened and viewed regardless of the application software or operating system, provided you have PDF reader software such as Adobe Reader. A PDF file preserves the original document's layout, typography, graphics, and images. It consistently displays and prints the document the same every time.

A PDF document can be viewed via Adobe Acrobat Professional, Adobe Acrobat Reader, Adobe Creative Suite, iTunes, iPhoto, and a host of alternative downloadable readers.

A PDF form is typically used to create paper-based forms. It is converted from third-party application documents, such as Microsoft Word, via a PDF converter, such as Adobe Reader. For example, when you are creating a PDF from Microsoft Word, you select Print and then choose the option Print to PDF.

Adobe LiveCycle Designer ES renders PDF forms in a structurally different way than traditional PDF files because they are based on Adobe's XFA.

For more information, visit http://en.wikipedia.org/wiki/Pdf.

> *The TDS format is the Adobe LiveCycle Designer Template format. This format enables you to save a form as a template from which to create new forms. Templates are covered later in this book.*

The XDP format

Within Adobe LiveCycle Designer ES, documents can be created and processed as the static PDF document, or they can be packaged into an XDP and processed as XML. XDP files contain the form data, templates, PDF documents, and other XML information.

The XDP format is the XML container that packages the PDF content and enables it to be transferred online via e-mail to a database or to other web services. It is compliant with standard XML tools, system interfaces, and standard web services.

An XML file is comprised of five distinct units of information:

- *XML form data*: This is the user data that is encoded to an XML database schema. This scheme is set up at the time of form creation.
- *XML form template*: This contains a map of the data to the PDF form and all of the form's intelligence such as calculations and data validation.
- *XML configuration information*: The form template uses this as a reference for web and database services and SOAP connections.
- *Other XML information*: This contains custom XML information such as scheme files to facilitate validation, XML digital signatures, content metadata to facilitate archiving, and information used by custom digital applications.
- *PDF document*: XPD files maintain the original document's layout, typography, and images.

Use a PDF when file size is important and the document has lots of graphics and images, and use XDP when you require interactivity or when the form data needs to be manipulated scripting or XML tools. For example, when you are creating a form that is to be printed and filled in by hand, you should save the form design as a static PDF document. When the intention of your form is to be completed electronically and features scripts and calculations, you should opt to save your form in the XPD format.

The LiveCycle Designer ES interface

Adobe LiveCycle Designer ES offers an intuitive and multifaceted interface that is configurable to accommodate multiple types of users. The first thing when LiveCycle Designer launches is the Welcome to Adobe LiveCycle Designer dialog box, as shown in Figure 1-5.

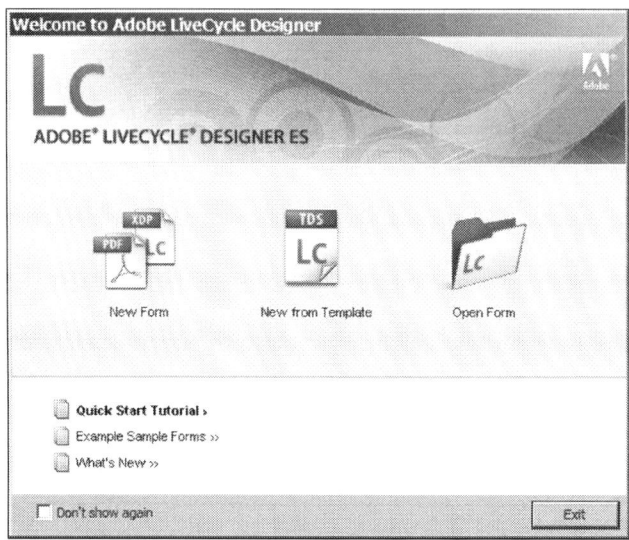

Figure 1-5. The Welcome to Adobe LiveCycle Designer dialog box

The Welcome to Adobe LiveCycle Designer dialog box provides three simple ways to get started creating and customizing forms. To create a blank form, you can click the first option, the New Form icon. This opens the New Form Assistant dialog box, which prompts you to select a method to create a form (see Figure 1-6). Some of the options are using a blank form, a template, a spreadsheet, a PDF form, and a Word file.

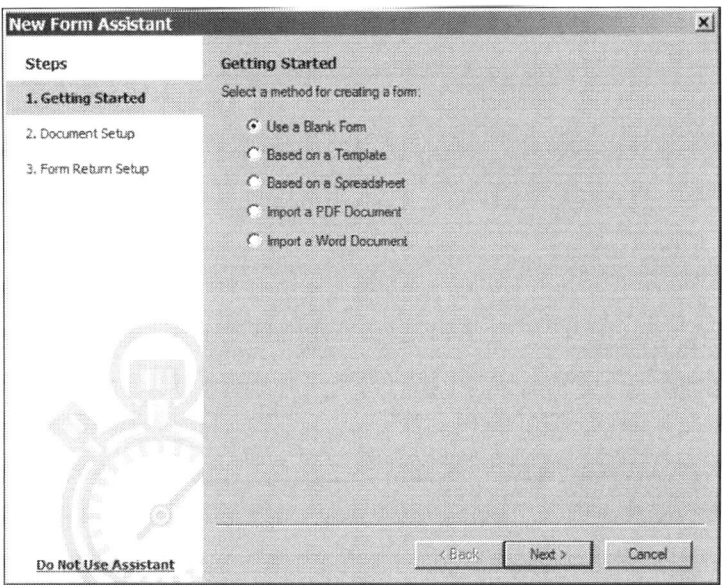

Figure 1-6. New Form Assistant dialog box

You can also create a form from a predesigned template by clicking the New from Template icon. This also launches the New Form Assistant dialog box and presents a list of predesigned templates from which to choose (see Figure 1-7).

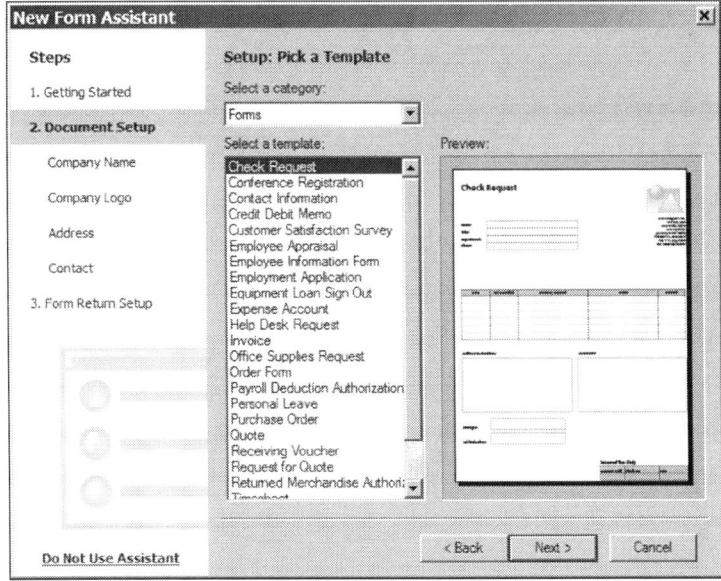

Figure 1-7. The New Form Assistant dialog box for choosing a predesigned template

9

If you want to modify an existing form, you can open the file by clicking the Open Form icon. The Open dialog box displays, as shown in Figure 1-8, allowing you to navigate to an area on your hard drive where the form resides. You will learn more about the types of file formats you can work with throughout the following chapters.

Figure 1-8. The Open dialog box

The options presented in the Welcome to Adobe LiveCycle Designer dialog box are also available in the application window's menu and toolbars. Clicking the Exit button in the Welcome to Adobe LiveCycle Designer dialog box displays the LiveCycle Designer workspace, as shown in Figure 1-9.

10

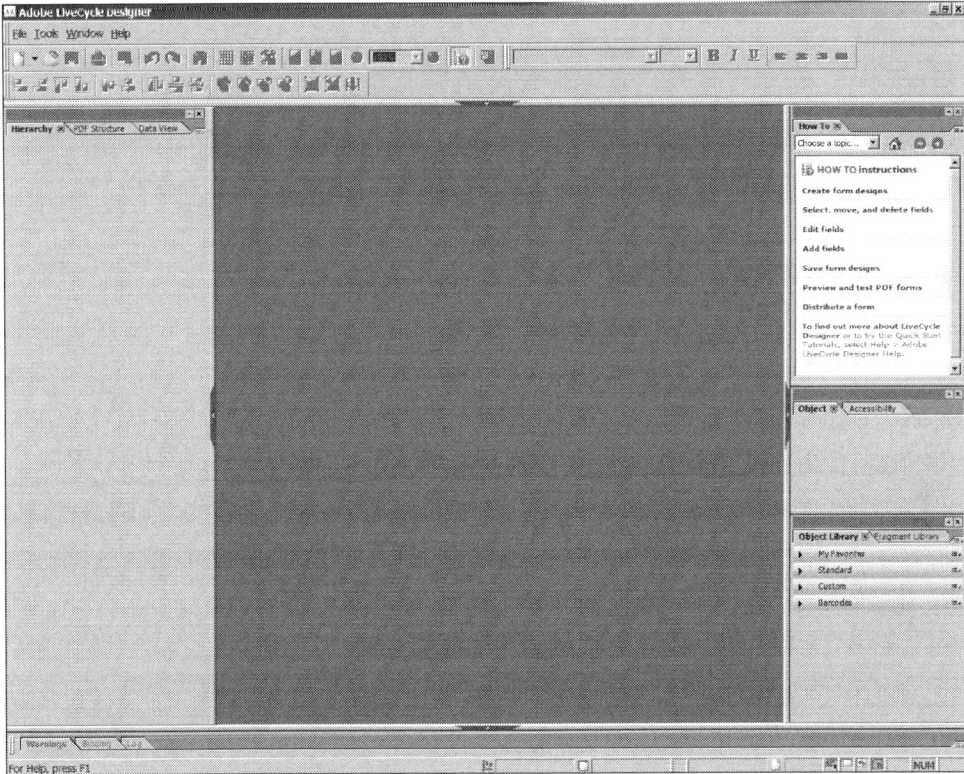

Figure 1-9. The default display of the Adobe LiveCycle Designer ES application window

The designer workspace

The **workspace** is the area where you create forms, manipulate various palettes, and work with other objects. When you launch LiveCycle Designer and exit from the Welcome to Adobe LiveCycle Designer dialog box, the workspace is empty, and some of the palettes are blank. Figure 1-10 shows an example of how the workspace displays with an active form. You will learn how to create a new form later in this chapter—seeing firsthand how the workspace appears when a form is active.

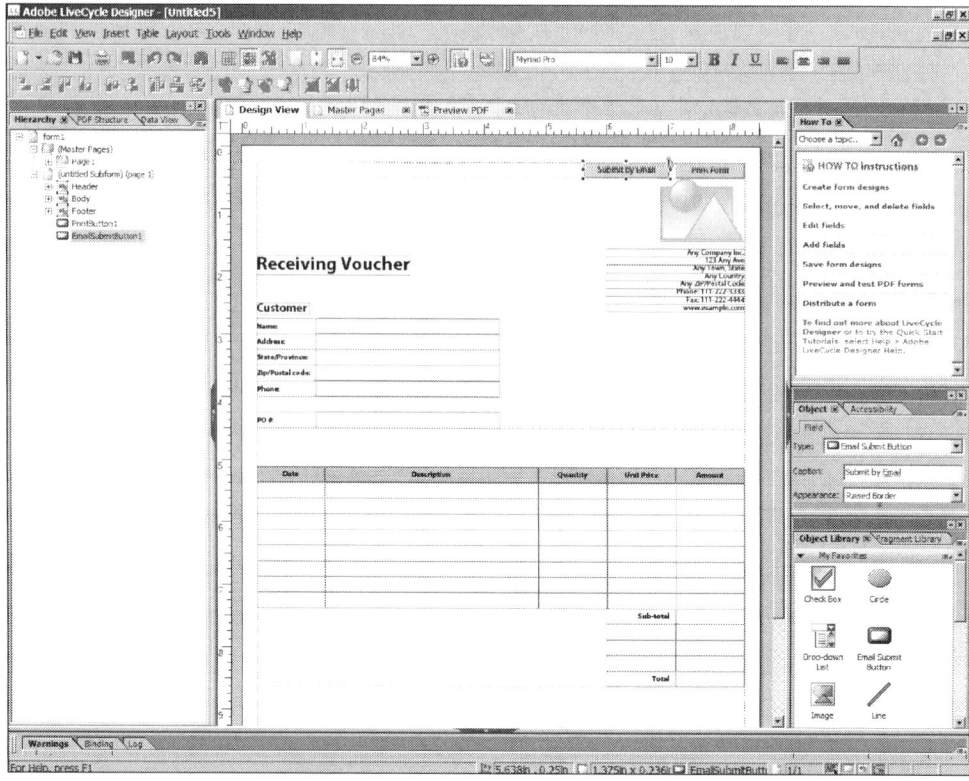

Figure 1-10. The LiveCycle Designer workspace with an active form

Palettes

Palettes are mini-windows in the workspace that provide access to commands, options, and common properties to objects. Palettes are designed to provide easy access and organization for tools most often used. You can arrange and remove active palettes to better suit your particular work environment.

> *Most palettes are empty by default because an object is not selected. Some palettes display information only when a file is open in the workspace. The view or object that is selected determines what kind of information a palette displays.*

As you work with different objects on a form, the palette will change its display options based on the object selected. For example, in Figure 1-11 you can see a form in the workspace that has the e-mail button selected. The Object palette then displays the properties of the e-mail button.

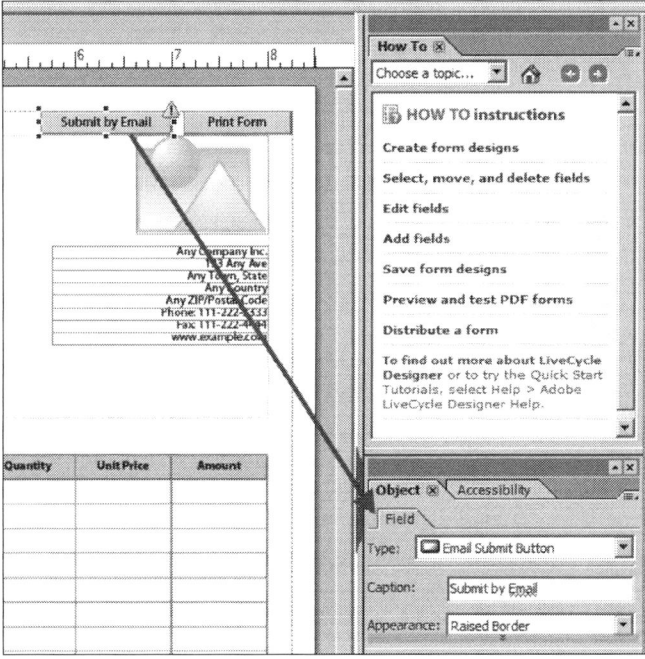

Figure 1-11. The e-mail button is selected in the workspace, which then updates the Object palette with the e-mail button's properties.

In Figure 1-12, you can see the same form displayed. However, the image is selected. The Object palette updates and displays the properties of the image.

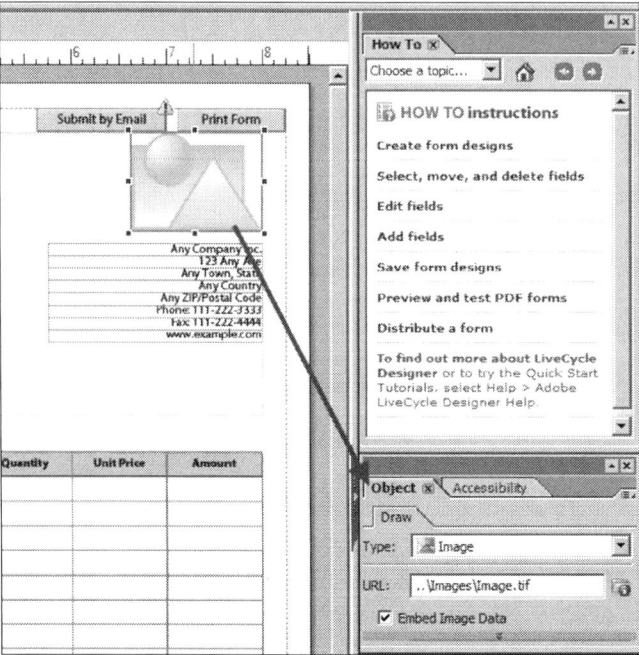

Figure 1-12. The Image object is selected in the workspace, and the Object palette updates to reflect the image properties.

The default palettes

The default palettes that display when Adobe LiveCycle Designer is first launched can be moved, reorganized, or even deactivated. All the palettes available are accessible from the Window menu, as shown in Figure 1-13. You will learn more about each of these palettes in later chapters. However, this section provides a brief description of the default palettes.

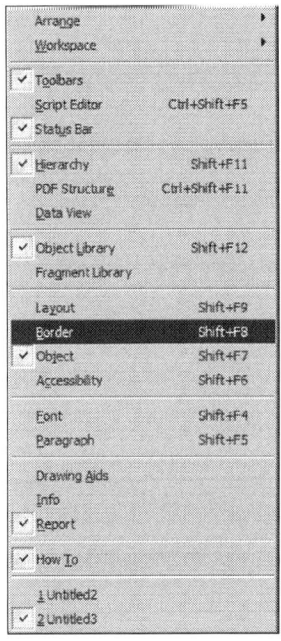

Figure 1-13. The Window menu listing the available palettes. The check marks denote which palettes are active.

Hierarchy palette: Displays information and structure about the document on which you are working. This includes sections and objects such as subforms and the master file. As your forms become more advanced, the Hierarchy palette becomes useful in navigating, renaming, and organizing sections of a form.

PDF Structure palette: Displays the structure of the PDF document such as heading, paragraphs, and form elements. It defines the tabbing and reading order of a document for accessibility issues.

Data View palette: Displays information about the data source associated with a form. The Data View palette remains blank until you establish a data source.

Object Library palette: Displays a collection of form objects that you can drag and drop onto the work area. Probably utilized most, the Object Library palette also allows you to organize objects in the following categories: My Favorites, Standard, Custom, and Barcode. The Object Library palette is not the same as the Object palette because it displays the available form objects you are able to insert into your form. The Object palette displays the properties of a selected object.

Object palette: Displays the properties of a selected object such as a form field or text. For instance, if a check box form element is selected, the Object palette will reflect the properties available for the check box.

Fragment palette: Displays form fragments that you have created so that you can use them in multiple forms. Fragments are basically snippets of reusable form components. You can create parts of forms and reuse them with other forms. When the fragments are modified, used fragments will update in documents as well.

Accessibility palette: Provides the ability to define custom text for an object for accessibility issues. When a Microsoft Active Accessibility (MSAA)–compliant reader reads the form, it will display the custom text. Adobe LiveCycle Designer ES provides full support for W3C-standard XML schemas, which means it can be easily integrated with existing applications and systems.

How To palette: Displays a screen of help topics and provides access to Adobe LiveCycle Designer help documentation.

Layout Editor

The Layout Editor is the main workspace where the design of the form takes place. Four tabs appear at the top of the area:

Design View tab: This tab displays the form design.

Master Pages tab: This tab displays master pages that can be applied to the form design.

XML Source tab: This tab displays XML source code that dictates the form design architecture and its objects.

Preview PDF tab: This tab displays a PDF preview of the form currently in the workspace.

By default, only the Design View tab is displayed when you open a new document. If you have Adobe Acrobat Writer or Reader installed on your computer, the default will switch to the Design View and PDF Preview tabs being displayed.

To display the hidden tabs, select View from the toolbar, and select the tab you want to view.

Design View tab

Design View is the initial mode displayed, as shown in Figure 1-14. It shows the form's content design. The first time Adobe LiveCycle Designer ES launches, Design View will display a blank page ready for objects to be dragged onto it.

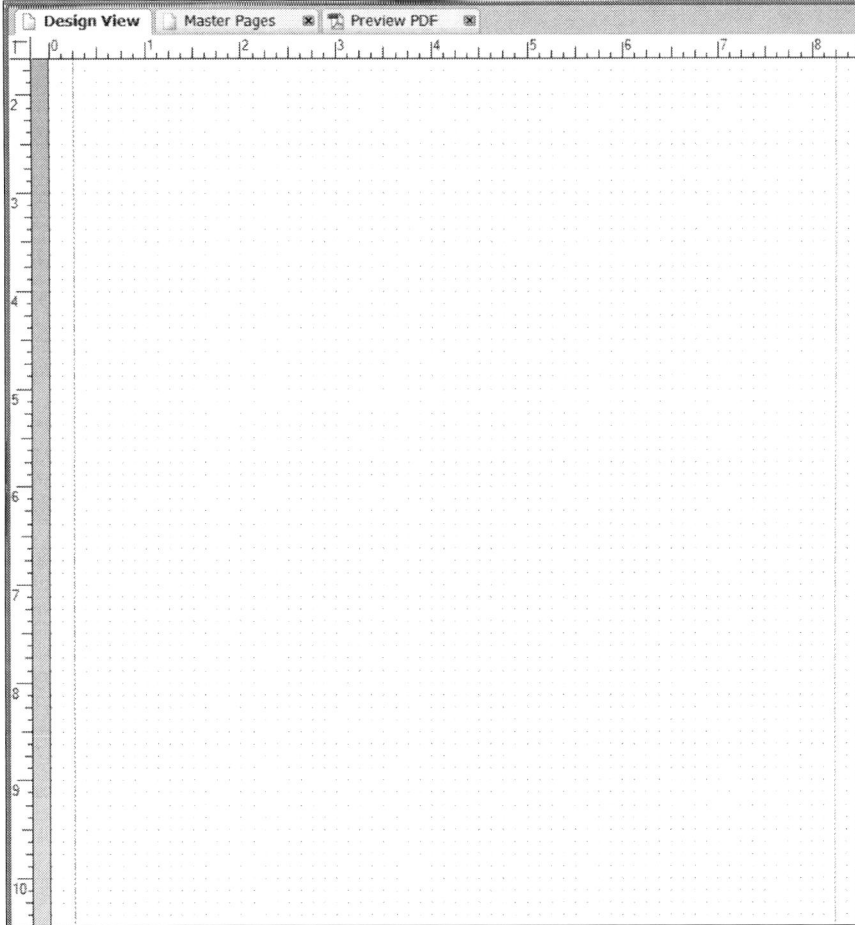

Figure 1-14. Design View is the first tab displayed in the workspace.

If you are creating a form from a master page, the objects that appear on the master page will be displayed, but you will be unable to select them or edit them in Design View.

Design View is the visual editor area where you design and view the form. Here you will drag and drop your form objects from the Object Library palette to create the actual form page.

Master Page tab

The next tab is the Master Page tab of the document. The Master Page tab acts as a universal wrapper that includes information to be shared across the various body pages in your PDF document. Master pages specify the layout for the form design. Objects placed on the master pages will appear in the same position throughout the body pages. You will work in detail with master and body pages in the next chapter.

Preview tab

The Preview PDF tab is displayed only when Acrobat, Adobe Reader, or a PDF reader is installed. This allows you to preview what the form will look like in a PDF reader or a web browser, as well as test the functionality of the form as you build it.

Use the Forms Properties dialog box to set options for previewing interactive and static PDF forms. To access the Form Properties dialog box, select File ➤ Form Properties. If you have created an interactive, dynamic form but the Form Properties dialog box is set to preview a static PDF form, your dynamic form will be rendered static, and you will be unable to view the form's interactivity. Instead, you should ensure that the Form Properties dialog box is set to preview interactive forms, which will allow you to test the interactivity of your form.

Script Editor

As you become more advanced working with LiveCycle Designer, you'll begin to work with scripting options for each form object. The Script Editor is where you create, modify, and view scripts of a particular object in a form. You can view a single line of code or multiple lines depending on your needs, as shown in Figure 1-15. There are two types of scripting languages you can work with in LiveCycle Designer: FormCalc and JavaScript.

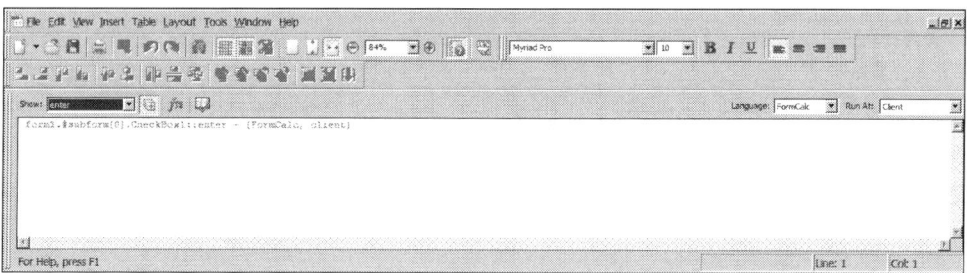

Figure 1-15. The Script Editor

LiveCycle Designer uses the Adobe-developed FormCalc as its default scripting language. FormCalc was developed by Adobe for users who do not have advanced programming skills but are familiar with spreadsheet software. FormCalc supports a wide variety of environments such as date and time strings, mathematics, finance, logic, and some web services. It is used to calculate fields much like a spreadsheet program such as Microsoft Excel. To find out more about FormCalc, visit http://help.adobe.com/en_US/livecycle/es/FormCalc.pdf.

LiveCycle Designer supports JavaScript by providing properties and methods that give JavaScript programmers access to field and object values. You will work more with the Script Editor in Chapter 4.

By default, the Script Editor is not displayed. You can activate the Script Editor from the Window menu by selecting Window ➤ Script Editor from the menu bar, as shown in Figure 1-16.

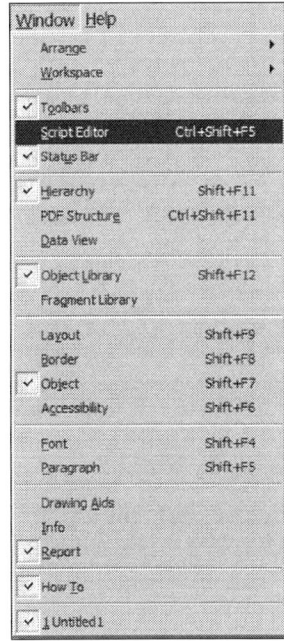

Figure 1-16. To activate the Script Editor, select Window ➤ Script Editor from the menu bar.

Using menus and commands

The default toolbars that display in the application window are the Standard toolbar and the Layout toolbar. The Standard toolbar, as shown in Figure 1-17, offers all the common standard commands such as Save, Open, and New. The Layout toolbar, shown in Figure 1-18, offers the standard layout commands that enable you to align certain objects.

Figure 1-17. Standard toolbar

Figure 1-18. Layout toolbar

Other toolbars that are available are the Text Formatting, Table, and Tools toolbars. These toolbars are not active in the default display. You can activate these toolbars by right-clicking a blank area on a toolbar, as shown in Figure 1-19.

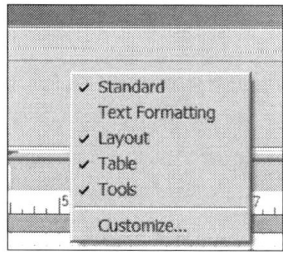

Figure 1-19. Right-click an empty space on the toolbar to activate and deactivate toolbars.

> *To customize a toolbar, right-click the toolbar to display a shortcut menu, and then select the* Customize *option.*

Keyboard shortcuts

As with most applications, LiveCycle Designer comes equipped with default shortcuts already defined. You can discover these shortcuts by accessing the Keyboard Shortcuts dialog box, as shown in Figure 1-20, by selecting the Tools ➤ Keyboard Shortcuts menu. Based on your needs, the Keyboard Shortcuts dialog box enables you to modify, remove, and create new shortcuts.

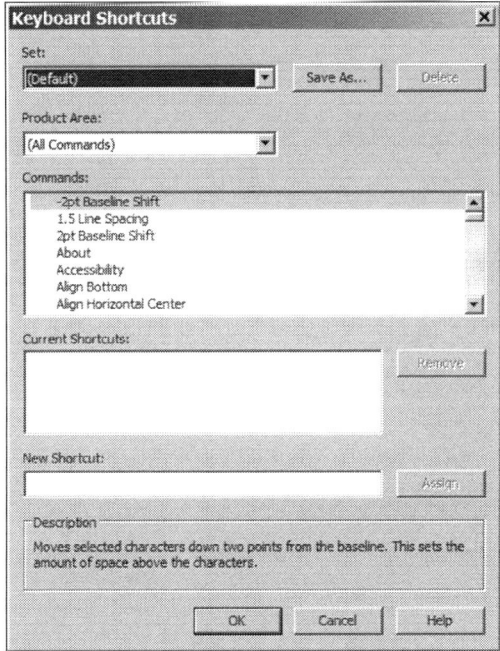

Figure 1-20. The Keyboard Shortcuts dialog box

To determine which shortcuts have already been assigned, you can select a command from the Commands section to display the shortcut keystroke in the Current Shortcuts box, as shown in Figure 1-21.

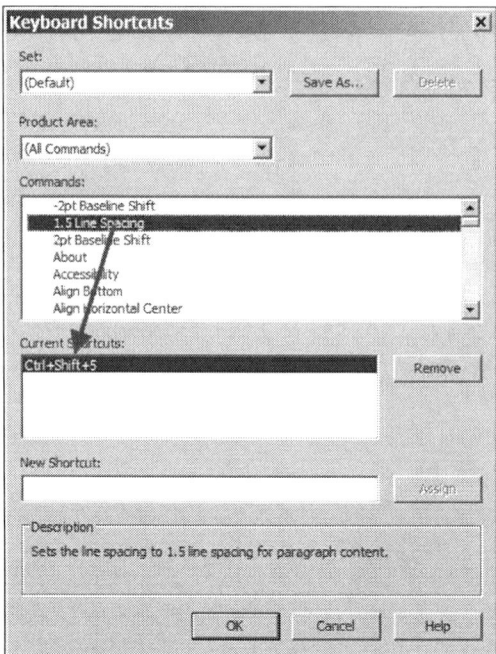

Figure 1-21. View which shortcut is assigned by selecting a command from the Commands section.

Now that you have a fundamental understanding of the basic tools and features of Adobe LiveCycle Designer, it is time to move onto creating your first form. In the following section, you will learn how to build a form using the New Form Assistant.

Creating your first form

Now that you have had an overview of the interface of LiveCycle Designer, you will create your first form. Palettes provide an easy way to manipulate your forms on a step-by-step basis without being required to know Adobe LiveCycle Designer ES explicitly. So, you'll now explore creating your first form using LiveCycle Designer's built-in New Forms Assistant.

There are a few methods for creating a new form, and depending on which method you select, you'll be presented with certain criteria. These include using the New Form Assistant or manually setting the options for your form. You will learn more about these methods in Chapter 3.

New Form Assistant

As previously discussed, when LiveCycle Designer is first launched, you are presented with the Welcome to Adobe LiveCycle Designer dialog box, which has three options for creating forms. If you choose to create a blank form or a form from a template, the New Form Assistant box displays. Alternatively, you can launch the New Form Assistant dialog box from the menu bar by selecting File ➤ New.

> *Clicking the* New *button in the* Standard *toolbar will not launch the* New Form Assistant *dialog box; instead, it will create a new, blank form. The difference is that the* New Form Assistant *dialog box will provide some basic questions regarding page options, e-mail submission options, and print form options.*

Create a New Form

The New Form Assistant dialog box provides step-by-step assistance through an interview process:

1. Launch LiveCycle Designer by selecting Start ➤ Programs ➤ Adobe LiveCycle Designer ES.

Adobe LiveCycle launches with the now-familiar Welcome to Adobe LiveCycle Designer dialog box.

2. Click the New Form icon.

The New Form Assistant dialog box displays, as shown in Figure 1-22. Use a Blank Form is selected by default.

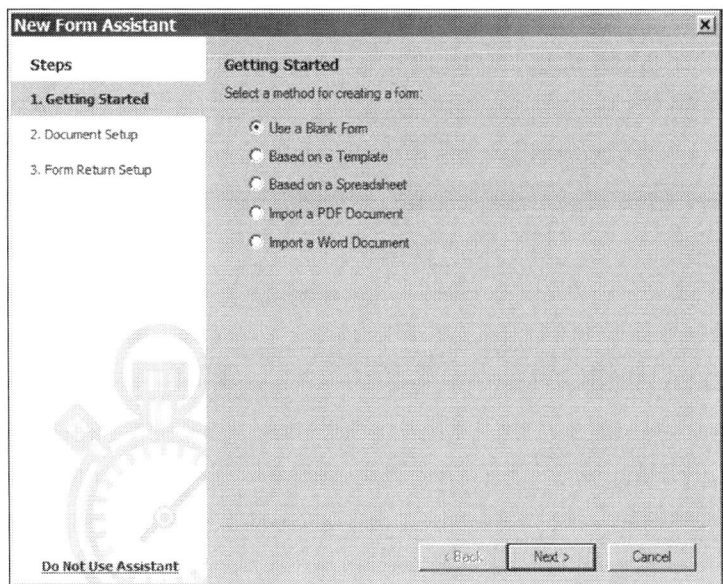

Figure 1-22. New Form Assistant dialog box

3. Click the Next button to continue.

The next section is Document Setup. Here you can change the page size, the orientation, and the number of pages you want to start with, as shown in Figure 1-23.

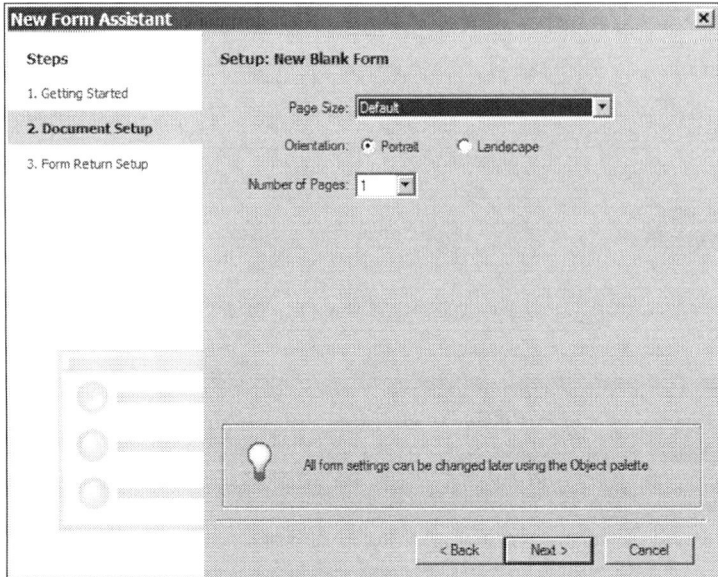

Figure 1-23. The Document Setup section

4. Keep the default settings for the Document Setup section, and click the Next button.

The Form Return Setup section, as shown in Figure 1-24, is where you have the option of adding an e-mail button and a print button. You can also enter the e-mail address where you want the form submission to be sent. You can also add these later.

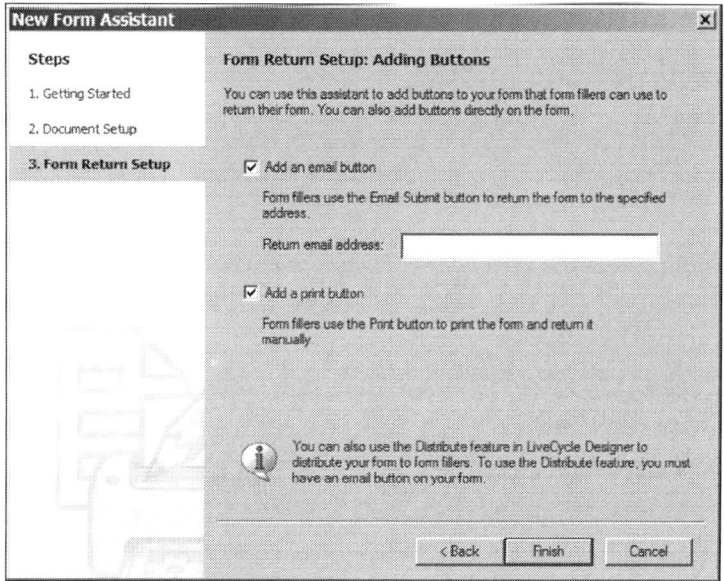

Figure 1-24. Form Return Setup section

5. Do not enter an e-mail address at this time. Click the Next button.

The form displays in the workspace with an e-mail button and print form button inserted in the top-right corner. Notice that the e-mail button has a warning icon attached to it, as shown in Figure 1-25. The warning icon indicates there is a problem with a particular object.

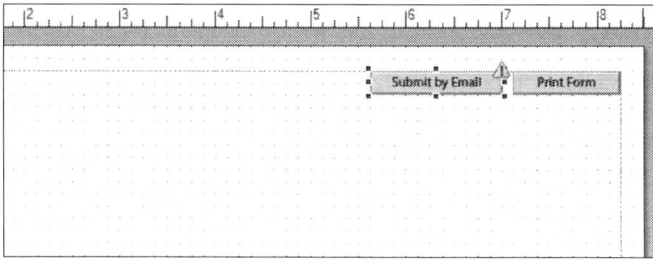

Figure 1-25. A warning icon indicates there is a problem with an object.

6. Hover your mouse over the warning icon next to the e-mail button.

A tooltip displays with an explanation of the error and a suggested remedy. In this case, you do not have an e-mail attached to the button (see Figure 1-26).

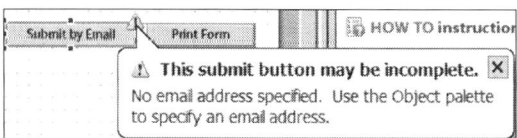

Figure 1-26. A tooltip alerting that the Submit by Email button has no e-mail address associated.

7. Fix the problem by entering an e-mail address in the Caption field of the Object palette, as shown in Figure 1-27.

Figure 1-27. Enter an e-mail address in the Caption field.

You've successfully created your first form. You will work much more with the Object palette throughout the course of this book. This exercise is to help you familiarize yourself with the Adobe LiveCycle Designer interface.

8. Exit the program without saving the file.

Summary

Adobe LiveCycle Designer ES is a form design program that simplifies the creation of forms. Using the point-and-click interface, you can create PDF forms that generate versatile and interactive forms that guide users to completion. You can also create dynamic data-driven documents customized for specific business needs.

Adobe LiveCycle Designer ES enables you to integrate forms into a number of standard databases, enterprise applications, and web services. Form recipients are able to fill out a form and submit the data online, fill out a form and print it, or print the form and fill it out by hand.

Chapter 2

UNDERSTANDING FORMS AND DESIGN

Forms are used to fulfil a number of information collection requirements in our society such as surveys, member registrations, financial transactions, feedback forms, competitions, e-commerce, and other data collection functions. They are a ubiquitous element in the conduct of data transactions in today's society.

A **form** is a document that allows a user to supply their information via a series of questions. Fillable (print-and-fill) forms collect data only, and interactive and dynamic forms collect or display structured data; they are the interface users interact with to supply you with the information you require. Form data can be submitted to a server electronically or filled out by hand and returned to the form originator.

A form's success is determined by the number of completed forms with accurate and useful information that you receive from users. The goal of a form is to have the user complete it and return the data to you. Therefore, you need to design your forms in a way that encourages a user to give you the information you are seeking.

In this chapter, you will investigate the issues you need to consider when building a form for the best user experience, and then you'll move on to basic form components and building exercises in Chapter 3.

Creating a design flow

Design Flow is a design methodology that is commonly applied when working with electronics. It defines the order of progress from initial concept to the final product. Design Flow can be applied when designing both static and interactive forms, and it can be broken down into four basic stages: concept and planning, design and build, quality assurance testing and deployment, and implementation.

Concept and planning

This first stage develops the "big idea" behind your form. It is the link between your original idea and the final form product. You need to examine your motivation for creating the form in the first place and consider precisely what you need your form to accomplish.

At this stage, your research will help you determine whether you need to create a static PDF form, an interactive form, or a dynamic form.

Design and build

In the second stage, you begin to give your concept a physical shape. Map out your form questions by topic, and begin to assemble a natural intuitive flow to your form on paper. It is at this stage you specify key aspects of your form, such as form and object properties, accessibility, page orientation, and size and font properties. Remember to save your form as you build it.

You now should consider what information you need to obtain from the users to be able to receive orders, process their payment, and deliver the orders. This may seem intuitive and very basic information to be mentioning, but it enables you to begin to map out the detailed level of questions you require. The following exercise will take you through the steps to arrive at a consolidated form design.

Quality assurance testing

This is a critical stage of your form's design flow. Quality assurance is methodically and systematically testing to ensure that your form looks and behaves the way you intended. Via test scripts, quality assurance testing ensures that errors are caught before your form is distributed to your audience. **Test scripts** are instructions that you create to help you test your form. For example, if you require a field to accept only numerals, entering letters should cause an error message to be displayed. If your form design fails your test script, you must return to the design and build stage of the design flow.

Deployment and implementation

When you are satisfied that your form passes your testing script, it is time to implement it. Publishing your interactive form to a shared folder will allow other people to complete it and return the data to you electronically; it will also allow your static form to be downloaded for printing and filling in manually.

Implementing the design flow of your form

I will now walk you through the first two of the four stages of the Design Flow methodology to create an order form. I will thoroughly cover the later two stages, quality assurance testing and deployment and implementation, in Chapter 5 and Chapter 6.

Concept and Planning: A form's "big idea" should consist of a defined statement of your form's purpose. To demonstrate this, let's assume you want to create a form that will enable you to receive orders of supplies that you are able to process and fulfil. In this case, the form's "big idea" statement might be as follows:

The purpose of this form is: To enable us to receive orders that will enable us to process payment and fulfil the order with one customer interaction.

Design and Build: You now need to consider exactly what information you need from your users and how it should be laid out.

1. Research forms that other departments and companies use to accomplish the same result. From this you will be able to determine what information you should consider including in your form.

   Through research, you have discovered that there are six key areas to an order form. You will now refine and expand upon these areas to define.

2. Create a document that clearly states your purpose. List the six key areas shown in Figure 2-1. These become your form sections.

The purpose of this form is:

To enable us to receive orders that will enable us to process payment and fulfil the order with one customer interaction.

1. Date of order

2. Customer details

3. Delivery details

4. Order details

5. Payment details

6. Record that the order has been fulfilled.

Figure 2-1. A simple document that breaks down your form sections

3. You now need to consider the information that the user is required to submit that will allow you to capture all the necessary details in order to fulfil the order. List under each heading the information you need to obtain (see Figure 2-2).

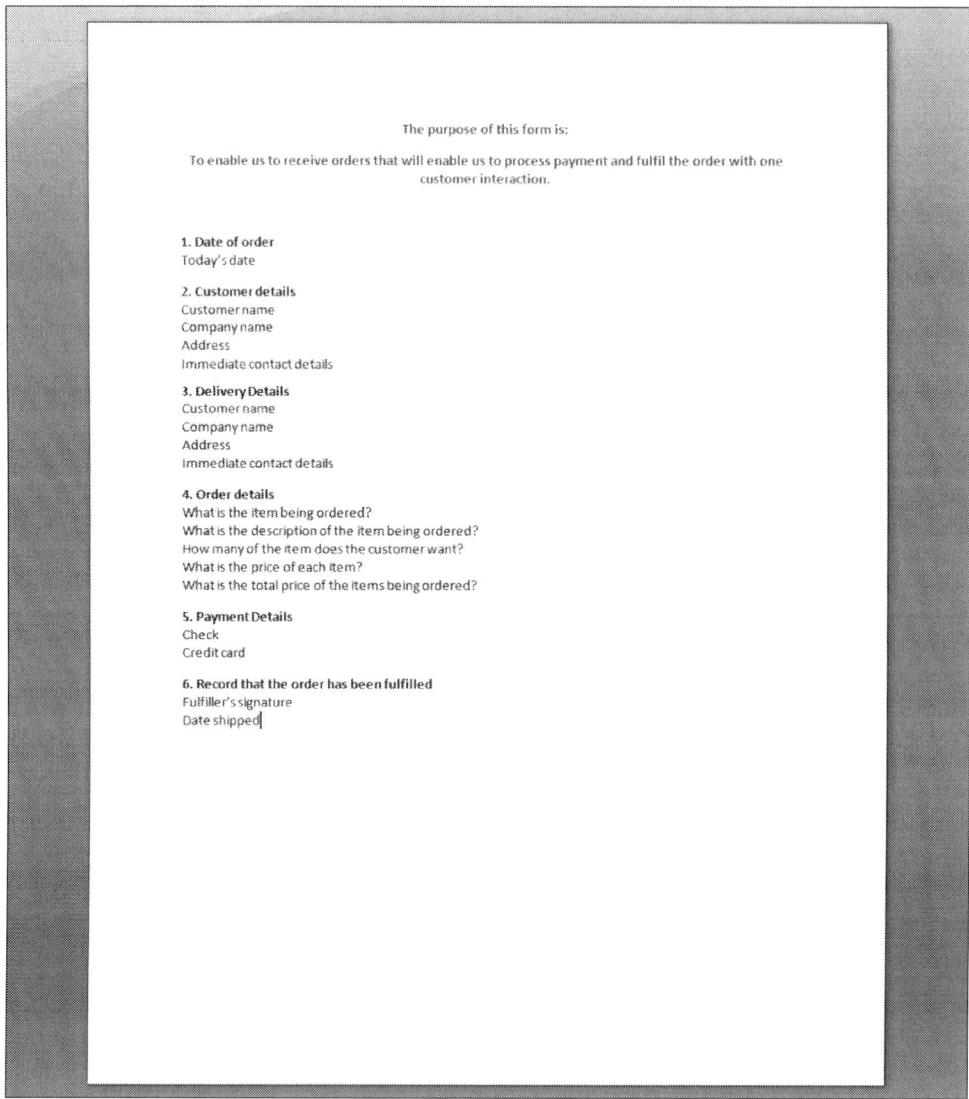

The purpose of this form is:

To enable us to receive orders that will enable us to process payment and fulfil the order with one customer interaction.

1. Date of order
Today's date

2. Customer details
Customer name
Company name
Address
Immediate contact details

3. Delivery Details
Customer name
Company name
Address
Immediate contact details

4. Order details
What is the item being ordered?
What is the description of the item being ordered?
How many of the item does the customer want?
What is the price of each item?
What is the total price of the items being ordered?

5. Payment Details
Check
Credit card

6. Record that the order has been fulfilled
Fulfiller's signature
Date shipped

Figure 2-2. Beginning to define form fields by identifying required information

4. Continue to define each section of the form by breaking headings down until there is no more information required for each one.

5. Consider the kinds of objects that supply the information you require and that require the least amount of effort on the user's behalf. List them next to each required field (see Figure 2-3).

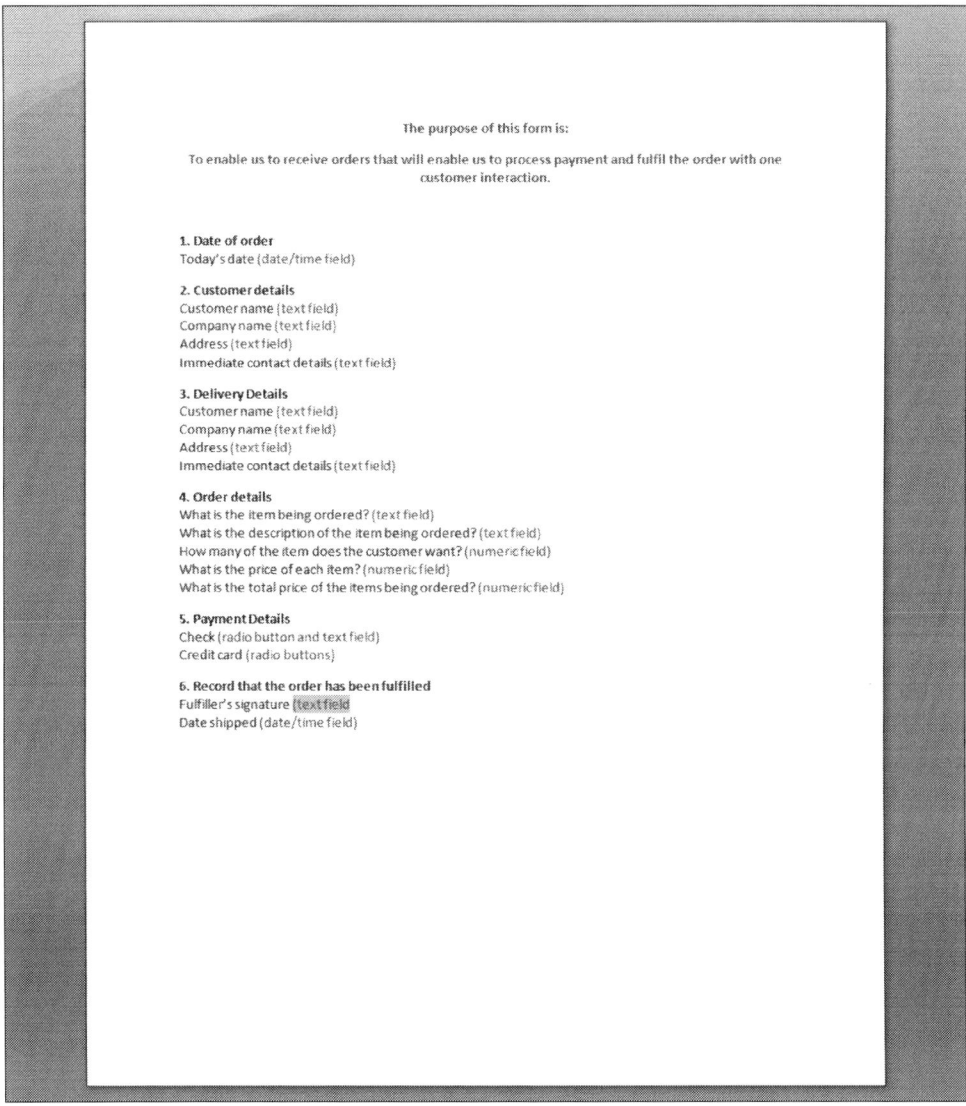

The purpose of this form is:

To enable us to receive orders that will enable us to process payment and fulfil the order with one customer interaction.

1. Date of order
Today's date (date/time field)

2. Customer details
Customer name (text field)
Company name (text field)
Address (text field)
Immediate contact details (text field)

3. Delivery Details
Customer name (text field)
Company name (text field)
Address (text field)
Immediate contact details (text field)

4. Order details
What is the item being ordered? (text field)
What is the description of the item being ordered? (text field)
How many of the item does the customer want? (numeric field)
What is the price of each item? (numeric field)
What is the total price of the items being ordered? (numeric field)

5. Payment Details
Check (radio button and text field)
Credit card (radio buttons)

6. Record that the order has been fulfilled
Fulfiller's signature (text field)
Date shipped (date/time field)

Figure 2-3. Aligning object types against form questions

You now have enough information to be able to build your form in Adobe LiveCycle Designer. In the coming chapters, you will discover how to apply scripts such as calculations, date/time fields, and text fields.

Designing forms to be filled out

Forms are a common method of conveying information to a variety of technologies including web services, databases, and enterprise applications, and forms provide an intuitive graphic user interface for users to provide data in the format required. To ensure that your target users understand how to progress through your form, you should be aware of a number of design and usability considerations.

Forms provide user interfaces for companies both internally and externally. Adobe LiveCycle Designer ES allows you to integrate business forms with your corporate intranet and streamline your business processes. For example, a time sheet for employees is traditionally printed out, filled in, and filed by hand. Adobe LiveCycle Designer ES can help you streamline this business process by hosting the form on your corporate network, allowing people to complete and submit it electronically.

Alternatively, you may want your form to be the interactive part of your website, where users can request more information, ask questions about your brand, or try your product. Adobe LiveCycle Forms ES can also fulfil these functions via downloadable interactive PDFs on your website or via rendering the form as HTML in conjunction with Adobe LiveCycle Forms ES and incorporating it as part of your website.

Principles of form design

A form's design provides the visual guidance required for a user to navigate through it to completion. The layout and look and feel are as important as written instructions because they dictate the way the user will interact with your interactive, dynamic, or static PDF form.

A good form design is possible if you keep in mind two simple values: simplicity and consistency.

Simplicity and openness lead to completion

Simple, intuitive design and easy-to-understand instructions are key to successfully navigating through a form. A clear and concise explanation of the form and its goal should be followed by form questions displayed in a logical order and a layout that implements that order.

Your introduction should let the user know why they are being asked to fill out the form, what information you'll be requesting from them, and why you are requesting it. You need to let them know the benefit of completing the form and what they can expect in return. If the form is long, you should also let them know approximately how long it will take for them to complete it. From your introduction, you should assemble your questions in a structured and logical manner. Group questions by topic.

The credit debit memo shown in Figure 2-4 has four sets of information that are clearly grouped by topic: date, payment type, billing details, and shipping details.

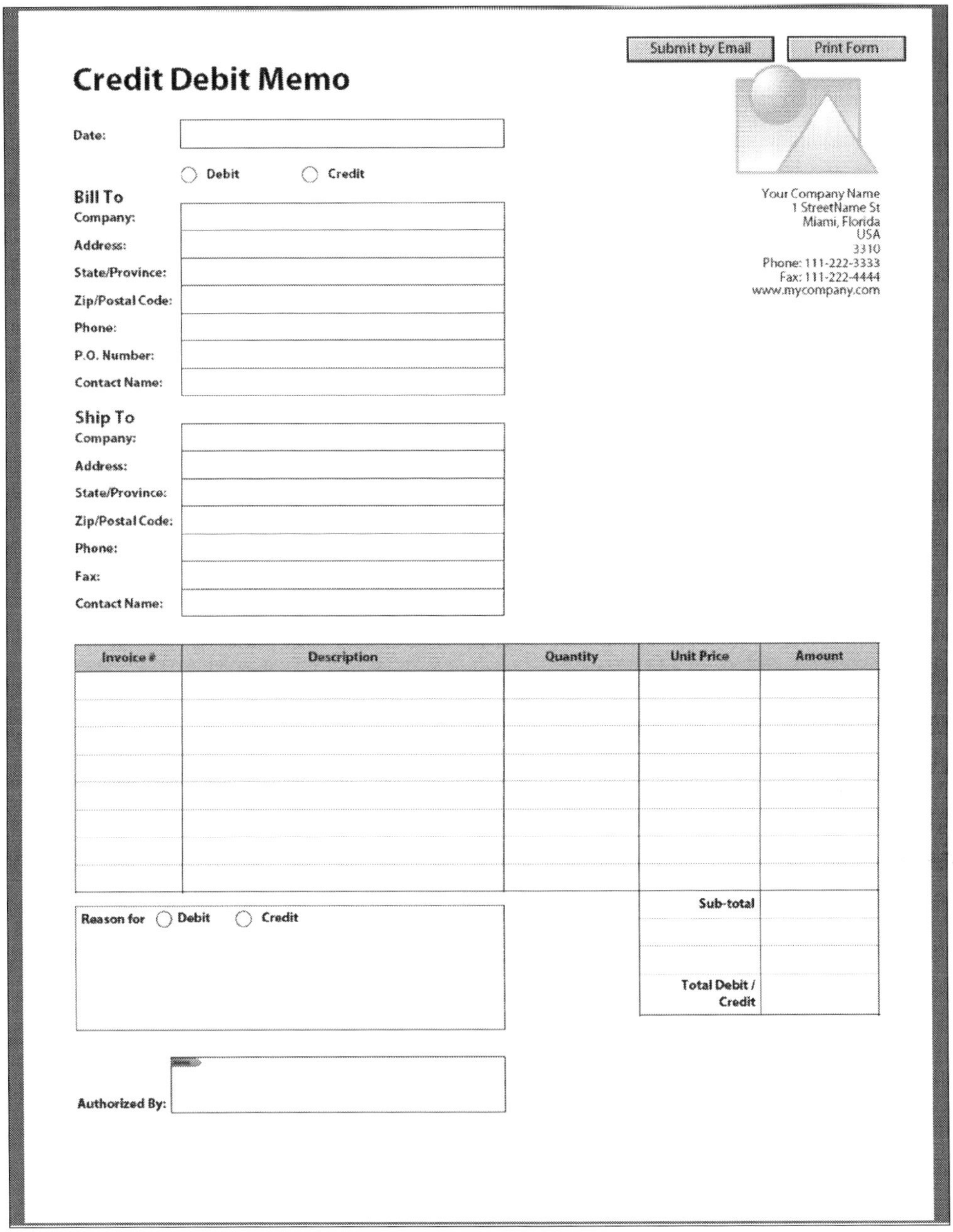

Credit Debit Memo

Submit by Email   Print Form

Date: _____

○ Debit   ○ Credit

Bill To
Company: _____
Address: _____
State/Province: _____
Zip/Postal Code: _____
Phone: _____
P.O. Number: _____
Contact Name: _____

Ship To
Company: _____
Address: _____
State/Province: _____
Zip/Postal Code: _____
Phone: _____
Fax: _____
Contact Name: _____

Your Company Name
1 StreetName St
Miami, Florida
USA
3310
Phone: 111-222-3333
Fax: 111-222-4444
www.mycompany.com

Invoice #	Description	Quantity	Unit Price	Amount
			Sub-total	
			Total Debit / Credit	

Reason for ○ Debit ○ Credit

Authorized By: _____

Figure 2-4. An example of grouping a form's questions by topic

You can simplify interactive forms even further. Identify predictable answers, and prefill the answers within form objects such as drop-down menus, radio buttons, and check boxes. You will become familiar with form objects in Chapter 3.

Adobe LiveCycle Designer ES allows you to create dynamic forms that have expandable fields that accommodate more data than a fixed layout form. Users can add and remove sections as required. You are able to hide questions and information until it becomes relevant to the user.

Implementing a dynamic interactive form simplifies the form design from the user perspective without putting any limitations on the data entry. Dynamic interactive forms will be discussed in greater detail in Chapter 4.

Consistent layouts guide users through a form

Design consistency helps users complete your form. A form should follow a logical progression and guide the user through a preferred route of form completion.

The user must intuitively know how to progress through your form via established conventions. This will allow them to move easily from one section to another and allow them to focus on the information they are providing.

LiveCycle Designer enables you to keep the look and feel consistent throughout the document with master pages that enable you to fix the background and layout of the form design. They are the blueprints you use to control the overriding look and feel of the form document.

When establishing visual consistency, create the information hierarchy first.

Here are some basic tips for maintaining consistent form layouts:

- Express similar objects in similar ways. For example, use drop-down objects for a user to select predetermined answers such as their country of origin.
- When writing your form questions, use the same tone and voice throughout.
- Use the same font for all field labels.
- Denote required fields the same way throughout the form. Traditionally, mandatory fields are marked with an asterisk (*) or are highlighted in bold or in a bright color.

Grouping Information in tables

Tables provide an obvious way for you to organize your information into structured groups of related information. You can create two kinds of tables: tables that have a fixed number of columns and rows and tables that have fixed columns only. Fixed column tables are able to add rows depending on the amount of information being entered into the form. This consistency and regularity in data display ensures that users understand what is expected of them and that the data will always display the same way. They are a valuable addition to a dynamic form, because they allow the form to expand according to the amount of information the user is entering. Fixed columns and rows tables are used in static forms, where the amount of data that the user is entering is predetermined, or they are printed to be filled out by hand.

Create a Table with the Insert Table Dialog Box

To create a table using the Insert Table dialog box, follow these steps:

1. Open a new, blank form in Adobe LiveCycle Designer ES.
2. Select Table ➤ Insert Table from the default toolbar.
3. The Insert Table dialog box that appears offers you two options (see Figure 2-5):
   - Create Simple Table
   - Create Table Using Assistant

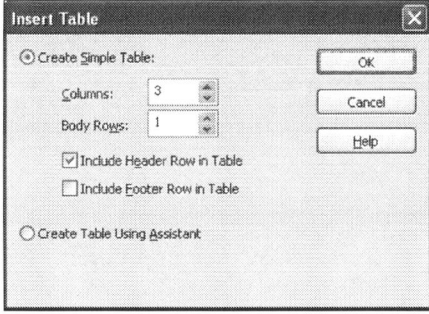

Figure 2 5. Insert Table dialog box

4. Ensure the Create Simple Table button is selected, and click OK.
5. Your table will appear in Design View in the layout area.

Create a Table with the Table Assistant

To insert a table using the Table Assistant, follow these steps:

1. Select Table ➤ Insert Table from the default toolbar.
2. In the Insert Table dialog box that appears, select Create Table Using Assistant. The Table Assistant dialog box appears (see Figure 2-6).

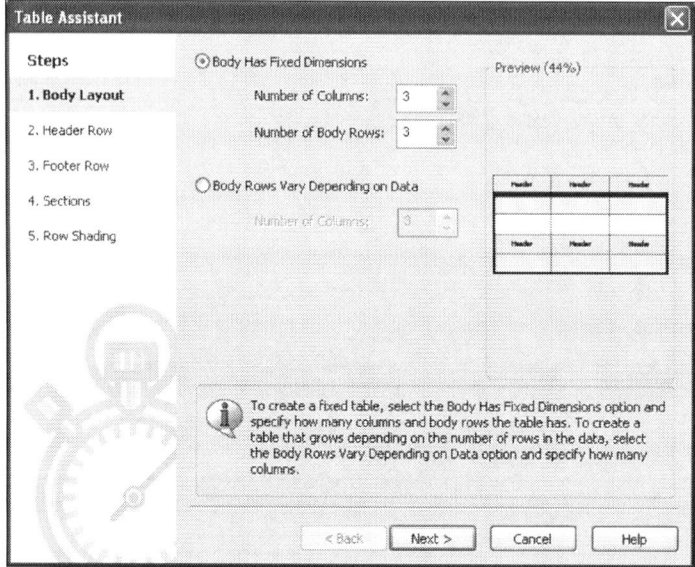

Figure 2-6. Creating a table with the Table Assistant

3. Decide the amount of columns and body rows your table needs. As you add or subtract rows and columns, you will see the preview section on the right side of the Table Assistant change. Choose Body Has Fixed Dimensions, and click Next. You will investigate the other option later in the book.

4. Follow the prompts through the screens to establish the header and footer rows, define sections, and define shading (see Figure 2-7).

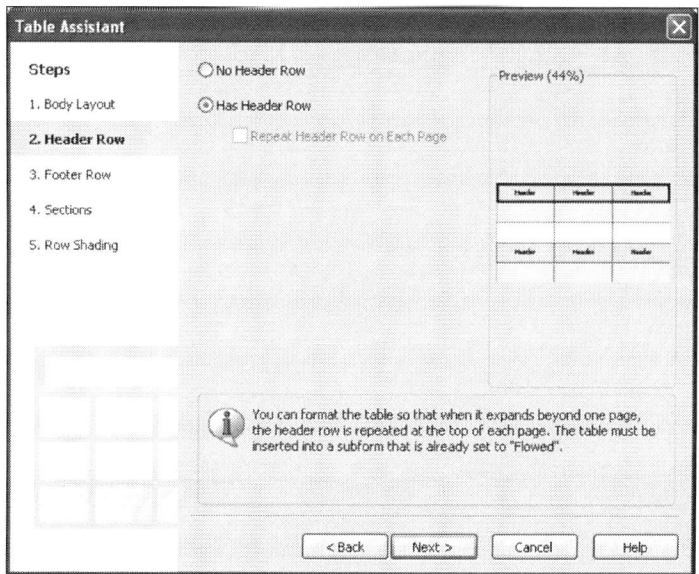

Figure 2-7. Determining header rows in the Table Assistant

Aesthetics impact form usability

Aesthetics and usability impact the success of your form. Usability determines the actual usage of an application, but user impressions of how easy the form is to use are directly influenced by its aesthetic design.

Therefore, for a form application to be successful, the aesthetics need to support the function of the form.

We have seen this particularly impact the online world in the past decade. As technology has made leaps and bounds, our ability to design compelling and interactive web applications has expanded. Initially websites were designed with simple, visually unappealing interfaces. These early sites were daunting to users who perceived them as being difficult to use. As technology has changed, sites are now designed to be beautiful and usable, and they have had much more success in terms of users interacting with them.

This principle can be applied to your form designs. Use your questions and crucial information as the skeleton for your design, and build inviting, intuitive interface around this.

Regardless of where in your business you implement them, designing clear, intuitive, attractive forms will ensure that more forms are completed than worked around in business processes or than abandoned on the Internet.

Useful design tips

Design flow, form design principles, and aesthetics all impact the usability of your form. Let's investigate specific design tips that will enhance the user experience and guarantee users will more accurately complete your forms.

Be clear and explicit about the purpose of the form. If the user has arrived at the form through a series of other forms or website links, there may be some ambiguity about the exact reason for the form's existence.

Structure questions according to importance

Decide where it will be most effective to position your most important questions on the form. Often your questions will lead with the form user's contact details and then branch into other topics. List your questions in defined and logical blocks. This will focus the user's concentration and help ensure that the data they provide is correct.

Figure 2-8, a customer satisfaction survey, illustrates how structuring your questions in order of most relevant to least relevant can contribute to guiding the user through the form. Following the contact and professional details are a series of questions designed to elicit details of the customer journey from the initial purchase of goods or services, the impressions of the delivered goods and services, and the pricing before beginning to extract details of customer ideas on improving service.

Accordingly, you should ensure that you treat your users as real people, not database entries. Provide instantaneous visual feedback, and ensure that your message is always in context. LiveCycle allows you to easily incorporate validation and error messages to be displayed where the actual error occurs, thus ensuring that the user receives feedback as they work through the form. You will investigate validation, error messages, and user feedback thoroughly in Chapter 6.

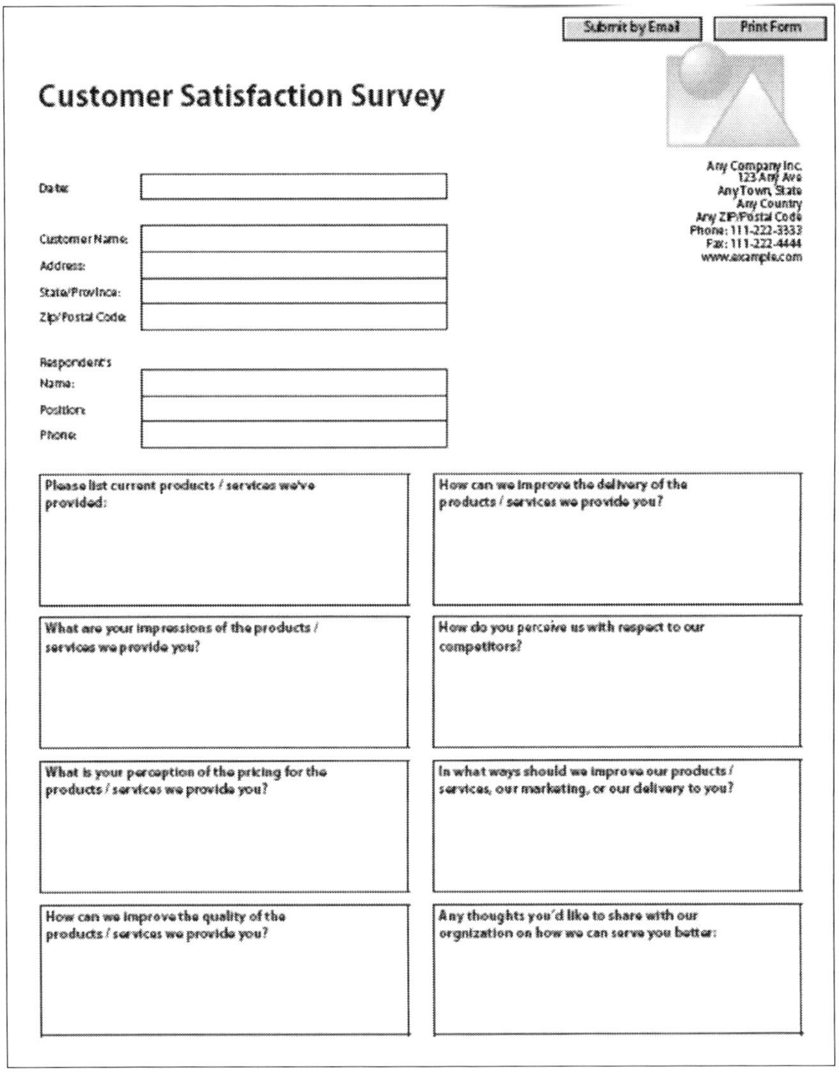

Submit by Email | Print Form

Customer Satisfaction Survey

Any Company Inc.
123 Any Ave
AnyTown, State
Any Country
Any ZIP/Postal Code
Phone: 111-222-3333
Fax: 111-222-4444
www.example.com

Date:

Customer Name:
Address:
State/Province:
Zip/Postal Code:

Respondent's
Name:
Position:
Phone:

Please list current products / services we've provided:

How can we improve the delivery of the products / services we provide you?

What are your impressions of the products / services we provide you?

How do you perceive us with respect to our competitors?

What is your perception of the pricing for the products / services we provide you?

In what ways should we improve our products / services, our marketing, or our delivery to you?

How can we improve the quality of the products / services we provide you?

Any thoughts you'd like to share with our orgnization on how we can serve you better:

Figure 2-8. Customer satisfaction survey

Smart defaults ensure consistent data formatting

Prefill data where possible, and don't make the form user enter information more than once. Use data fields similarly throughout the form. For example, if you require the user to select dates in a particular format, add a Date/Time Field. This allows the user to choose the date from a calendar, but you can specify the format in which the information is returned to you (see Figure 2-9).

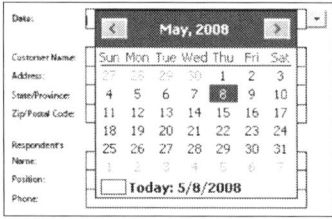

Figure 2-9. Date/time format

Use spatial relationships to your advantage

The relationship between your form labels and form fields provides clarity at a microscopic level in your forms.

Justify your form labels appropriately. **Justification** is the alignment of the content on the page in relation to the margin. Content is justifiable to the left, the right, or the center of the page. Left justification for body copy in forms is the most common.

Regardless of whether your form is a print-and-fill form or an interactive form, the length of the responses depends on the length of the field. It is visually interruptive to the user if your fields are smaller than the answer you require. For example, the bottom field in Figure 2-10 is better because it's long enough for a user to type an e-mail address.

Figure 2-10. Set data expectations with appropriate field lengths.

Emphasize important actions

Interactive forms have an advantage over print-and-fill forms because the user can instantaneously submit the data to you upon filling out the form. Since the goal of a form is to get the user to submit their data to you, the call to action to submit their data is of extreme importance.

Ensure that your call to action to submit data, regardless of whether this is via e-mail to the form originator or a submit button, is clearly denoted. Submit buttons are usually at the end of the form so that as soon as a user has filled it out, it is clear for them what their final action should be.

Thank your user for entering the form, and tell them what the next steps will be after their data is received.

The effect of typography on forms

When a user views a form, they subconsciously absorb the overall patterns and layout of the page before they consciously read the information on the page. I have already established that setting a hierarchy is important in form design because it helps take the user on the journey to form completion. Typography and font choice are important in this visual hierarchy because they help the form user understand the relationship between text, images, and form objects.

There are five generic font families: monospace, cursive, fantasy, serif, and san-serif. The first three listed are used sparingly, if at all, on forms and interactive web pages. It is the serif and san-serif families we will concentrate on.

Serif fonts, sometimes called Roman fonts, are thought to have emanated from the Roman inscriptional capitals. There are two main theories about how they came to be as they are today.

The first, which is also the most widely accepted, is that the Roman letters were painted onto a stone slab with a brush, and then stone carvers carved the brush marks out of the stone. The brush marks left flares at the ends and corners of the letters, and these were also incorporated into the carvings.

A second theory is that serifs were conceived to give neatness to letters carved in stone. Carving sharp corners in stone slabs is labor intensive and difficult. Serifs may have been invented as a way to mask these imperfections.

Serif fonts are thought to be the easiest to read out of all the font families, and because of this, they are widely used in traditional printing. They are a sound choice for lengthy texts such as books, magazines, and newspapers. Serifs are thought to help distinguish each letter and, thus, make it easier to read blocks of text.

Figure 2-11 shows Times New Roman, a serif font.

Figure 2-11. Times New Roman, an example of a serif font

San-serif fonts (*san* is French for "without") are known by many other names including Gothic, Egyptian, Antique, and Grotesque fonts and do not have the "serif" at the end of the letter strokes.

San-serif letterforms can be found from the fifth century in Greek and Latin texts. In about 1805 san-serif letters appeared in print mediums such as *European Magazine*. It was in 1919 that the san-serif letters began to be popular when the first of the Bauhaus schools of design, which eventually had a massive influence on modern architecture and design, opened in Weimar, Germany. (Bauhaus literally translates to "House of Building" or "Building School.")

Today san-serif fonts are widely accepted as the standard font for use online. They have a simpler shape than serif fonts because they consist of only the dominant strokes. This trait makes san-serif fonts easy to view onscreen, and they're a good choice for your forms.

Figure 2-12 shows Arial, a san-serif font.

Figure 2-12. Arial, an example of a san-serif font

Impact of typography on successful forms

Decide which font to use on your form by identifying where it is most likely to be used. If your form is text heavy and more suitable for printing and reading, use a serif font. If your form guides people with instructive messages as they progress through the form and it can be submitted online, use a san-serif font.

The following are some useful tips when considering the fonts to use on your form:

- The more fonts you have on a page, the harder it is for the user to comprehend. If a form looks difficult to fill out, users will likely abandon it.

- Users will abandon a form if they can't read it. The body and text of the instructions should be large enough that it is easily read. As a general guide, 11 points for most fonts is legible. If the font is a smaller type, for example, Arial Narrow, you can increase it to 12 points to make it easier to read.

- Strive to keep your headings consistent. You don't necessarily require a different font for headings. Use the same font for all headings, but change the size to denote that it is a heading. If your body font is an odd number, for example, 11 points, as a general rule make the heading font 3 points larger, for example, 14 points. If your body font is an even number such as 10 points, make the heading font 4 points larger, for example, 14 points.

- Use color sparingly. Just as red is universal for warnings, you should use red only to denote error messages in your forms, and you should avoid underline on printed documents unless you are referring to a URL. For online forms, use underline only to indicate a hyperlink.

- With the exception of acronyms, it is harder to read blocks of text if they are all in capitals than it is to read mixed cases. In the interactive world, all capitals can indicate the user is being condescended to or shouted at and may discourage your user from completing your form.

The Font palette in Adobe LiveCycle Designer ES allows you to manipulate typography. This is where you can define the font, its size and style, and the baseline shift (see Figure 2-13). The baseline shift feature allows you to lower or raise the baseline of letters and numbers.

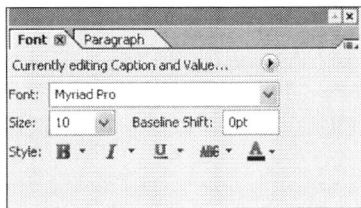

Figure 2-13. The Font palette

Understanding graphic design in forms

Graphic design uses text and images to present information visually. It uses a combination of design, typography, layout, and aesthetics—everything discussed in this chapter—to produce a document that visually communicates your message.

Today, graphic designers are an important part of any communications team because they form the bridge between the user and your goal. In this case, your end goal is getting the user to complete the form.

Information design is derived from traditional graphic design. It is simply preparing the information you want to impart to your user in a palatable way for them to digest and understand it.

Developing forms for people

Your form is primarily built for the user to be able to submit information to you in the format that you want it. When you are designing your form, you need to consider some critical factors to make your form a success.

User needs

Your form is the interactive interface that prompts the user to give you the information you want. When you are constructing your form, you need to keep in mind your audience. Structure the user interface, questions, and input fields with the person in mind, rather than the business system or database requirements.

There is a better chance of the user filling in your form to completion if you explain to them clearly and concisely why you require their data and the benefits they will receive from completing it. Be up front about data usage, and display your privacy policy.

Let the user know what information you are likely to require from them that they may not have at their fingertips.

Don't ask for information that the user doesn't have at their fingertips. If you direct the user away from the form, they will most likely not return.

Computers format data, users enter it

Set up your form field objects so that there is only one way the user can enter the data. This ensures that all data entered in forms is exactly as your system requires it.

Requests for data such as phone numbers can be ambiguous, because there are many different ways the user can provide the data. When confronted with a question like this, be very clear about the way you want the data to be entered (see Figure 2-14).

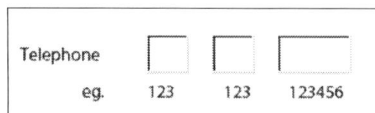

Figure 2-14. Demonstrate clearly how data is to be entered.

Mark mandatory fields clearly

Mandatory fields are the crucial elements of the information you are seeking from the user. For example, if your form performs the function of obtaining people's contact details so that they can be sent information about your business, their address, telephone number, and e-mail fields may all be mandatory.

You need to give the user visual cues as to which fields are required and a legend that explains to them what these cues mean.

Traditional ways of indicating mandatory fields are as follows:

- Using an asterisk (*)
- Adding "(required)" at the end of mandatory fields
- Dividing the form into two areas, optional and mandatory

Adobe LiveCycle Designer ES allows you to easily set mandatory field specifications via scripting properties. Using the Script Editor (see Figure 2-15), you can set both checks to ensure that the mandatory fields have been completed and also set up error messages to remind the user to complete the form before the data is submitted.

Figure 2-15. The Script Editor

The message that indicates the user has failed to complete a mandatory field should be expressed in a manner that is clear to the user which field is in error and how to correct it.

It is important to manage your user's expectations about the number of mandatory objects in your form and ensure that these visual cues are consistently adhered to throughout the form. To make the document clearer to the user, consider grouping mandatory fields together or separating the mandatory and optional fields with a visual divider.

Designing accessible forms

Accessibility means creating your form in such a way that people with disabilities can read, comprehend, progress through, and interact with it. Accessibility should not be confused with **usability**, which is the ease with which people can use your form. Accessibility is ensuring your form is available to a wide range of people with a wide range of computer environments and equipment.

Your form needs to be accessible to assistive technologies for people who are unable to see, unable to hear, or can't process some types of information; for example, they may not be able to read or comprehend text or be unable to use a keyboard or mouse. They may have a text-only, small screen, or they may have a slow Internet connection.

Tips for designing accessible forms

The previous typography and design tips will set you on the path to creating accessible forms, but there are a few specific tips that will ensure your forms are created to be as accessible as possible:

- Create clear and simple instructions for form completion. Tab order should support the progression of the form.
- Form design should be uncluttered and simple.
- The form should be able to be completed using only the keyboard or an equivalent assisted technology device.
- Include a text description along with any images in your form to ensure that screen readers can describe the image to users.

Designing forms for screen readers

Using the Adobe LiveCycle Designer CS Accessibility palette, you can define the information a Microsoft Active Accessibility (MSAA)–compliant screen reader will read out for each form object. It also allows you to change the order the screen reader reads the text. MSAA is a technology designed to enhance the way accessibility aids such as screen readers work with applications that run in Windows environments.

To view the Accessibility palette of an open form, select View ➤ Accessibility (see Figure 2-16).

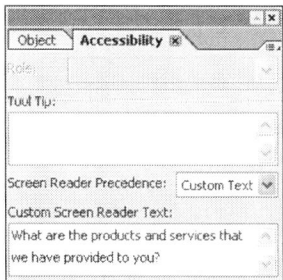

Figure 2-16. The Accessibility palette

The Accessibility palette is where you can specify options for screen readers such as custom screen reader text, object tool tips, field captions, and object names.

The shortcut to open the Accessibility *palette is Shift+F6.*

When you are creating a screen reader–accessible form, you need to understand the way screen readers read certain objects.

Screen readers read through the entire page, including all text and image objects. When the form is tabbed through, the screen reader reads the text for the active object. Therefore, the tabbing order is of extreme importance in ensuring the accessibility of your form. Ensure all text fields images and buttons are properly encountered in tabbing order. Tabbing order uses the Tab key on the keyboard to move between fields and buttons instead of the mouse.

Adobe LiveCycle Designer ES has the tabbing order set from left to right and from top to bottom, beginning in the upper-left corner of the page. It is best to set the tabbing order as one of the last steps when creating your form because your objects may change position. To view the tabbing order, select View ➤ Tabbing order (see Figure 2-17).

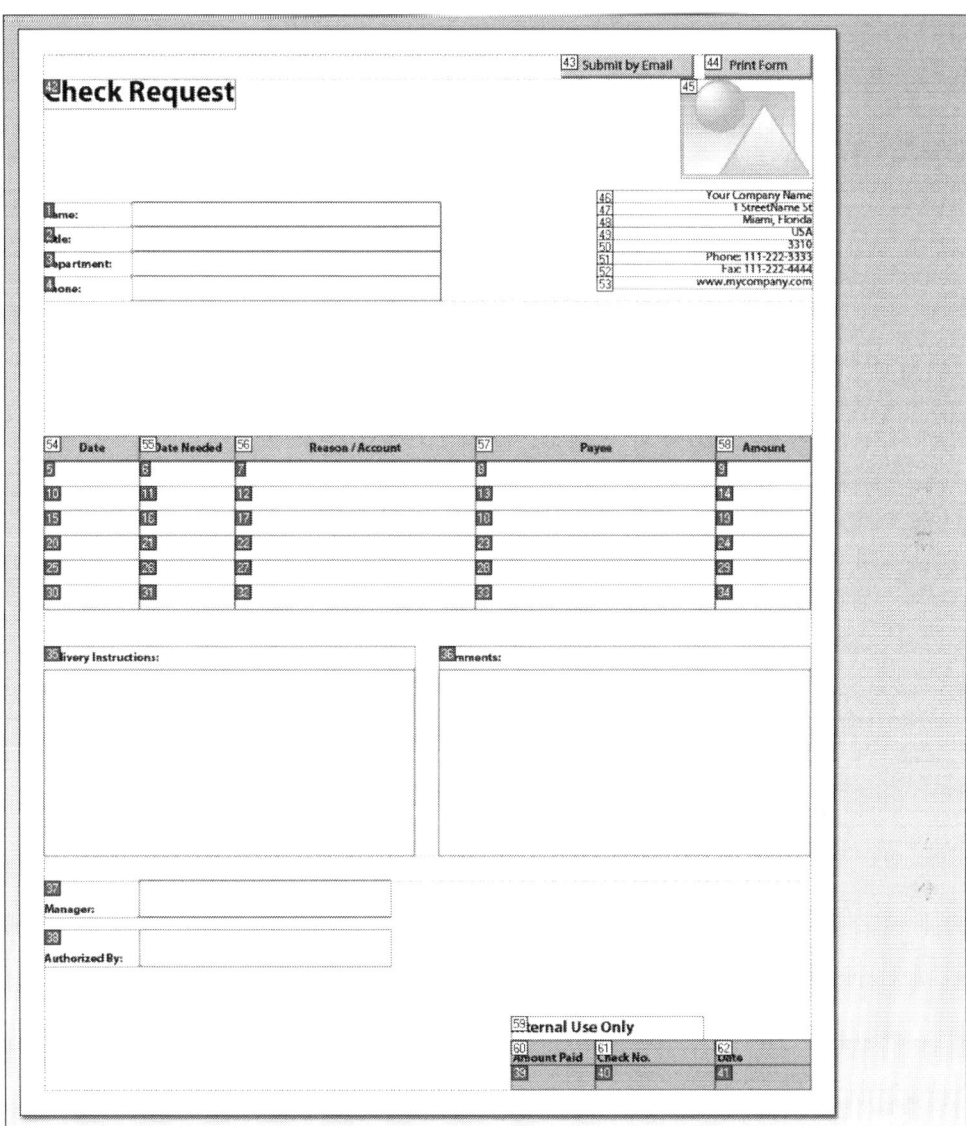

Figure 2-17. Viewing the tabbing order of your form

Radio buttons can be misinterpreted by screen readers depending on where the text is in relation to the form object. The screen reader expects the radio button or check box to come before the text. Rectify this by having the text after the radio button or check box (see Figure 2-18).

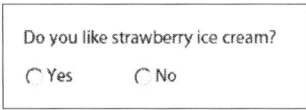

Figure 2-18. Text after radio buttons improves accessibility.

Screen readers read out the default item selected in list boxes and drop-down menus. Let the user know the options for the drop-down via the object tool tips in the Accessibility palette (see Figure 2-19). Educate the user to use the up and down arrows to navigate through list items and about which key to press to select the item they want.

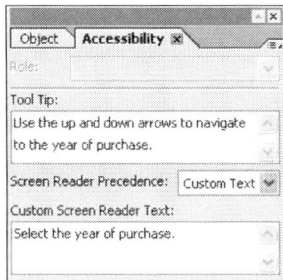

Figure 2-19. Specify a tool tip to instruct readers how to navigate through a drop-down list.

In addition to specifying text for screen readers, you must also create a tagged PDF form so that the screen reader can read the text. You do this by generating accessibility tags when saving the form design as a PDF file.

Data-handling needs

Data handling for interactive forms occurs through data binding in Adobe LiveCycle Designer ES. **Data binding** is where you "attach" a form field object with the corresponding object in the database.

Using data binding, you can set up a form designed to capture data from the user or a form that displays data to the user, for example, telephone bills.

As touched on in Chapter 1, Adobe LiveCycle Designer ES gives form designers the ability to integrate PDF forms into a variety of technologies such as XML schemas; enterprise applications including SAP, Microsoft, and Oracle; databases such as MySQL and Access, and standard web services.

Adobe LiveCycle Designer ES allows you to create forms that go beyond simple data capture. Using Adobe LiveCycle Designer ES, you can collect data entered on a form; populate form fields; and add to, validate, and define form field values using external data sources such as XML schema and data files, databases, and web services.

With data binding you can link a form object to the corresponding data field within a data file or a database. Via data binding you can connect to data sources such as XML schema, Object Linking and Embedding Database (OLEDB) data sources, XML data, and Web Service Definition Language (WSDL) files. When you bind a form object to a data source field successfully, it will appear in the Data View palette.

Binding fields in a form to its data source creates a relationship between the form design and the form data. This relationship enables you to do many things with the information associated with the form design such as capture, present, and move data; process data; and print information. Adobe LiveCycle Designer ES allows you to use server-side or client-side binding. Client-side binding allows you to make immediate changes to the data and requires Adobe Acrobat or Adobe Reader to be installed on the user's computer. Server-side binding commits the changes to the data only after it has been submitted to the server. To do server-side binding, you must have Adobe LiveCycle Forms ES installed on a Microsoft server.

You can bind a field or a subform to a data source in Adobe LiveCycle Designer in four ways:

- Using the Data View palette to create new form objects
- Associating a node from the Data View palette with an existing form field
- Using the Binding Tab option in the Object palette to specify the binding node
- Allowing Adobe LiveCycle Designer ES to autogenerate bound fields into a subform

These methods will be expanded upon in Chapter 6 when you investigate advanced form design.

Overview of data validation

Adobe LiveCycle Designer ES offers other powerful tools such as data validation. **Data validation** is the process that is used to determine whether the data the user has entered has been entered accurately, that it is complete, and that it meets the specified criteria. Data validation can occur only on interactive forms.

These are types of validation:

- Field validation checks for data presence (something has been entered into the field) and that the data is in a specified format (for example, dates or e-mail addresses).
- Form validation, upon clicking the submit button, ensures the entire form is validated.
- Data formatting allows you to specify how data will look in your form and what format it will take when it leaves your form.

Ensuring data security

The security of your data is just as important in the form design process as the layout or the questions. Your users must be comfortable that their information will not be redistributed or publicly accessible.

Developing a data security process will ensure that the data you receive is controlled, that it has limited access, and that it is safe from corruption. Your data security process will help shape your privacy policy.

Adobe LiveCycle Designer ES provides the following security options for your form.

Security via digital signatures

A **digital signature** is a message signed by the sender's private key that can be verified by the sender's public key. Digital signatures simulate a traditional handwritten signature by employing a kind of cryptography. The signature indicates the verification of the message to which it has been applied. If an unauthorized person makes changes to the document without the proper authentication, all changes to the file will be still be communicated, but the document will contain an invalid signature.

Adobe LiveCycle Designer ES offers two ways to set a digital signature in a form: document signatures and data signatures. **Document signatures** safeguard the look and feel of the form objects and their values, and **data signatures** protect the data in transmission.

Insert a Document Signature

To insert a document signature into your form, simply drag the Document Signature field from the Object Library palette onto your form (see Figure 2-20).

Figure 2-20. Document Signature field

The Object palette displays the Document Signature tab (see Figure 2-21).

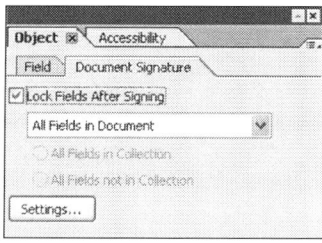

Figure 2-21. Document Signature tab

To sign the document signature field, a user simply fills out the form. When they are sure it is correct, they click the Document Signature field. The user must have a digital certificate from a certificate issuer to be able to sign the document.

Forms that use Document Signature fields often become very large over time, because each time the form is signed, it adds a complete copy of the PDF form to the document.

Add a Data Signature

Data signatures protect the integrity of the form during the online transmission of the data. To establish a data signature, add a standard submit button, an e-mail button, or an HTTP submit button, and choose Sign Submission in the Object palette. I'll discuss this in greater detail in coming chapters.

Using PDF security settings

You may want to restrict some of the capabilities that PDF documents usually have such as printing, not requiring a password to open the document, adding comments and signatures, and copying in your PDF form.

Adobe LiveCycle Designer ES allows you to restrict these capabilities through the PDF Security tab.

Restrict a PDF Document's Capabilities

To restrict normal PDF document capabilities, follow these steps:

1. Select File ➤ Form Properties.
2. Click the PDF Security tab.
3. The Permissions area has a number of options that allow you to restrict the capabilities of the PDF document (see Figure 2-22).

Changing the text access can affect people who use screen readers. To enable screen readers to be used, you must have text access enabled. This is set as a default in Adobe LiveCycle Designer ES.

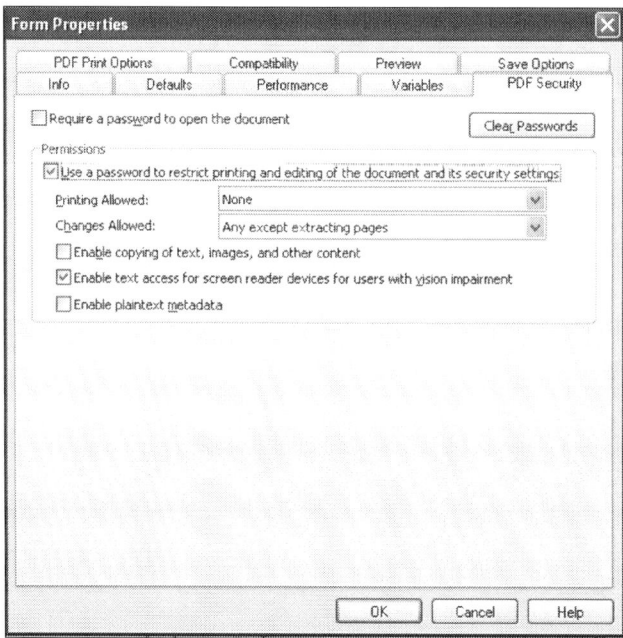

Figure 2-22. PDF Security tab in Form Properties

Setting passwords for security

A password field will control who has access to your form. Adobe LiveCycle Designer ES allows you to set character masking on the password field of your form. **Character masking** enables users to enter their password, but instead of seeing the characters, it is masked with a character such as an asterisk.

A password can be included in your form without necessarily being a mandatory part of the user experience. You can create messages to prompt users to enter a password, and you can specify whether the password is arbitrary, advised, or mandatory. Scripting can validate all user input.

Privacy

Data privacy defines the relationship between the data's collection and its distribution to eligible channels and the legal issues that can arise between these two steps.

Form users have a legal right to expect reasonable privacy of their data and that it will be kept within the boundaries of the privacy policy under which the form they complete is executed. A **privacy policy** is a legal notice associated with your form that states explicitly how the data a user enters will be used, who will access it, and the security procedures in place to prevent unauthorized people from accessing it.

Privacy issues may arise wherever a user has submitted a form that contains personally identifiable data about them.

The contents and details on a privacy policy vary from country to country. It is best to obtain legal advice if you are collecting data from users regardless of whether your form is available for public consumption.

Summary

This chapter covered a number of valid considerations that you need to take into account when creating forms for internal or external consumption. The design of your form will impact the success of it and the number of people who will complete it. Designing accessible forms will ensure a broad range of users will be able to navigate, understand, and ultimately fill them out. Security, privacy, and data-handling policies are as important to the form as the actual building of it.

In Chapter 3, you will become acquainted with the building blocks of forms and learn how Adobe LiveCycle Designer ES contains many preconfigured tools that will streamline your form-building process.

Chapter 3

UNDERSTANDING THE ELEMENTS OF FORM STYLE: COMPONENTS, TEMPLATES, AND MASTERS

It is now time to move past design theory and become acquainted with the actual working components of a form. Templates and master pages create the overall look and feel of the form, and fragments enable you to group objects. Objects are the basic building blocks that allow users to submit data.

This chapter is designed to give you an overview of components that are needed to build your form (see Figure 3-1). Although these exercises may seem basic, it is important to understand their contributions to the overall form design.

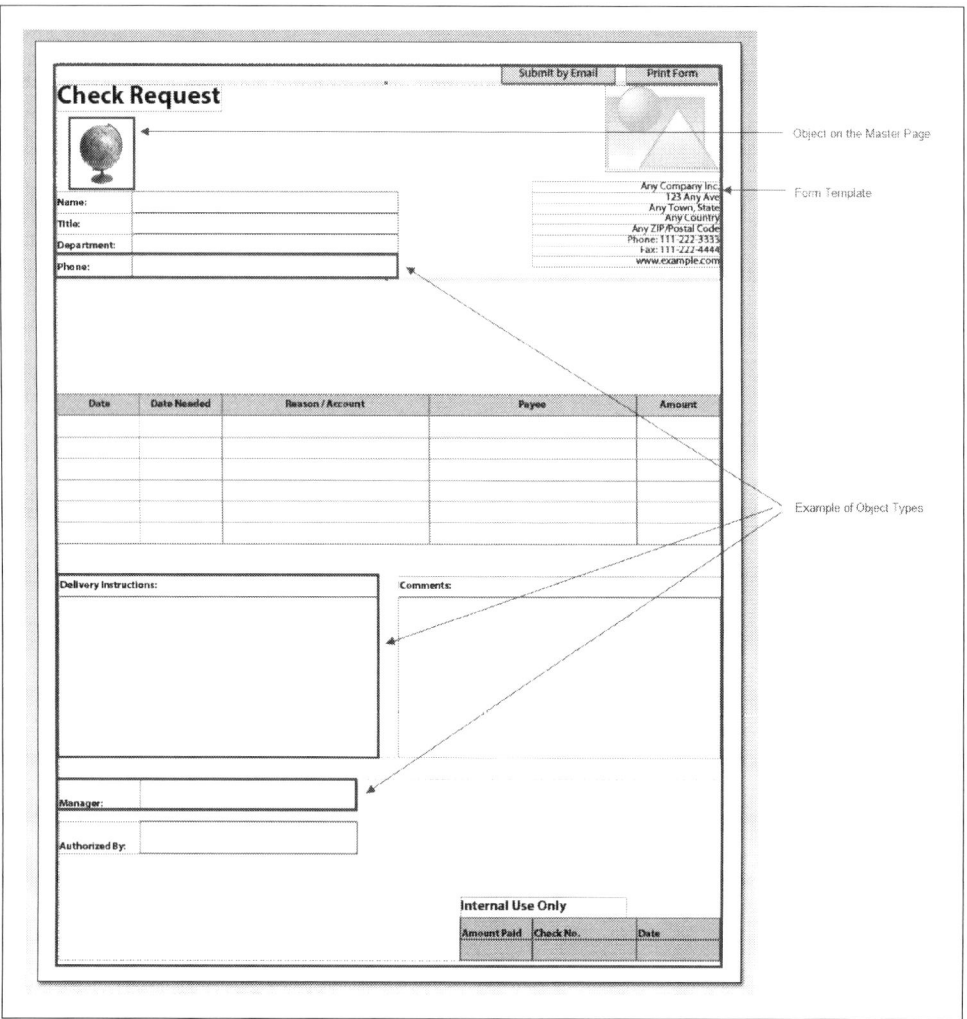

Figure 3-1. A form is created from templates, master pages, fragments, and form objects.

Understanding objects

Objects are the fundamental building blocks of every form. They are the smallest functional components in a form, and they fulfill a number of direct data entry functions.

Investigating the Object Library palette

In Adobe LiveCycle Designer ES, you interact with objects via the Object Library palette. To add an object to a form, simply choose the object you want to add from the Object Library palette, and drag it onto the layout area of the form. You will use objects to create a form in Chapter 4.

Each object provides some piece of functionality to your form, such as a place to enter text or a button to e-mail the form. As you create your form, you select objects and add them to the body or master pages of the form design. You will find all the available objects in the Object Library palette.

The objects in the Object Library palette are grouped into categories. The My Favorites category contains the objects you use most often. The Standard category contains objects that are common to many forms, and the Barcode category contains standard bar-code objects. In addition, a number of predefined custom objects are available in the Custom category. You will now look at the individual objects in each category.

My Favorites category

The My Favorites category of the Object Library palette contains the form objects you will use the most, according to Adobe. You can find everything you need to build a form using generic fields (see Figure 3-2).

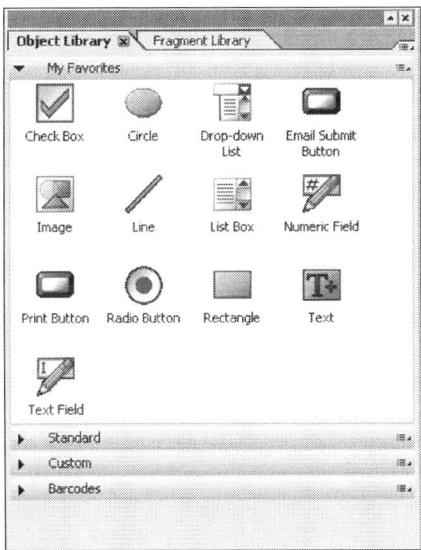

Figure 3-2. The My Favorites category of the Object Library palette is prepopulated with form objects that are commonly found in forms.

Check Box object: This allows users to select an individual choice by clicking a check box.

Circle object: This is a drawing object. It allows you to draw an ellipse, circle, or oblong on the layout area. Drawing objects offer an easy way to enhance your forms graphically.

Drop-down List object: This offers the user a list of predefined selections from which users can select a single choice. Drop-down lists display only the selected choice or the default selection. Users must click the list to see the other options.

Email Submit Button object: This is a standard button that has properties already predetermined. These properties allow the user to click the button to submit the data directly to you.

Image object: This allows you to add an image to a form. You used this object earlier in this book when you edited a master page.

Line object: This is another drawing object. It allows you to draw a solid, dashed, or dotted line anywhere on the layout area. Line objects are an easy way to create visual dividers between information.

List Box object: This is similar to the Drop-down List object in that it offers the user a list of predefined selections from which they can select a single answer. The difference between the two is List Box objects display all the choices on the form page, possibly with the addition of the scrollbar depending upon the size of the list, and Drop-down List objects display only a single choice after selection.

Numeric Field object: This allows you to specify numeral-only data validation; that is, these will not accept any characters from the alphabet.

Print Button object: This allows the user to print the form. It has a script included on the button click event that immediately prints the form when the user clicks it.

Radio Button object: This allows you to present the user with a number of mutually exclusive options succinctly. The group of radio buttons can be toggled between on and off. Only one radio button in the group can be on at any time. I touched briefly on radio buttons in Chapter 2.

Rectangle object: This is another drawing object. It allows you to draw rectangles or squares that have either sharp 90-degree corners or soft, rounded corners anywhere on the layout area.

Text object: This allows you to add headings, instructional paragraphs, and blocks of text to your forms.

Text Field object: This allows users to enter blocks of textual information into your form. Users are able to cut and paste the information from other documents into this field, and they can display fonts in different sizes, colors, and typefaces. You can specify text boxes to receive a limited amount of characters or to wrap and expand in dynamic forms. They are the most flexible data entry field in forms.

Standard category

The Standard category (see Figure 3-3) in the Object Library palette contains all the commonly used form fields, including all that are included in the My Favorites category by default plus the following.

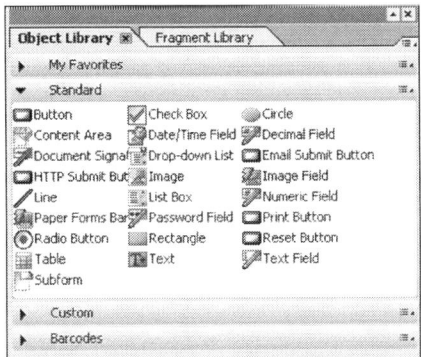

Figure 3-3. The Standard category of the Object Library palette contains all the typical objects that can be used on your form.

Button object: This allows users to commence actions such as submitting form data, running a web service operation or a database query, and printing the form.

Content Area object: This allows you to apply a new content area to a master page.

Date/Time Field object: This allows you to standardize the data the user enters for the date. It allows the user to either enter the date manually or choose the date from a pop-up calendar.

Decimal object: This is similar to the Numeric object. The Decimal object allows you to specify numbers in a decimal format and set the number of characters before and after the decimal point.

Document Signature object: This allows you to authenticate the identity of the user and the contents of the form. It is a security checkpoint that ensures that the form is not tampered with.

HTTP Submit Button object: This is a preconfigured object that allows you to create buttons to enable users to send their data via an HTTP post.

Image Field object: This allows you to display images that can be changed in interactive forms. These images can be bound to a database, or they can be bound through scripting.

Paper Forms Barcode object: This allows you to electronically capture information that the user has entered into an interactive PDF form. When the user returns the form to you, the bar code is updated, and it can be scanned using a scanning device and automatically decoded.

Password object: This allows you to control access to the form by applying a password to it.

Reset Button object: This is another preconfigured button object that allows the user to clear all the fields in the form by clicking the Reset Button object.

Table object: This allows you to insert a table into your form, thus allowing for fast and neat layout formatting.

Subform object: This enables efficient grouping of form objects into subforms.

Custom category

The Custom category (see Figure 3-4) has a number of preformatted objects that are useful globally. This category streamlines the form creation process because you do not need to create these objects. You are able to customize preexisting objects in any of the Object Library categories and save them in the Custom category, where you can implement them across multiple forms. This will be covered in Chapter 5.

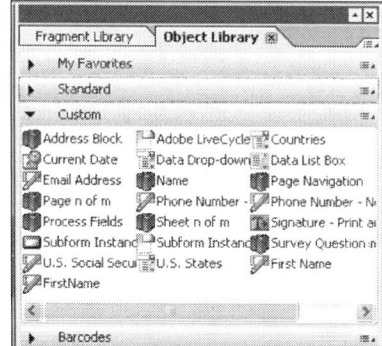

Figure 3-4. The Custom category of the Object Library palette stores custom form objects.

Address Block object: This is a group of text objects that is preconfigured to show addresses in the U.S. Postal Service–approved format.

Adobe LiveCycle object: This enables the form to communicate outside of the PDF.

Countries object: This is a list that is prepopulated with country names.

Current Date object: This is a time/date object preconfigured to display the current date.

Data Drop-down object: This is similar to the Drop-down List, but it populates with choices from a database.

Data List Box object: This populates with choices from a database like the Data Drop-down object. The difference is all of the choices are displayed in the form, where the Data Drop-down object displays only a single choice at a time.

E-mail Address object: This is preconfigured to validate e-mail addresses that the user enters.

Name object: This creates a group of objects that displays name information.

Page Navigation object: This is a group of buttons that allows the user to easily navigate between pages of a form.

Page n of m object: This allows the user to know where they are in the process of a form by displaying the current page and the total page count.

Phone Number – UK object: This formats data to display as a UK phone number. You can specify this object to display with a different country's phone number formatting.

Phone Number – North America object: This formats data to display as a North American phone number.

Process Fields object: The allows you to specify interaction with the rest of Adobe LiveCycle ES.

Sheet n of m object: This allows the user to know where they are in the process of a form by displaying the current sheet and the total sheet count.

Signature – Print and Sign object: This is a preformatted field that shows a signature field at the conclusion of the form. It allows a user to print and sign the form.

Subform Instance Controls – Add object: This allows you to add a button to the form that enables the user to add one line of a subform upon clicking. You will investigate this further when you create a dynamic form.

Subform Instance Controls – Insert, Remove, Move object: This allows you to add a button to the form that enables the user to insert, remove, or move one line of a subform upon clicking. You will investigate this further when you create a dynamic form.

Survey Question object: This is a group of radio buttons that allows you to ask a survey question in the form.

US Social Security object: This allows you to add a field that is preconfigured to accept only U.S. Social Security numbers.

US States object: This allows you to insert a drop-down list prepopulated with U.S. states into your form.

Barcodes category

The Barcodes category (Figure 3-5) allows you to easily insert predefined bar codes into your form. Bar codes are used profusely throughout business processes and information exchanges globally.

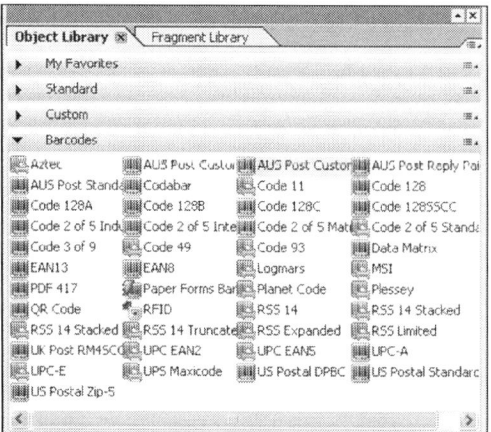

Figure 3-5. The Barcodes category in the Object Library palette contains predefined objects for bar codes.

Understanding content areas

Content areas provide a definition of the overall boundaries of your form layout area via anchor points.

For static and interactive forms, it's generally unnecessary to modify a content area. It is when you are designing dynamic flowable forms that these become very important.

Content areas are regular design objects and can be found in the Library palette.

Editing content area in master pages

Content areas are edited via the Master Pages tab of the layout editor. They are defined by a rectangle on the master page.

When a form is created in Adobe LiveCycle Designer ES, it is automatically assigned a default content area. Figure 3-6 shows the three-tab view of the design area, with the Master Pages view displaying in full. Note that the image that has been placed on the master page is replicated on the Design View tab and the Preview PDF tab, while the text object placed on the Design View tab is reflected only in the Preview PDF tab.

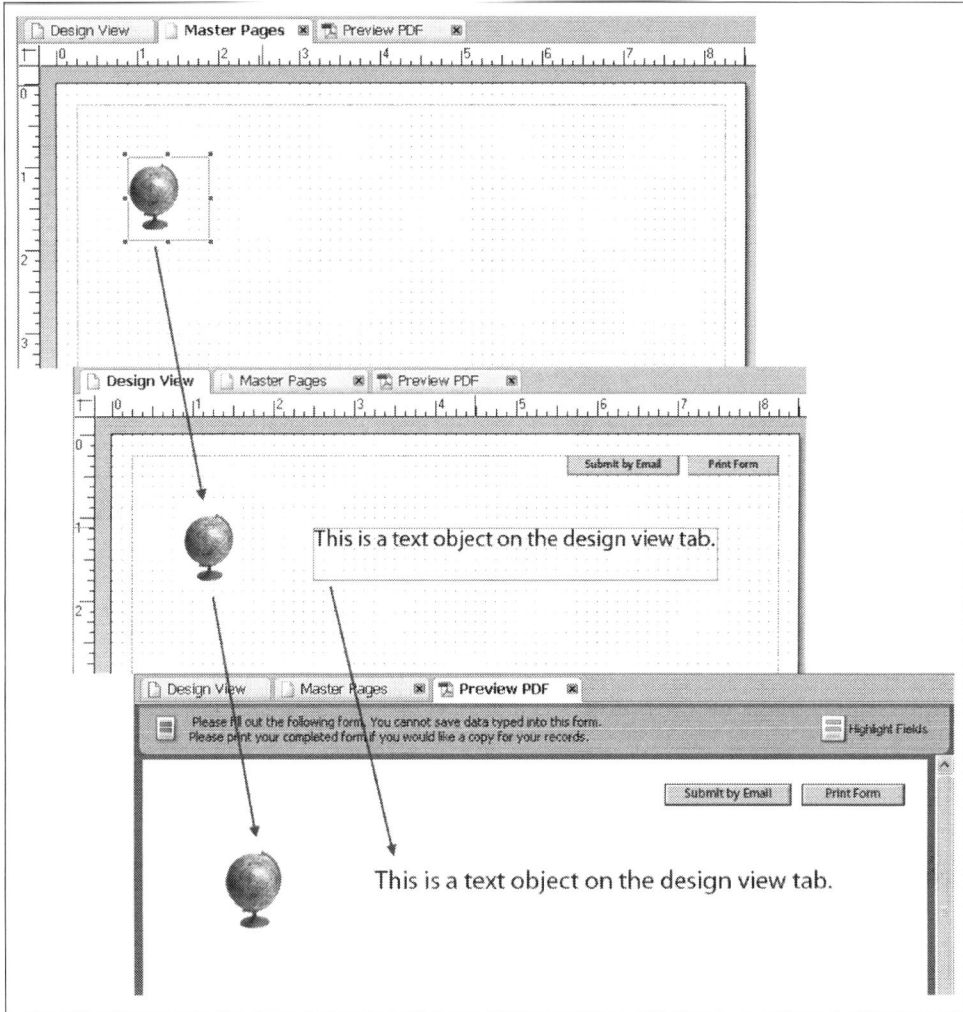

Figure 3-6. An object that has been placed on the master page also displays in the Design View and Preview PDF views.

Replicating design across multiple projects with templates

A **template** is a page that provides the basic form structure design. It's a premade layout, usually designed for specific purposes and themes, that has a set color scheme and outline. Adobe LiveCycle Designer ES contains a number of premade form templates that you can use to get started building forms quickly.

Templates contain form design page layouts and the objects used in the form's design. They differ from master pages in that they affect the unique form objects on the page, while the master page affects the overall look and feel of the page.

Templates allow you to specify form layout preferences and file settings such as headers and footers, embedded images and watermarks, and formulas and equations. Templates are timesavers and help ensure consistency across design, form objects, and user experience throughout your family of forms. The default templates in Adobe LiveCycle Design ES can be used as a premade form, or they can be customized with your information to create new forms.

Figure 3-7 illustrates the difference between a master page (left) and the form template (right). In a nutshell, templates are edited in the Design View area. They affect only one page of the form. Master pages possess design or field objects that can be edited only in the Master Pages view and can be applied to every page of your form.

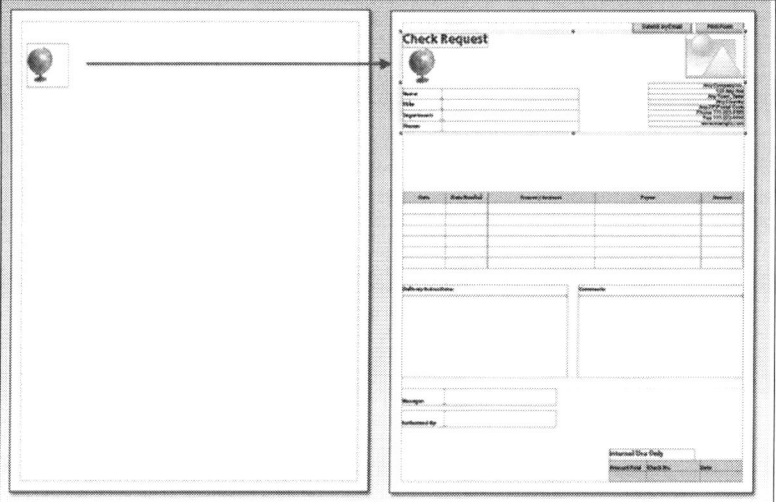

Figure 3-7. The master page and the form template of the same form

Understand the role of the Template Manager

The Template Manager contains sample templates that come with Adobe LiveCycle ES. Any templates you create are saved in the Template Manager. Designer templates are saved as TDS files. They can contain components such as layouts, formatting, scripts, and form settings.

Create a form based on a preexisting template

Building a template is similar to building a form design. In LiveCycle Designer, the New Form Assistant is the easiest way to create a new template. If you prefer not to use the assistant, select Tools ➤ Template Manager.

This opens the Template Manager dialog box where you can select the template you want to use. In the following exercise, you will use the New Form Assistant to create a personalized contact information form.

1. Open the New Form Assistant by selecting File ➤ New.

2. In the New Form Assistant dialog box, select the option Based on a Template, and click Next (see Figure 3-8).

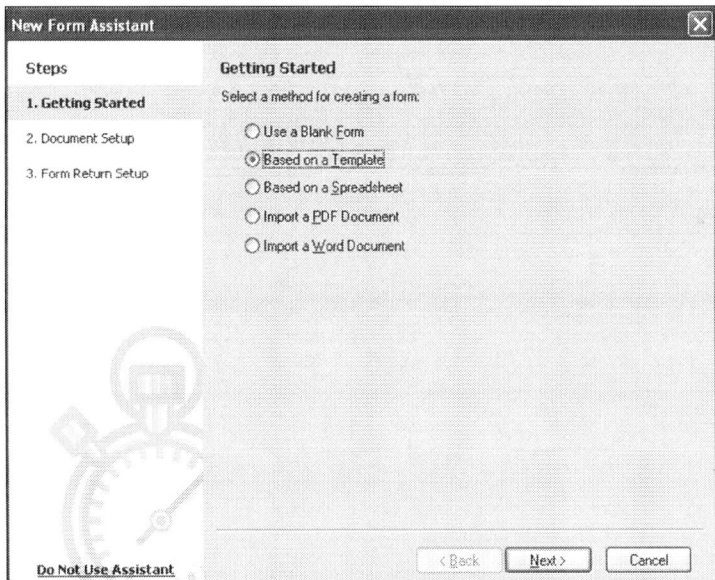

Figure 3-8. Building a form based on a template in the New Form Assistant

3. The second screen of the New Form Assistant offers a number of options. Here you can choose from a number of prebuilt templates that you can customize to suit your needs. Choose Contact Information, and click Next (see Figure 3-9).

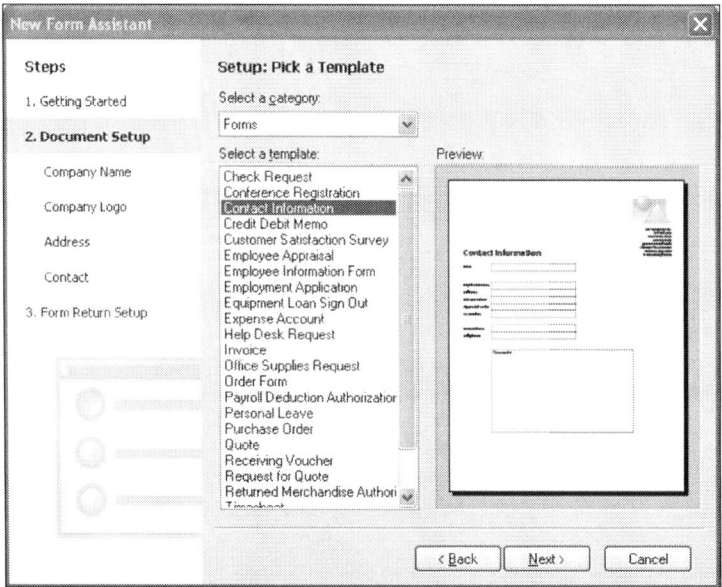

Figure 3-9. Choose Contact Information in the New Form Assistant.

4. On the Company Name screen, enter your company's name, and click Next (see Figure 3-10).

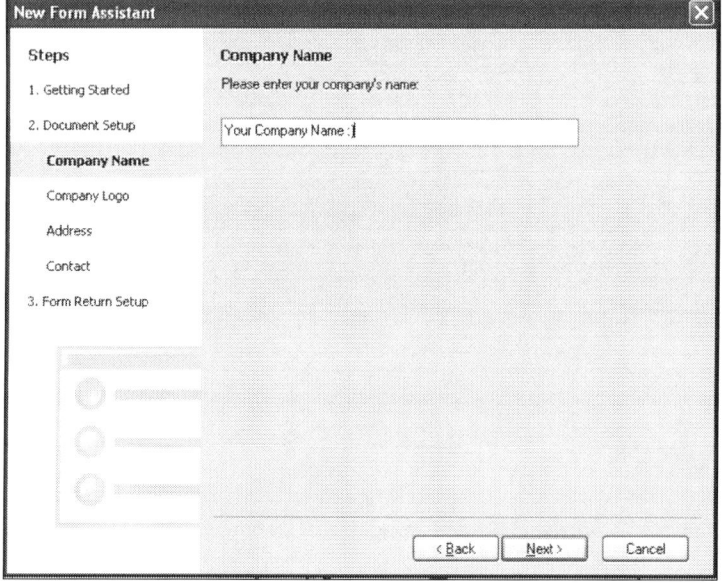

Figure 3-10. Enter your company name.

5. On the Company Logo screen, browse to where your logo is, and click Next (see Figure 3-11). If you choose not to upload a logo, the Adobe LiveCycle Designer ES default image will appear on your form.

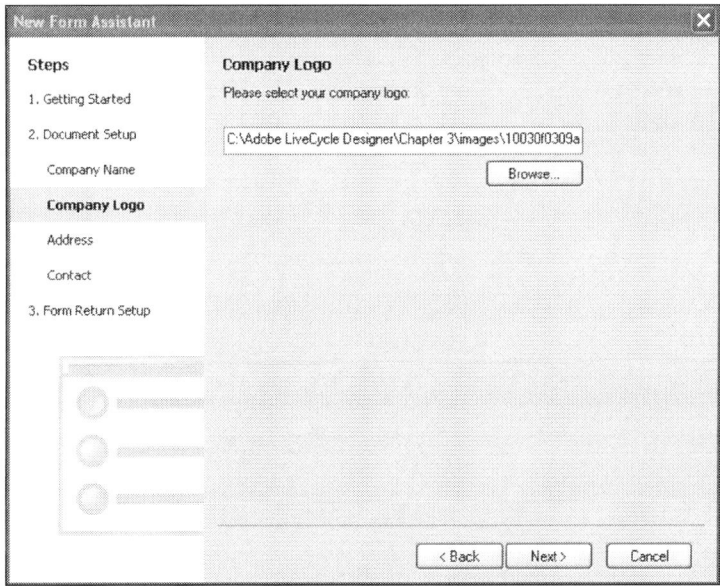

Figure 3-11. Upload your company logo.

6. On the Address screen, enter your company details (see Figure 3-12). This will appear in the masthead of your form design.

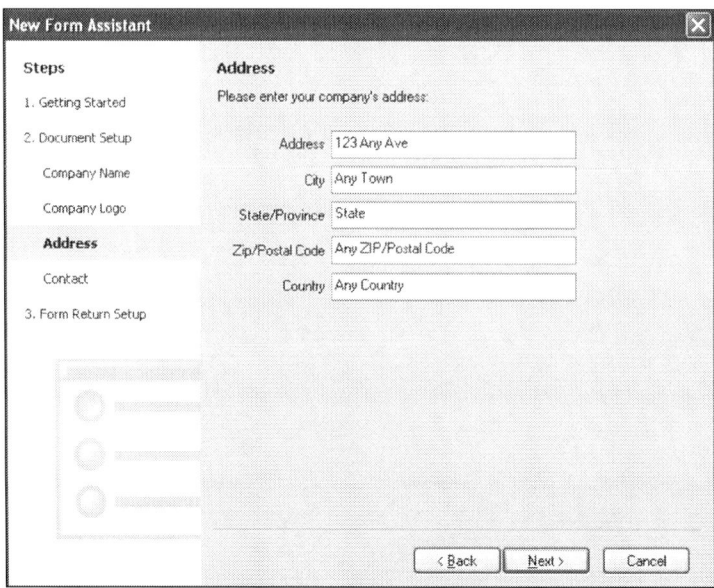

Figure 3-12. Enter your company's address details on the Address screen.

7. Finally, on the Contact screen, enter your telephone and website details (see Figure 3-13).

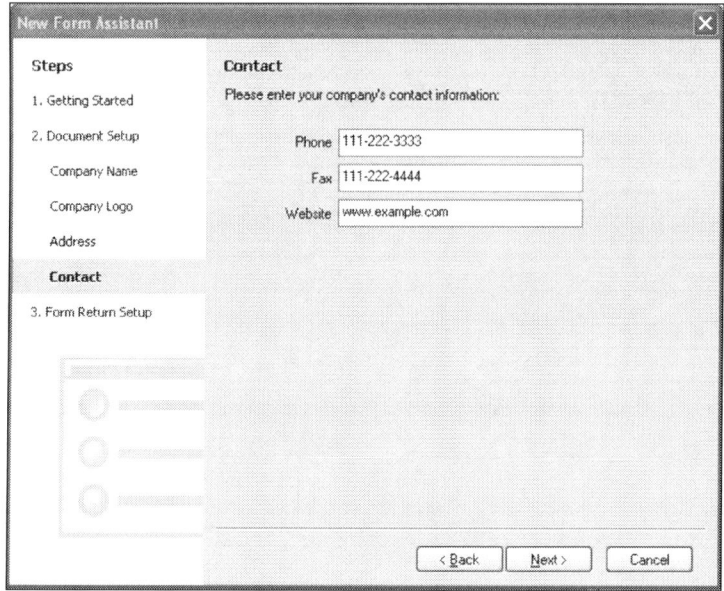

Figure 3-13. Enter your contact details.

8. The final step to setting up your form is to select the kinds of calls to action and buttons that you want on your form. Add an e-mail button, a print button, or both, and click Next (see Figure 3-14).

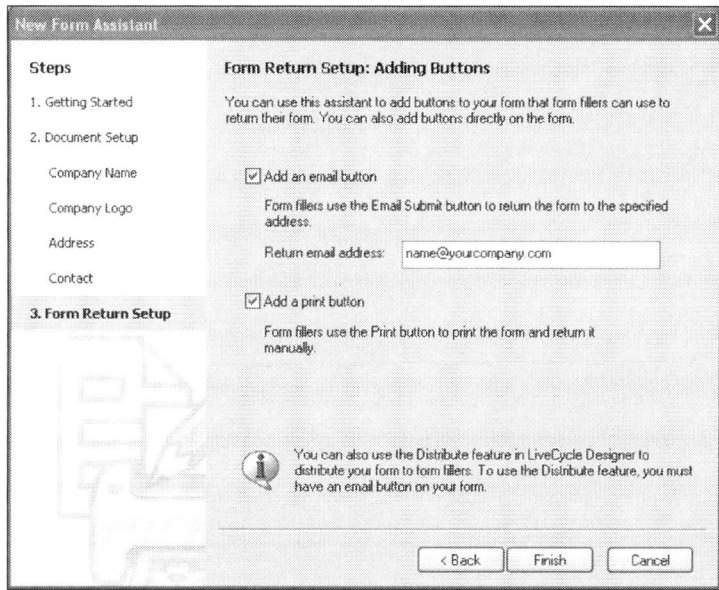

Figure 3-14. Adding buttons in the New Form Assistant

9. Your form template is now complete. You will see the finished product on the Design View tab. To save this as a template, select File ➤ Save As. In the Save as Type list in the dialog box, choose Adobe LiveCycle Designer ES Template (*.tds), and then click Save.

Using the Template Manager

As you saw when you were creating your customized contact details form in the previous exercise, Adobe LiveCycle Designer ES contains a variety of premade templates. These are saved in the Template Manager. You can also save any form templates that you create in the Template Manager.

Access a saved template

To access the Template Manager, open the New Form Assistant by selecting File ➤ New. Click the Do Not Use Assistant link at the bottom of the dialog box. The Template Manager will appear. Use the tabs at the top of the Template Manager to browse to the template on which you want to base your form (see Figure 3-15).

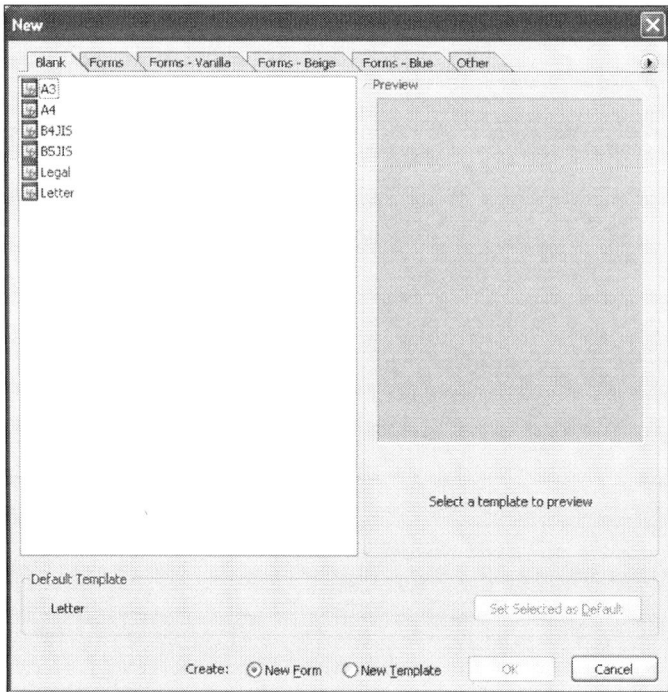

Figure 3-15. The Template Manager

Importing a template into the Template Manager

You can import any Adobe LiveCycle Designer ES template (TDS file) into the Template Manager. Doing this enables you to streamline your work process because the Template Manager enables you to move and categorize forms from a single dialog box.

Import a saved template

To import a template that you have created into the Template Manager, follow these steps:

1. Select File ➤ Open, and navigate to the template you want to open. Click Open.

2. In the Template Options dialog box, choose one of these options:

   - Select Edit This Template to edit the template in Adobe LiveCycle Designer ES.

   - Select Create A New Form Based On This Template to create a PDF form based on the template you are opening.

   - Select Copy This Template Into The Template Manager to add the template to the Template Manager (see Figure 3-16).

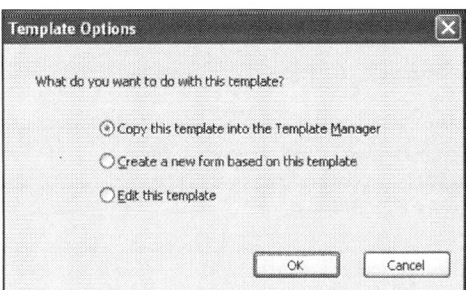

Figure 3-16. The Template Options dialog box enables you to copy templates into the Template Manager.

Defining a consistent look with master pages

Master pages are responsible for the overall layout and look and feel of your form. Every form contains at least one master page. They can provide the background, define content areas, and house the images and text that are required to display on every page. They are designed to house repetitive objects that you require on one or more pages of your form such as logos, headers, footers, page numbers, and date/time stamps.

A form has one or more master pages. You can apply a single master page to many forms. Refer to Figure 3-1 at the beginning of the chapter to see the difference between master pages and templates.

The Master Pages tab is hidden by default. To view it, select View ➤ Master Pages (see Figure 3-17).

Figure 3-17. The Master Pages tab is hidden by default.

Master pages are timesavers because they enable you to create a layout once and apply it to many pages.

Use the Master Pages tab to view, add, and delete master pages. You can also rename master pages, select the size and orientation of master pages, and reorder their sequence.

All new form designs are created with a default master page that is applied to the first page. Adobe LiveCycle Designer ES creates a blank master page for you by default. You create your own master pages when you have a specific look and feel in mind for your form design. Unless you create a new master page, all the pages of the form will be based on the default. If most of the pages in your form design require a certain amount of standardized or fixed content, you can place that content on master pages to provide a consistent background and make editing easier. For example, you can arrange text, images, and geometric shapes on a master page to have them appear in the same location on multiple pages.

We will learn more about master pages in Chapter 4.

Fragments

Adobe LiveCycle Designer ES has a range of tools such as **form fragments**, which allow you to maintain consistency throughout your form.

A form fragment is a piece of a form you can reuse. You can create a form fragment by selecting the part of the form that you want to preserve to use on other forms and saving it as an XPD file. Adobe LiveCycle Designer ES allows you to import the XPD format into other form designs.

Create a form fragment

To create a form fragment, follow these steps:

1. Select a number of objects on your form by holding Shift down and clicking each object you want to select.

2. Right-click the objects, and select Fragments ➤ Create Fragment (see Figure 3-18).

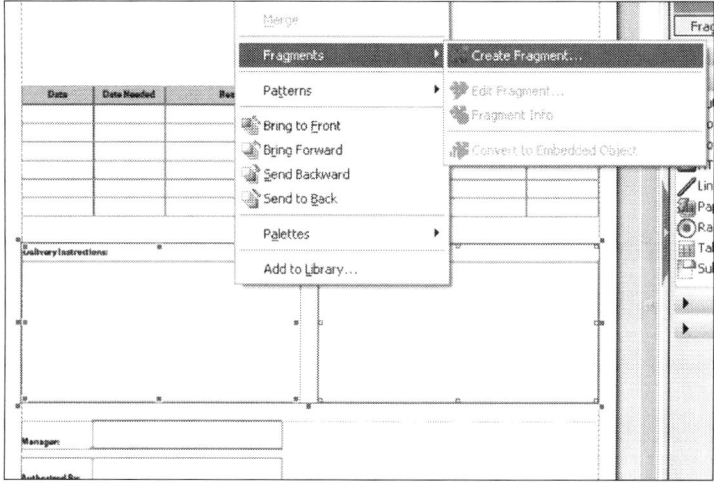

Figure 3-18. Creating form fragments in LiveCycle Designer

3. Accept the default name, or specify a new name for your fragment in the Name box.

4. Choose the method to save your fragment. You can opt to select an XPD file that is saved into the Fragment Library or to select Create New Fragment in Current Document to save the form fragment in the current file (see Figure 3-19).

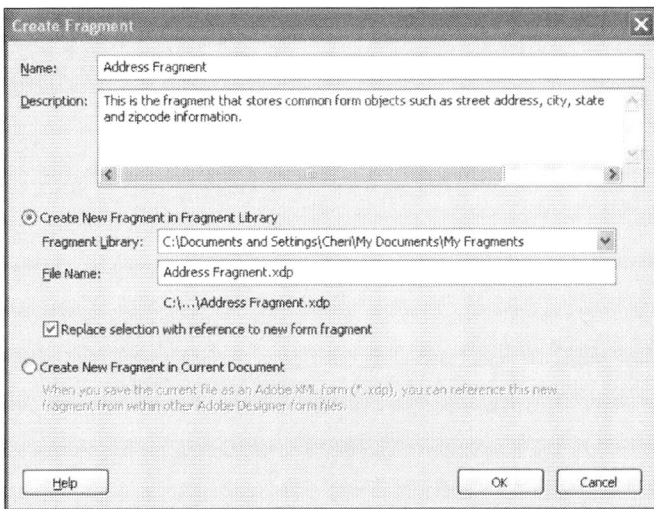

Figure 3-19. The Create Fragment dialog box

Setting common fragments within your forms means you have to update only the master fragment. All forms that reference that fragment will automatically be updated.

Learning about body pages

Body pages are the blank canvas on which you build your form. They are the extant functioning pages of the form. Most of the form objects that are relevant to a particular form are housed on body pages.

Just as master pages dictate the layout and background, body pages dictate its functioning. Each body page contains a subform that covers the entire page by default (see Figure 3-20).

Figure 3-20. A body page is the blank canvas on which your form is built.

Summary

In this chapter, you learned about the building blocks of forms, from integrated form components such as templates and master pages to objects that are the individual form building blocks.

You now know the difference between templates and master pages, and I have demonstrated the way they can streamline and standardize your form-making processes.

In Chapter 4, you will design forms using these components and learn how to edit and manipulate them to build truly powerful and integrated forms.

Chapter 4

LEARNING THE FUNDAMENTALS OF DESIGNING FORMS

Now that you are acquainted with the basic form components, you will move onto actively working with these components. This chapter will step you through the fundamentals of designing forms; creating and opening them; using the Template Manager, expanding on what you learned about it in Chapter 3; and opening and manipulating existing templates. Along the way, you will investigate useful tools such as the Hierarchy palette and ways to manipulate different form objects. These objects are the basis for more sophisticated form building.

Creating, opening, saving forms

When Adobe LiveCycle Designer ES launches, the Welcome to Adobe LiveCycle Designer dialog box (see Figure 4-1) appears and offers you three options for creating and opening forms.

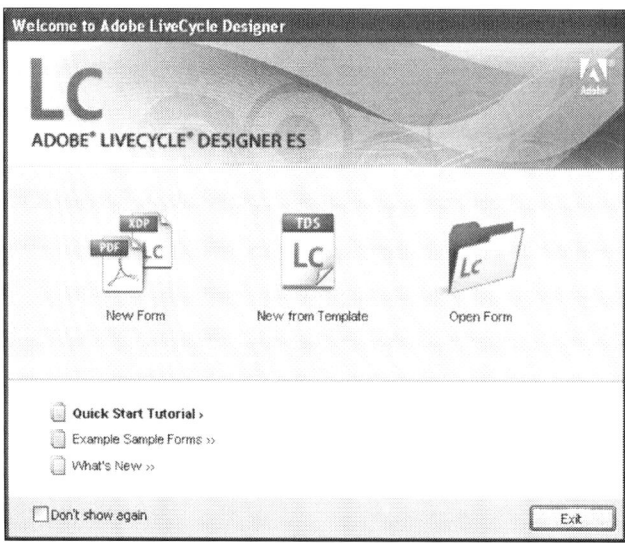

Figure 4-1. The Welcome to Adobe LiveCycle Designer dialog box

Creating and opening forms

If you choose either New Form or New from Template, the New Form Assistant will appear and guide you through the steps to opening a form (see Figure 4-1). If you choose Open, a dialog box will open that allows you to browse to the form you want to open on your computer or network.

You can also choose not to have the welcome screen display by checking the Don't Show Again box or elect to begin the Quick Start Tutorial, view some example sample forms, or find out the latest developments in LiveCycle Designer.

Saving forms

If you are operating LiveCycle Designer as a stand-alone application, you can save your form design as an Adobe static PDF document (.pdf), an Adobe dynamic XML form (.pdf), an Adobe XML form (.xpd), or an Adobe LiveCycle Designer template (.tds). In the coming chapters, I will define when you should use each type of file.

Save a form

To save a form, follow these steps:

1. Choose File ➤ Save As.
2. Browse to the location you want to save the file.
3. Name your file.
4. Decide the file format to save your form as.
5. Click Save.

Working with the Template Manager

As touched upon in Chapter 3, templates are the form elements that provide the overall structure of the form. You work with templates via the Template Manager. You probably encounter form templates in many facets of your everyday life. For example, consider the forms you might encounter at the Department of Motor Vehicles. They have many forms, but all of them require the same basic details such as your name and contact details. These forms, though they are all essentially for different purposes, may have been derived from the same template.

The Template Manager is preloaded with a number of LiveCycle Designer sample templates. Templates that you create can also be saved in the Template Manager for easy access when you want to use them.

You use the Template Manager to preview templates and to select the templates on which you want to base your form design. You can also rename, add, and delete templates and groups through the Template Manager.

To access the Template Manager, select Tools ➤ Template Manager. Alternatively, you can begin to use templates by selecting New from Template from the Welcome to Adobe LiveCycle Designer dialog box.

Using the Template Manager menu

The Template Manager menu (Figure 4-2) allows you to manipulate templates without having to browse to their locations on your computer.

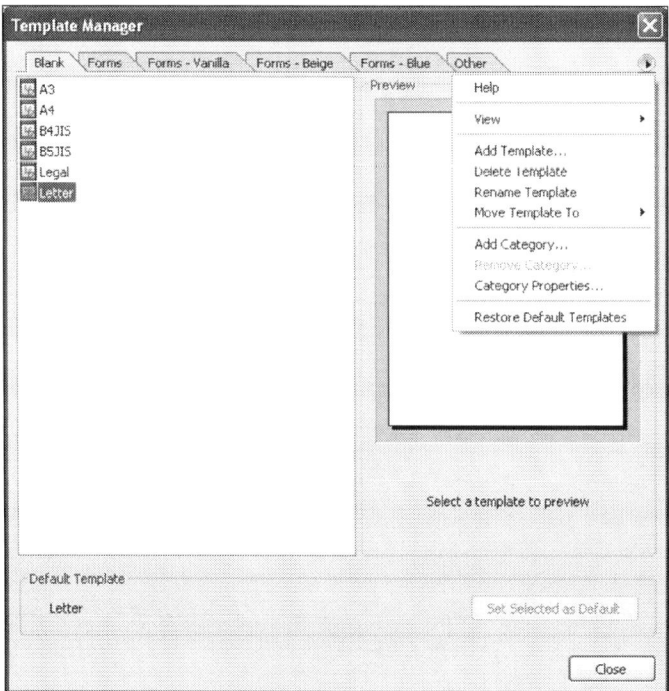

Figure 4-2. The Template Manager menu

View: This allows you to select how you want the templates to display within the manager. Selecting View ➤ List displays the templates as a list, and selecting View ➤ Large Icons displays fewer templates in the manager but larger and clearer icons.

Add Template: This allows you browse to a template to add it to the manager.

Delete Template: This allows you to delete a template from the Template Manager and your computer.

Rename Template: This allows you to change the name of a selected template.

Move Template To: This allows you to move templates between the tabs of the Template Manager.

Add Category: This allows you to add and name a new tab in the Template Manager.

Remove Category: This allows you to remove a tab from the Template Manager.

Template Category Properties: This allows you to rename a template category and change its location on your computer.

Working with existing templates

To create a form from an existing template, follow these steps:

1. Select File ➤ New. The New Form Assistant will open.
2. Select the Based on a Template Option for creating your form.
3. Select the Employment Application form template (see Figure 4-3).

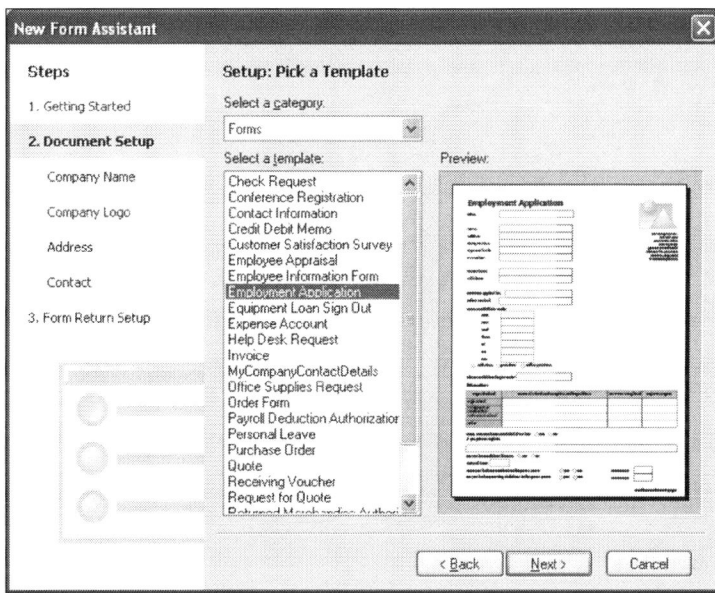

Figure 4-3. Previewing the Employment Application template in the New Form Assistant

4. Follow the prompts to enter your information into the template.
5. Click Finish on the final screen, and your Employment Application form will open in Design View, as shown in Figure 4-4.

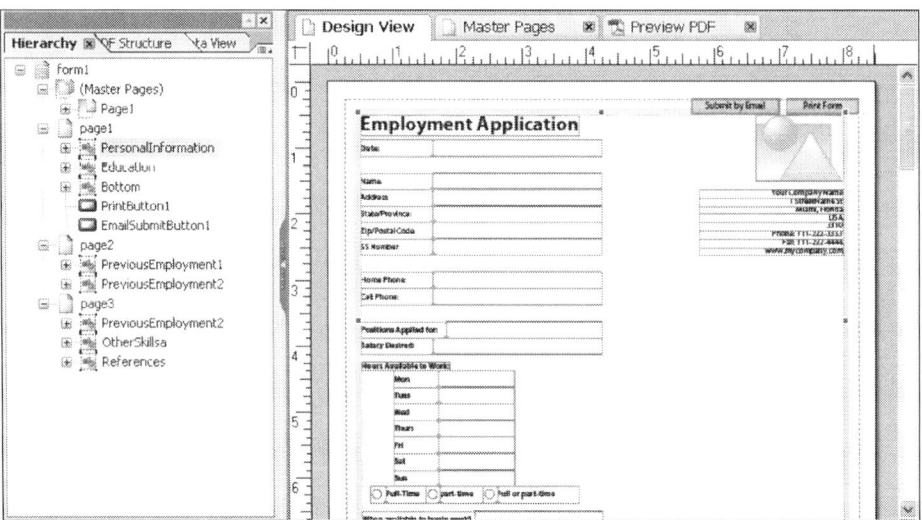

Figure 4-4. The Employment Application template in Design View

You have opened the Employment Application template. Now you can add, move, and remove objects on the page to further customize the template to your needs.

To save the employment application as a form, follow these steps:

1. Choose File ➤ Save As.

2. Browse to the location you want to save the file. In this case, I suggest creating a LiveCycle Test folder on your local drive.

3. Name your file.

4. At the Save as type prompt, choose to save the form as an Adobe static PDF (.pdf).

5. Click Save.

You opted to save the file as a static PDF form because the user options are only Print and Email. When the data submission process becomes more sophisticated and utilizes databases or web services, the other save options become applicable.

Working with form properties, information, defaults, and options

Form properties define certain traits, aspects, and behaviors of your form. In the following sections, you will learn how to set properties in the Form Properties dialog box. This is particularly important because though form properties are not shared with the user, from a form designer perspective it is immensely helpful to be able to view information about the form, such as when it was created, why it was created, and who created it.

You can change form properties in the Form Properties dialog box. To access this dialog box, select File ➤ Form Properties.

The Form Properties dialog box contains nine tabs that allow you to manipulate your form's settings:

- Information tab
- Defaults tab
- Performance tab
- PDF Security tab
- PDF Print Options tab
- Compatibility tab
- Preview tab
- Save Options tab
- Variables tab

Information tab

The Information tab allows you to enter information about the form (see Figure 4-5). Here you can add a description; update the author, department, and contact details; and update the date and version information. You can also change the name of the file and the title of the form. You are also able to enter the date the form was created and who created it.

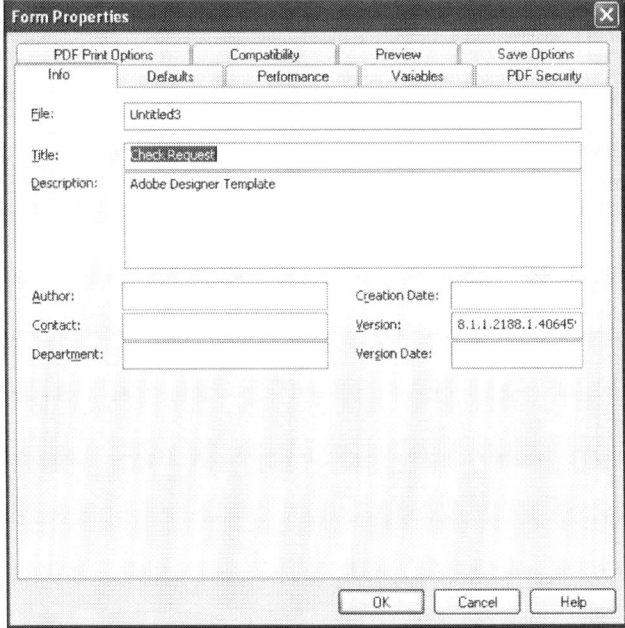

Figure 4-5. Updating the Information tab

Defaults tab

The Defaults tab (see Figure 4-6) is where you can specify standard settings and override default settings.

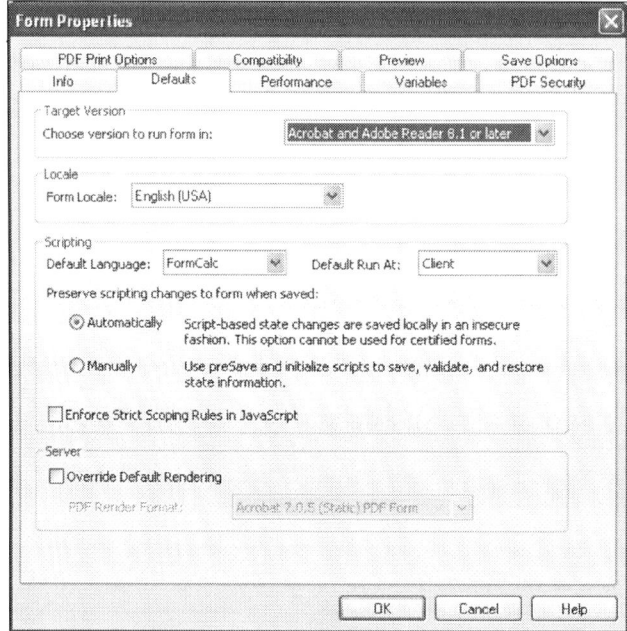

Figure 4-6. Changing and specifying form defaults on the Defaults tab

The Target Version section allows you to choose in which version of Adobe Acrobat and Acrobat Reader the form will run. As you create your form, Adobe LiveCycle Designer ES continually validates the form against the target Adobe default. Ensure that you have the same Adobe Reader software installed as the target version, or you will get errors when you preview the form on the Preview PDF tab.

Performance tab

The Performance tab allows you to designate print caching options, which will improve server-side processing and the print performance and server properties of your form. Be aware that selecting too many print options makes your form file size larger, which can degrade client-side performance.

Selecting Allow Form Rendering To Be Cached on Server (see Figure 4-7) improves performance by caching a PDF form on the server and reusing it for subsequent renderings.

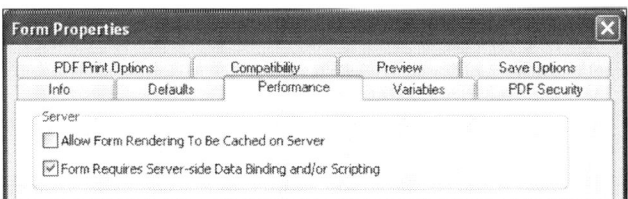

Figure 4-7. Specifying performance options

Form Requires Server-side Data Binding and/or Scripting should be selected only when the form includes database or web service binding and server-side scripting.

PDF Security tab

The PDF Security tab allows you to change the security settings of your form by setting passwords on features such as printing and allowing users to modify the PDF form. This tab enables you to disable form features such as printing, requiring a password to open (as shown in Figure 4-8), allowing comments and signatures, and preventing the copying of text and images. It is important to note that changing PDF features such as copying can impact the accessibility of a form. You will investigate passwords in depth in Chapter 5.

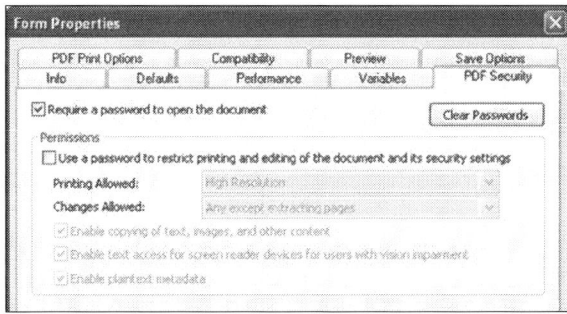

Figure 4-8. Specifying password requirements

Printing Options tab

The PDF Print Options tab (as shown in Figure 4-9) is where you set printing properties for your form design. You are able to specify that a print screen opens when the form launches to prompt users to print it immediately upon opening, to enable duplex printing, and to specify the number of copies that are printed by default as well as to set default printers on a network.

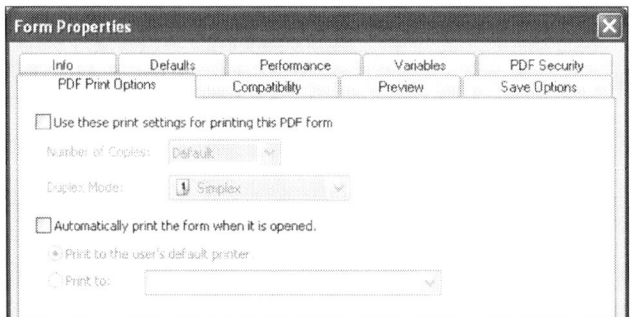

Figure 4-9. Choosing default printing options

Compatibility tab

This tab allows you to update forms that were created in an earlier version of Adobe LiveCycle Designer ES. Updating forms may result in the copy format changing. The form Compatibility tab (as shown in Figure 4-10) offers options to automatically correct this for you.

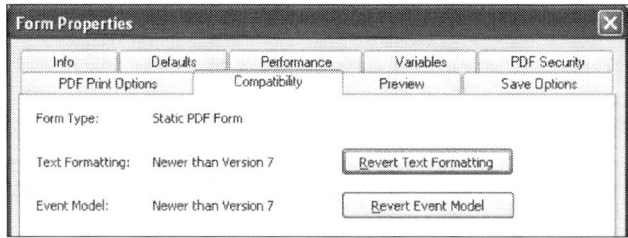

Figure 4-10. Updating text between LiveCycle Designer versions

The Text Formatting section of the Form Compatibility tab allows you to update text formatting to newer than Adobe LiveCycle Designer ES 7.0 or revert it to an earlier edition.

The Event Model section of the tab allows you to ensure that there are no event conflicts between the version of LiveCycle Designer the form was created in and the version it is being opened in.

Preview tab

The Preview tab (shown in Figure 4-11) offers options for previewing your form on the PDF Preview tab. You can preview it as an interactive form, a one-sided or two-sided print form, a static PDF form, or a dynamic XML form.

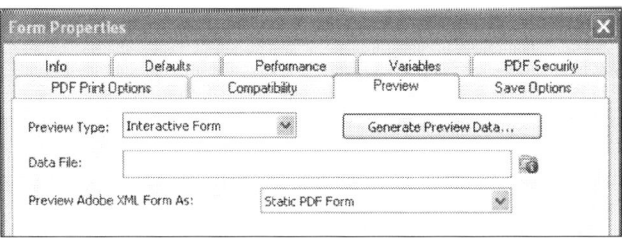

Figure 4-11. The Preview tab

Save Options tab

The Save Options tab (see Figure 4-12) allows you to specify the manner in which your PDF form is saved: as a static PDF form (.pdf) or a dynamic XML form (.pdf). Saving the form as a static PDF form renders it one time only. It is viewed in Adobe Reader. If you save a dynamic form as a static PDF form, it will be rendered as static and will no longer display dynamic behavior. Static PDF forms can be both interactive and noninteractive.

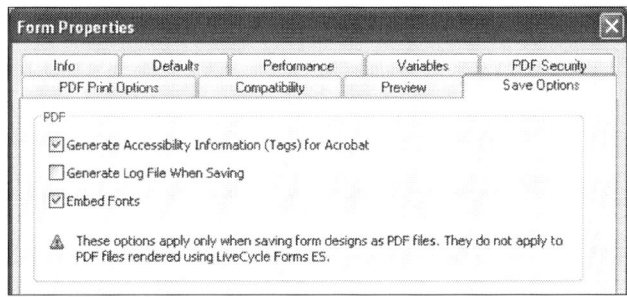

Figure 4-12. The PDF Save Options tab

Saving the form as a dynamic PDF preserves any expandable and flowable behavior in the form design.

Form Variables tab

The Variables tab (as shown in Figure 4-13) is where you are able to add, rename, and delete form variables. A **variable** is a proxy for information that can be changed or updated in the future. Unlike other scripts, variables are not defined in the Script Editor. Scripting variables are defined in the Script Editor and are created in JavaScript or FormCalc scripts. You will learn about this in Chapter 6.

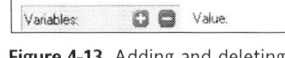

Figure 4-13. Adding and deleting variables in the Variables tab

Working with master and body pages

As we learned in Chapter 3, master pages define the background and layout of your form. Every form contains at least one master page. They can provide the background, define content areas, and house images and text that that are required to display on every page, allowing body pages to house working form fields.

A good way to think of master pages is to envisage a company's letterhead. Every letter sent by that company may be different, but they possess the same elements in the same places such as the company logo, address, and contact details.

In the same way, you can apply a single master page to many forms.

Adding master pages

You can add master pages by using the Hierarchy palette or the Insert menu. The Hierarchy palette is displayed on the left side of the screen. If you cannot see it, select Windows ➤ Hierarchy.

To add a master page, right-click the Master Pages node in the Hierarchy palette, and choose New Master Page, as shown in Figure 4-14.

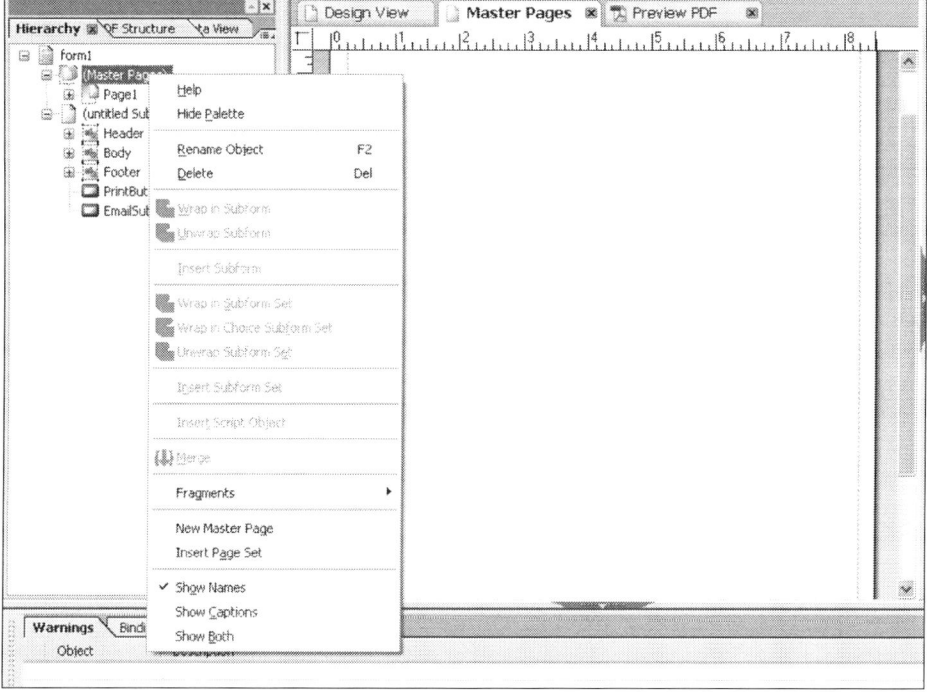

Figure 4-14. Hierarchy palette

Editing master pages

Master pages are edited in the Master Page tab of the layout area. If you do not specify a master page, Adobe LiveCycle Designer ES automatically applies a default master page to your form.

Apply an image and footer

In this exercise, you will edit the master page of the contact details form you created earlier in this chapter. You will apply an image and footer to this template. Follow these steps:

1. Open the Contact Details template through the New Form Assistant.

2. Click the Master Page tab in the layout area. The Contact Details master page is an Adobe LiveCycle Designer default master page, as shown in Figure 4-15.

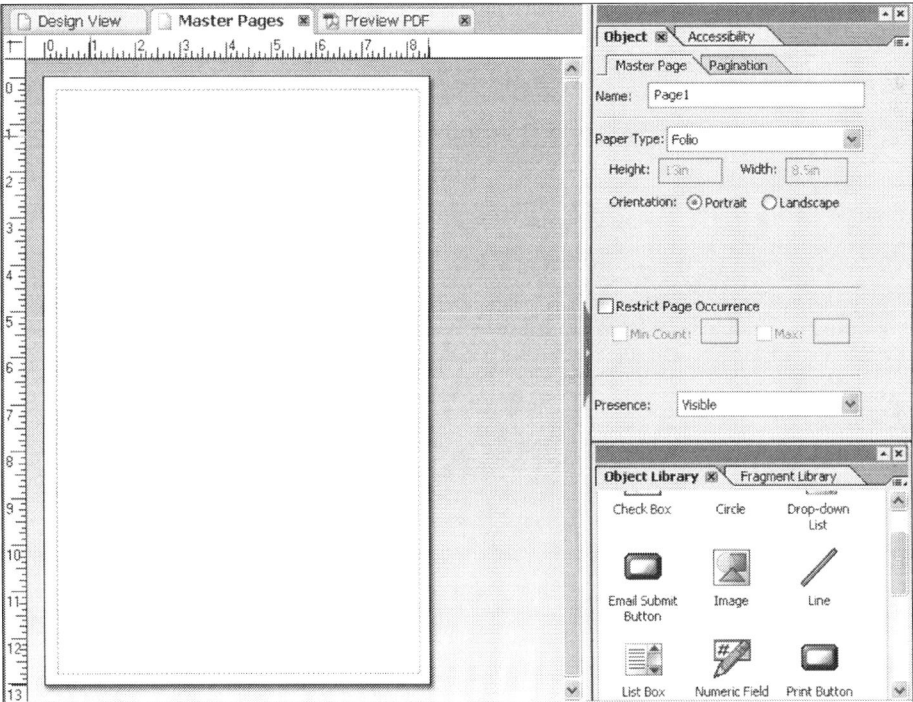

Figure 4-15. The master page of the Contact Details form

3. Locate the image object in the Object Library palette, and drag it into the master page. Position it in the upper-left corner.

4. Double-click the image object on the master page, and browse to the image you want inserted into the form.

5. Locate the Text object in the Object Library palette, and drag it into the master page. Position it at the bottom of the page in the center. Double-click the Text object to change the text. Type the words **The very best of the very best** in the text field.

6. Click the Design View tab. Your form will display with the image and the footer, as shown in Figure 4-16.

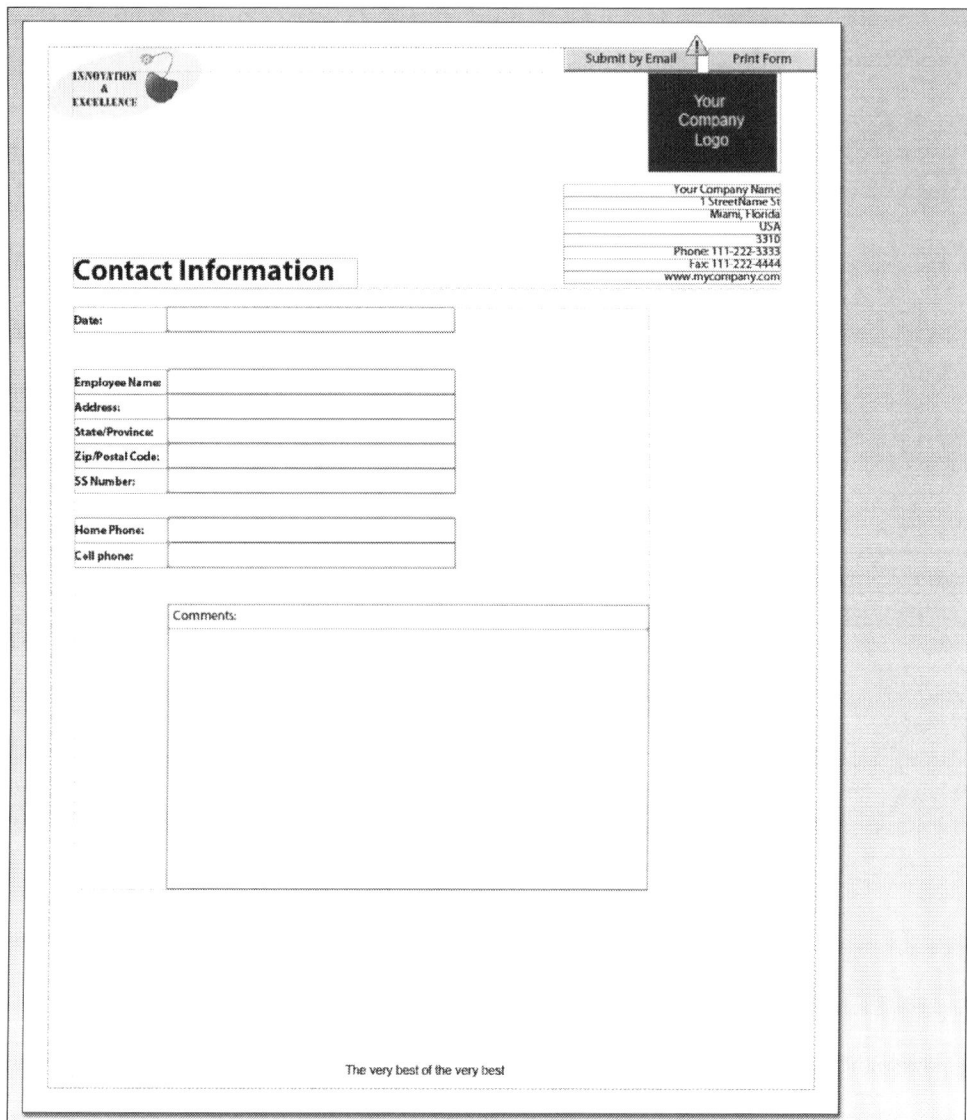

Figure 4-16. Contact information form with image and footer displayed from master page

Using body pages in your form

Body pages are the actual working pages of the form. They contain all the form objects that are relevant to a particular page. Master pages dictate the layout and background of your body pages.

As noted in Chapter 3, it can be helpful to think of a body page as a blank canvas. The artist or form designer then chooses objects to appear on the body pages that will become the form.

Each body page contains a subform that covers the entire page by default. A subform defines the form objects' positioning on the body page; this will be expanded on in Chapter 6.

You can view and edit your body pages in Design View.

Adding and deleting body pages

Body pages can be added and deleted via the Hierarchy palette or the Insert menu.

To add a body page, right-click the Body Page node in the Hierarchy palette and choose New Page.

To delete a body page, you can simply right-click anywhere on the page in the layout area and select Delete, or you can right-click the Body Page node in the Hierarchy palette and choose Delete.

Renaming body pages

Adobe LiveCycle Designer ES automatically assigns default names to your body pages. The default name is (untitled Subform) (page 1) for page 1, (untitled Subform) (page 2) for page 2, and so on. These names can be confusing and unintuitive when dealing with forms that contain many pages. You can rename a body page in Adobe LiveCycle Designer ES in two ways.

Renaming body pages in the Hierarchy palette

To rename a body page in the Hierarchy palette as shown in Figure 4-17, follow these steps:

1. Right-click the page node, and select Rename Object.

2. Enter the chosen name for your page.

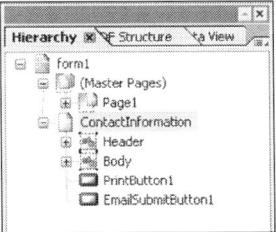

Figure 4-17. Renaming body pages in the Hierarchy palette

When you rename a page, spaces are not allowed.

Renaming body pages in Design View

To rename a body page in Design View, follow these steps:

1. Ensure that the Design View tab is selected.

2. Click anywhere in the page layout.

3. Click the Binding tab in the Object palette.

4. Rename your page in the Name field, as shown in Figure 4-18.

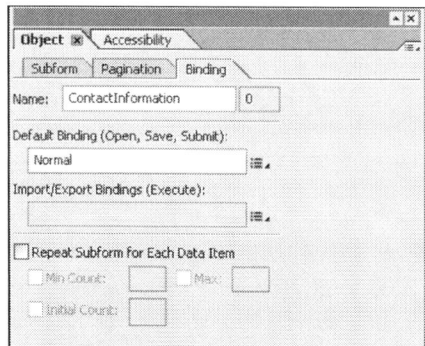

Figure 4-18. Renaming body pages on the Binding tab of the Object palette

Moving between and reordering body pages

Adobe LiveCycle Designer ES has a number of simple and user-friendly ways that you can use to navigate within forms that have multiple pages.

Moving between body pages

To move between body pages of forms that consist of multiple pages, simply use the scrollbar in Design View to scroll up and down to the required page. You can also jump to the required page by clicking on its node in the Hierarchy palette.

Reordering body pages

Adobe LiveCycle Designer ES allows you to reorder body pages in forms that have two or more pages by a simple drag-and-drop method in the Hierarchy palette. Specifically, to reorder pages in a form, simply select the subform of the page that you want to move in the Hierarchy palette and drag it to the desired position.

Setting the tabbing order

The tabbing order is one of the final tasks you need to complete when you are creating your form. You leave it until the final step of your form design to prevent having to set the tabbing order more than once. As you design your form, you may want to change object placement, and this affects tabbing order.

In the following exercise, you'll change the tabbing order so that the Employee Information heading is the first in the tabbing order and the Person to Notify fields are immediately after the employee contact details.

Set the tabbing order

To set the tabbing order, follow these steps:

1. Select View ➤ Tabbing Order. The default tabbing order will appear, as shown in Figure 4-19.

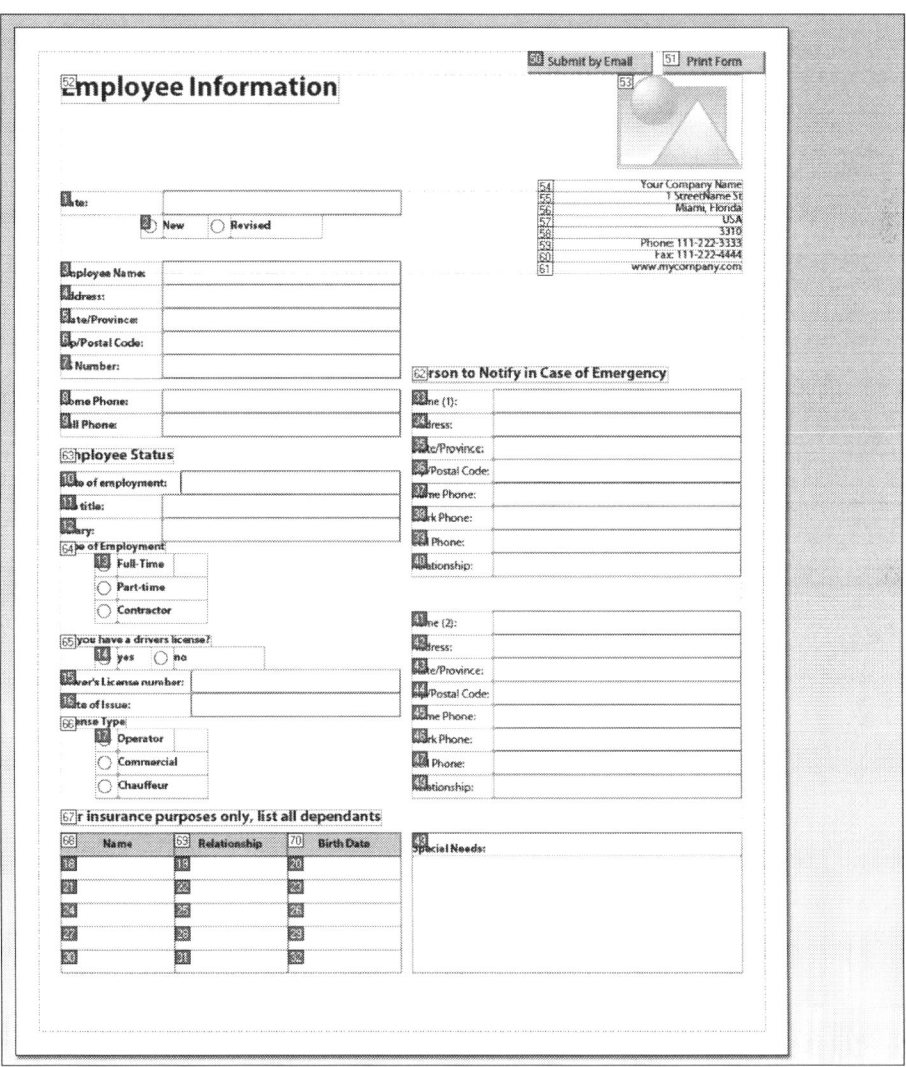

Figure 4-19. The employee information default tabbing order

2. Designate the Employee Information heading as first in the tabbing order by clicking it once. Notice that the tabbing order for the other objects then change, as shown in Figure 4-20.

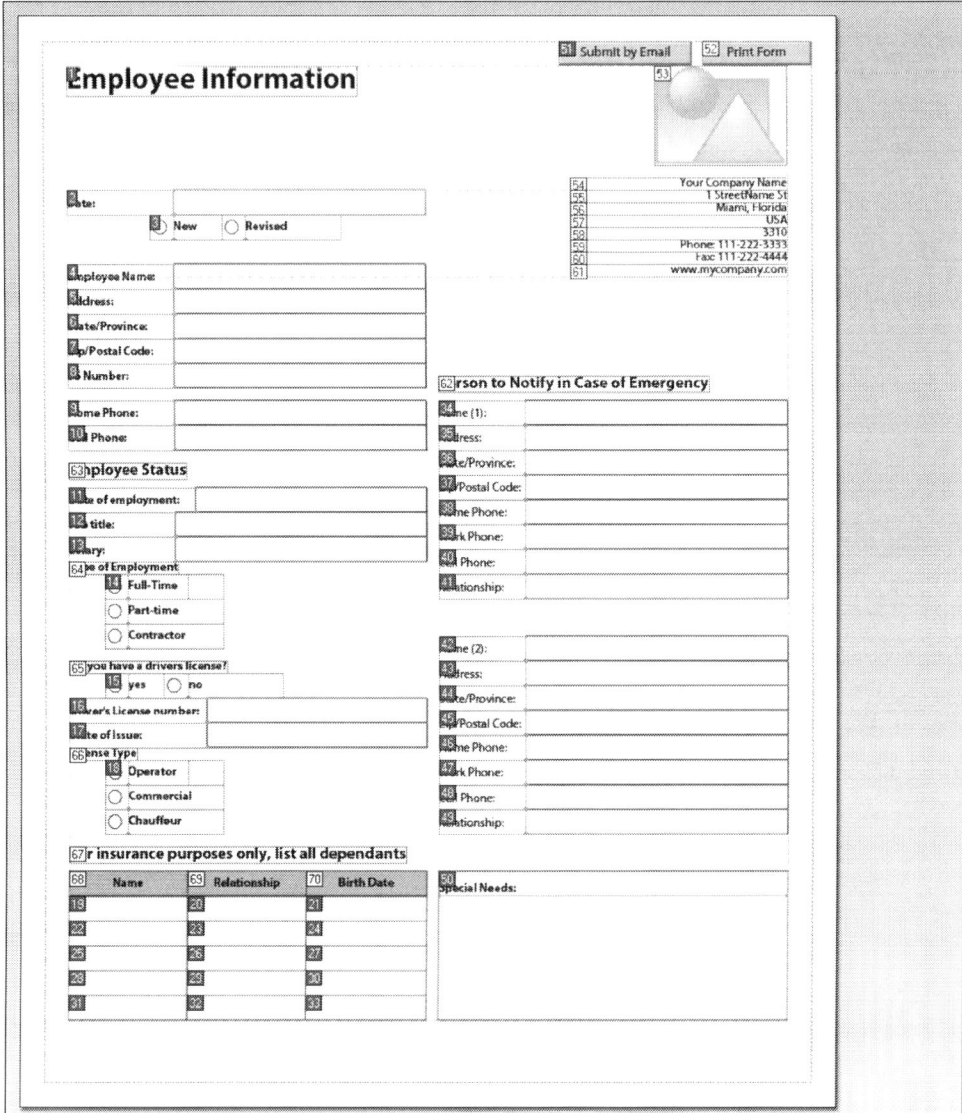

Figure 4-20. The form is updated to reflect the Employee Information heading as the first in the tabbing order.

3. Click the rest of the fields in the following order:

   a. Date

   b. New

   c. Employee Name

   d. Address

   e. State/Province

   f. Zip/Postal Code

   g. Home Phone

   h. Cell Phone

   You will not have seen any numbers changing on the fields.

4. Click Person to Notify In Case of Emergency. You will see that it is renumbered to 11, yet its following fields remain out of order.

   When you have renumbered all objects on the page, it will display as shown in Figure 4-21.

5. Click the remaining fields under Person to Notify in Case of Emergency until all the fields are in order.

6. When you are satisfied with the tabbing order, select View ➤ Tab Order to close the Tab Order view.

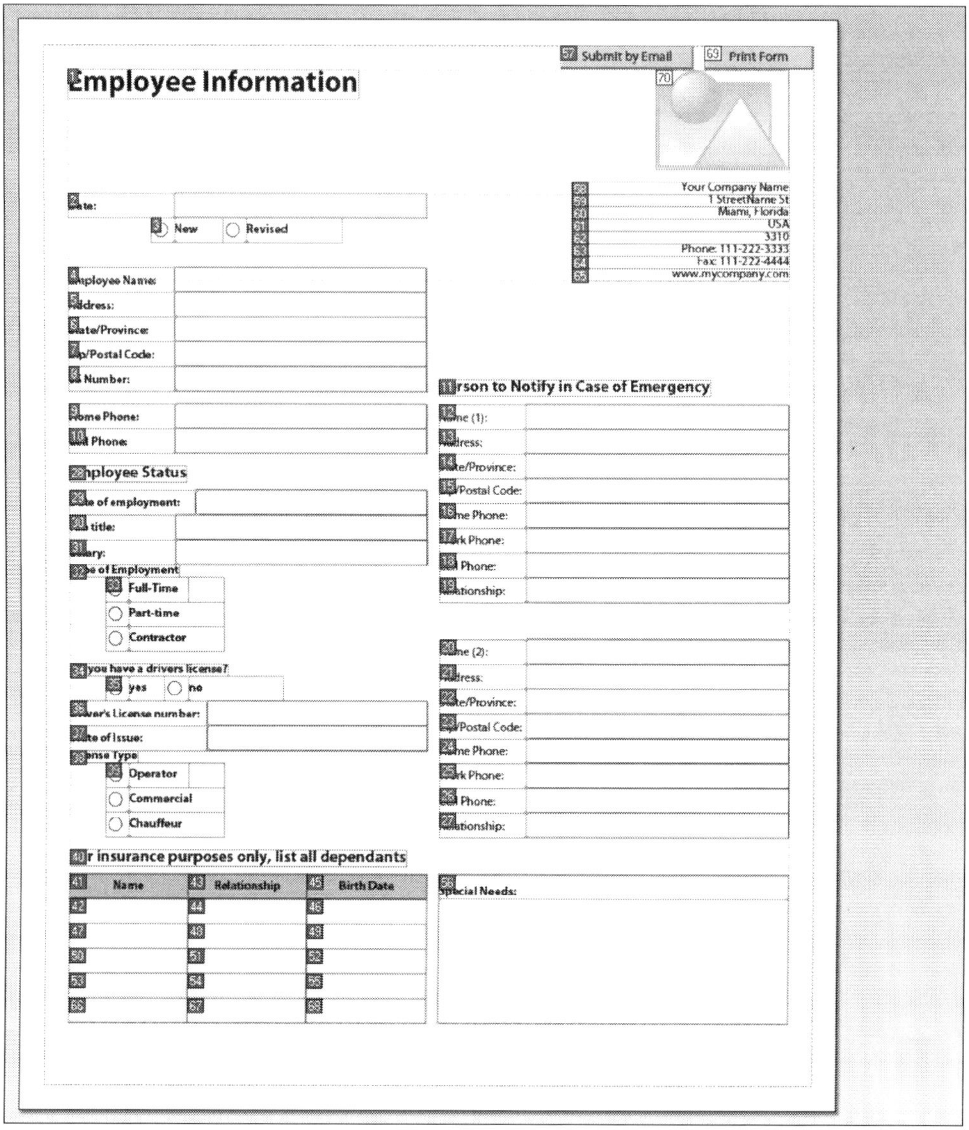

Figure 4-21. Changing the tabbing order

Manipulating objects

As you learned in Chapter 3, the fundamental building blocks of every form build are objects.

Objects are small, individual, functional components in a form and fulfill a number of functions, such as a place to enter text, a drop-down list from which to choose a selection, or a button to email the form to the form designer. Form objects are generally added to the body pages; however, if the object is going to be used in every page of the form or needs to be placed in a specific area, consider adding it to the master page of the form.

Each object provides some piece of functionality to your form, such as a place to enter text or a button to email the form. As you create your form, you select objects and add them to the body or master page of the form design. You will find all the available objects in the Object Library palette.

You will now build a basic contact form with objects and then manipulate those objects to make the form both intuitive and functional.

To begin, create a new blank form using the New Form Assistant. A blank form displaying only Submit by Email and Print Form buttons will be displayed.

Inserting objects

You can insert an object via drag and drop or the Insert menu. You will insert objects via drag and drop in this exercise.

Insert a drop-down list

To insert a drop-down list, follow these steps:

1. Drag a Drop-down list object onto the Design View of the layout area.
2. In the Object palette, rename the caption to Title.
3. Click the green + sign, and enter **Mr** in the text box that appears. Press Enter, and add the following to the text boxes that follow: **Mrs**, **Miss**, **Ms**, and **Dr**, as shown in Figure 4-22.
4. Click the layout area to close the Object palette for the drop-down list.

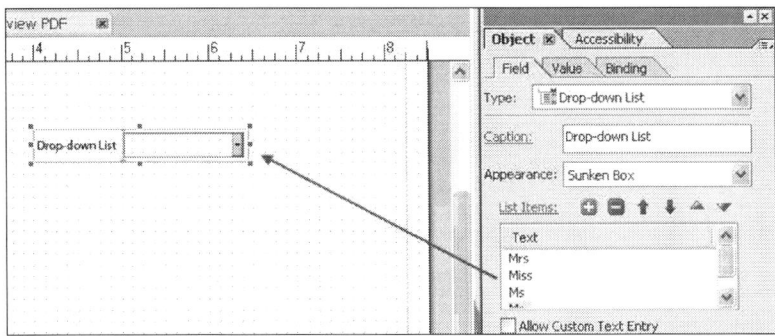

Figure 4-22. Using the Object palette to add options to a drop-down list

Insert a text field

To insert text fields, follow these steps:

1. Drag a Text Field object to Design View.

2. In the Object palette, rename the caption to **First Name**.

3. Click the layout area to close the Object palette.

4. Repeat this for the fields Last Name and Email.

Your form should now look like Figure 4-23.

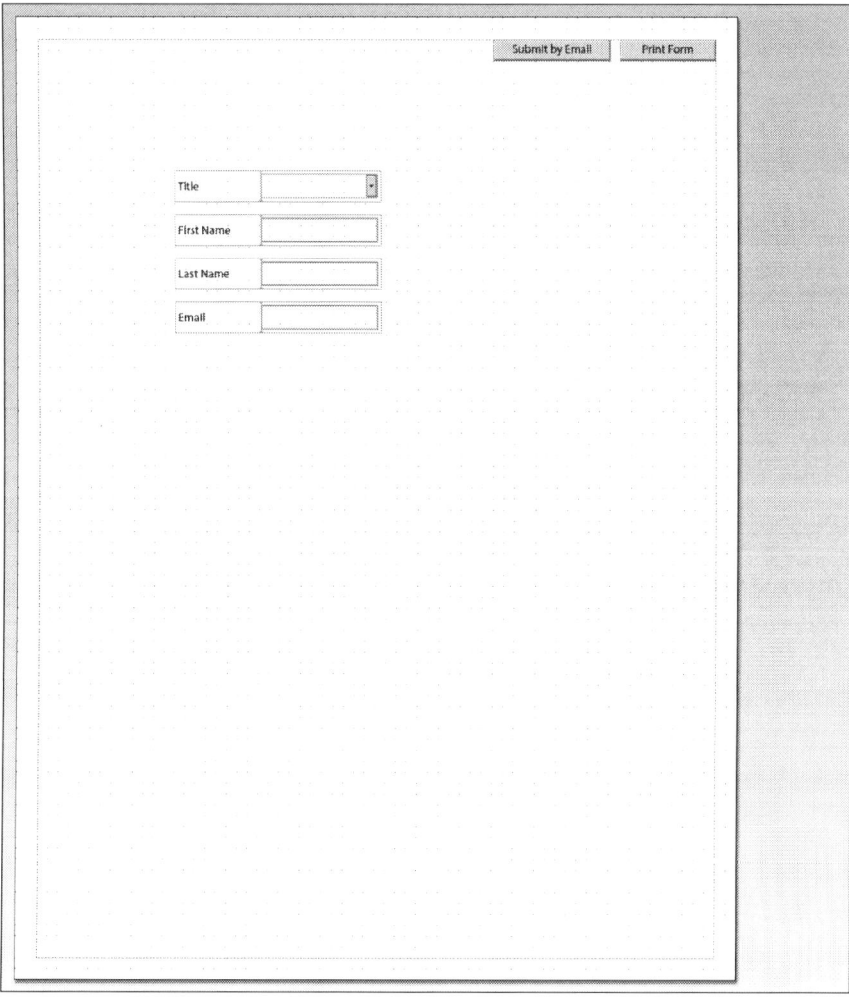

Figure 4-23. Your form with drop-down and text fields

Insert a numeric field

To insert a Numeric Field object, follow these steps:

1. Drag a Numeric Field object to the Design View.
2. In the Object palette, rename the caption to **Telephone Number**.
3. Click the layout area to close the Object palette.

Insert a list

To insert a List Field object, follow these steps:

1. Drag a List Field object onto the Design View tab of the layout area.
2. In the Object palette, rename the caption to Title.
3. Click the green + sign and add the words **Static PDFs** to the text box that appears. Press Enter, and add the Interactive PDFs and Dynamic PDFs text boxes.

   The drop-down list in Design View automatically populates with the values, as shown in Figure 4-24.

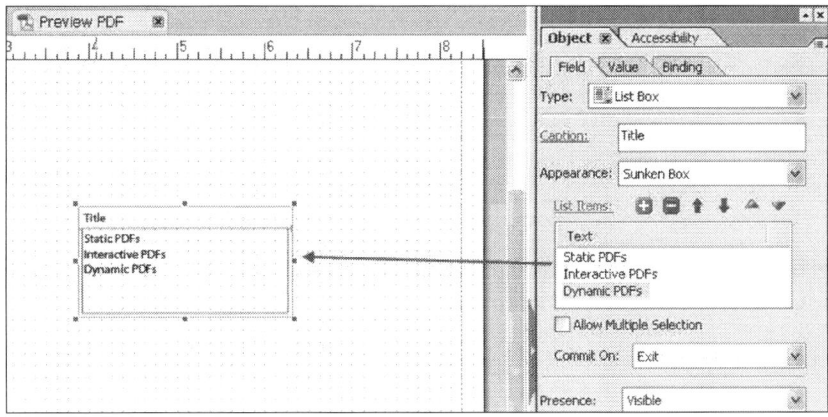

Figure 4-24. Using the Object palette to add options to a list box

4. Click the layout area to close the Object palette.

Insert a check box

To insert a Check Box object, follow these steps:

1. Drag a Check Box object to the Design View.
2. In the Object palette, rename the caption to **I would like to receive the latest news**.
3. Click the layout area to close the Object palette.

Your form should now look like Figure 4-25.

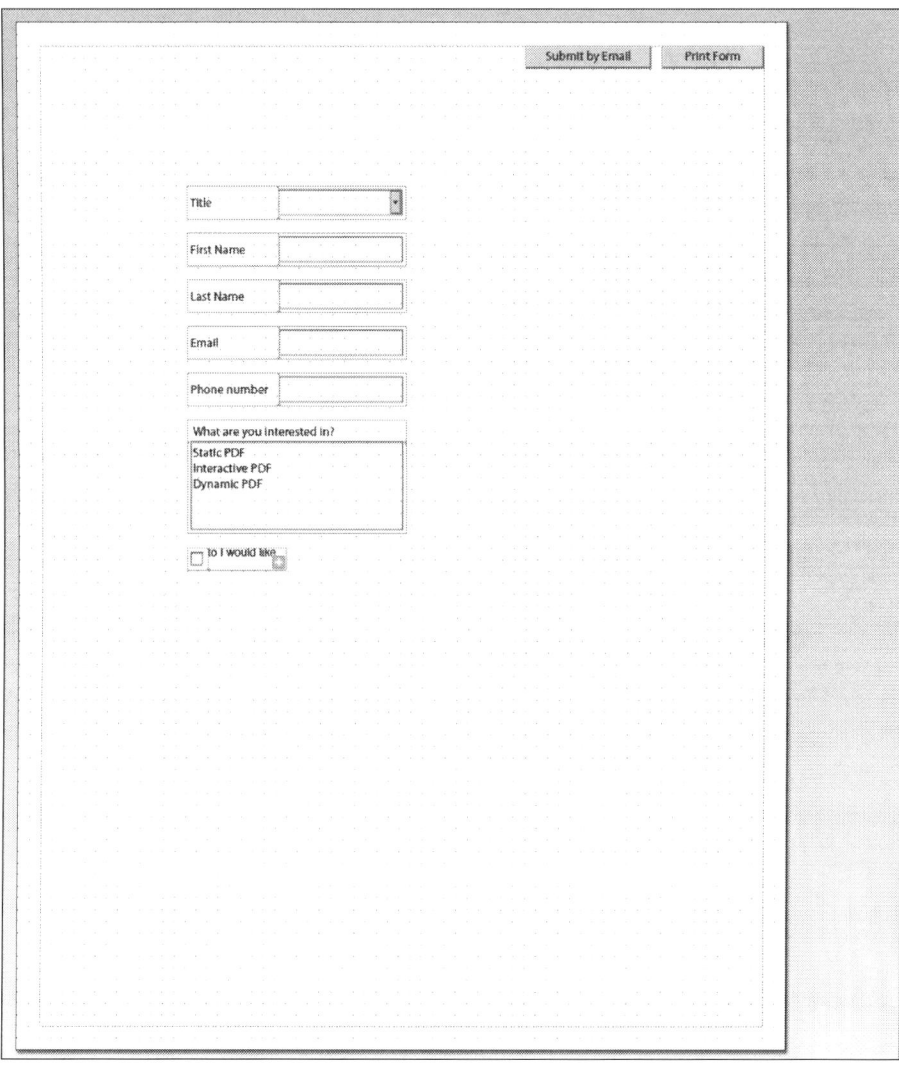

Figure 4-25. Your contact form with objects inserted

Moving objects

Now that you have the form objects inserted into the form design, it is time to move them to make the form more intuitive and easier to use. Interactive forms traditionally have the call to action—that is, the submit button—after the last form field question. Your form is going to follow that protocol.

LiveCycle Designer offers a number of ways to move objects including cutting an object and pasting it elsewhere, selecting an object and moving it via the arrow keys on the keyboard, and dragging and dropping. You are going to use the drag-and-drop method to move the form buttons to the bottom of the form.

Drag and drop buttons

To drag and drop the form buttons, follow these steps:

1. Click the Submit by Email button to select it.
2. Drag it with the mouse, and drop it under the Check Box object.
3. Repeat these steps for the Print Form button.

Your form should now look like Figure 4-26.

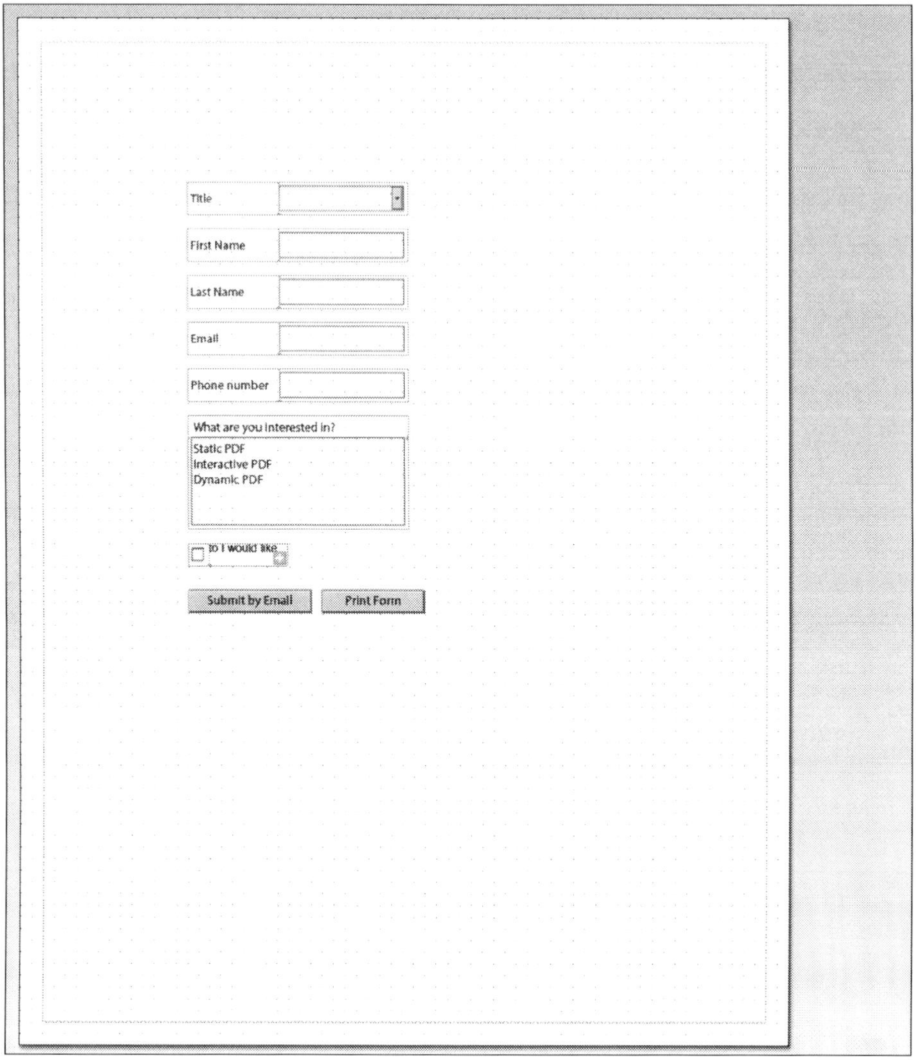

Figure 4-26. Your form with the buttons at its natural conclusion

Resizing objects

This contact form has one very obvious error in it. The check box caption is too large for the allocated text area. You will now correct this.

Resize a text area

To create a large enough area to view all the text in the caption, follow these steps:

1. Click the Check Box object. You will see six handles appear at each corner and in the middle of the long sides of the object.

2. Using the mouse, grab one of the handles, and extend the text area enough so you can view all the text, as shown in Figure 4-27.

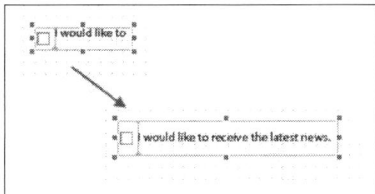

Figure 4-27. Using handles to resize an object's caption

Resize a button

You may want to make your call-to-action buttons larger. To do that, follow these steps:

1. Click the Submit by Email object. You will see six handles appear at each corner and in the middle of the long sides of the object.

2. Using the mouse, grab one of the handles, and extend the button area.

3. To change the button font size, double-click the button so that the text is selected, and change the size on the top-left corner of the Font Manager.

4. Repeat with the Print Form button.

Aligning objects

You can align objects to each other by selecting more than one. The Layout menu allows you to align objects in LiveCycle Designer.

Align objects

To align objects to each other, follow these steps:

1. Select the objects you want to align.

2. Select Layout ➤ Align, and choose Right.

The objects will align to the last object selected, as shown in Figure 4-28.

105

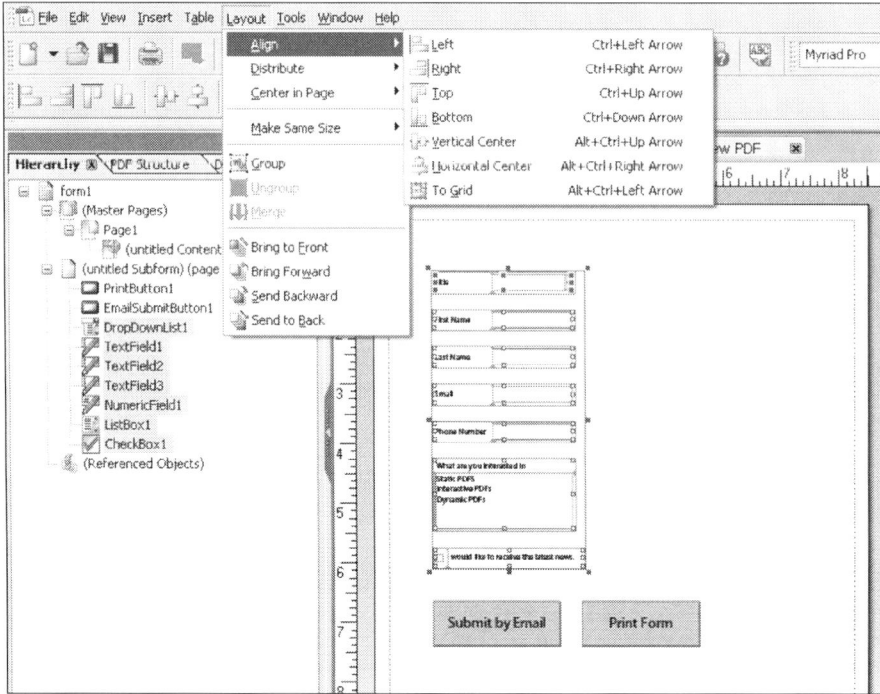

Figure 4-28. Aligning objects

You can also align objects to the layout grid.

Grouping objects

It is sometimes useful to group objects on a form design. This allows for easier formatting because you do not need to move the objects individually; rather, you can move them as a group. You can group objects via the Layout toolbar or the Hierarchy palette, as shown in Figure 4-29.

Group objects

To group objects in the Layout toolbar, follow these steps:

1. Select the objects you want to group.
2. Select Layout ➤ Group.

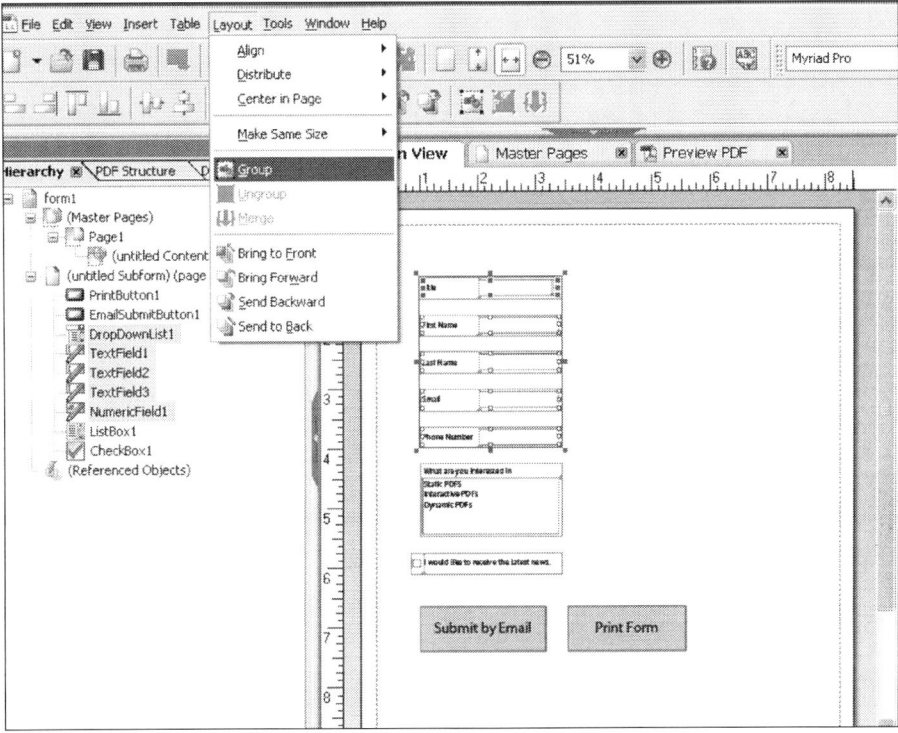

Figure 4-29. Selecting objects via the Layout toolbar

Summary

In this chapter, you learned the basics of designing in Adobe LiveCycle Designer forms, such as how to manipulate components like templates and master pages and how to import different file types. Next, you'll move on to in-depth form creation. Specifically, Chapter 5 will teach you how to create interactive forms using custom interactive objects, calculations, and scripts.

Chapter 5

UNDERSTANDING INTERACTIVE FORMS

Interactive forms capture data directly from users. The user fills out the form while connected to the Internet and submits their information online. You can configure an interactive form to integrate user data directly in your database.

Adobe LiveCycle Designer ES enables you to create interactive forms that the user can complete using Acrobat Professional, Standard, or Reader. Using LiveCycle Designer in conjunction with Adobe LiveCycle Forms ES enables you to output forms in .swf and .html files that you can then add to your website.

Interactive forms have many advantages over paper-based print-and-fill forms. They help eliminate duplication since data can be validated when the form is completed and submitted directly from the user to a database. And you can instantaneously distribute them to users via e-mail, an intranet, or the Internet.

In this chapter, you will be learning specifically about interactive forms. You will investigate interactive form objects, learn how to apply calculations and scripts, create interactive buttons, and process information from interactive forms.

Designing interactive forms

When designing interactive forms, it is important to understand the difference between interactive and static objects and how and when to apply interactive objects to your form. Interactive objects ensure a more satisfying and well-rounded user experience. In the following sections, you will investigate interactive objects and then do some exercises centered on specific interactive form objects, such as drop-down lists and date/time fields.

Exploring types of interactive objects

Interactive forms are composed of objects that explicitly define how users enter data and how the data they have entered is returned to you, the form designer. These objects include drop-down lists, radio buttons, and check boxes and can have calculations, scripts, and validation procedures applied to them. Interactive forms also typically have submit buttons.

Adobe LiveCycle Designer ES allows you to use FormCalc functions that are built into objects to maximize the interactivity of the object. You can also use JavaScript to customize the functionality of interactive objects.

Working with custom interactive objects

Custom objects are objects you create with characteristics you want to implement often in your forms. You create custom objects by defining the properties of a standard object with functionality such as calculations and scripts. You then save them in the Library palette. This helps streamline your form-building process because you can use these custom objects in multiple forms without having to customize or build them every time. You then drop and drag your custom objects from the Object Library palette onto Design View to use them.

When you are creating a custom object, you must determine what functionality you want the object to have. You can then base your object selection on this functionality. The following exercise will demonstrate step-by-step how to create a custom List Box object.

Adding a group to the Object Library palette

As you know, objects are stored in the default sections of the Object Library palette. You can create your own sections in which to save your custom objects by following these steps:

1. Select Add Group in the Object Library palette's menu (see Figure 5-1).
2. Name your group in the Add Library Group dialog box.
3. Click OK.

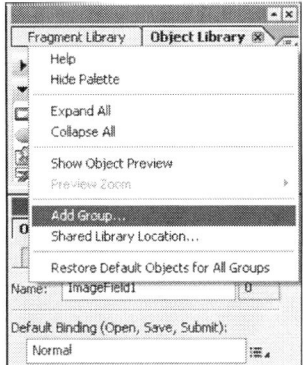

Figure 5-1. Adding a group to the Object Library palette

Creating a custom object

To create a custom object, follow these steps:

1. Open a new blank form.

2. Drag a List Box object onto Design View (see Figure 5-2).

As you discovered in Chapter 3, the List Box object offers the user a list of selections from which they can choose an answer. This object displays all the choices for the form questions, sometimes utilizing a scrollbar depending on the size of the list.

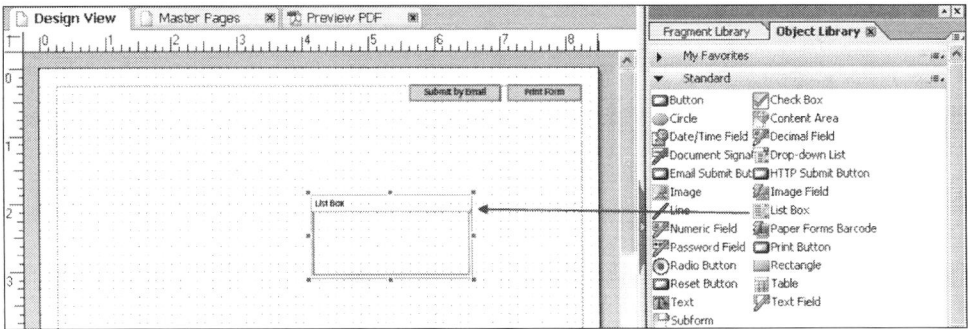

Figure 5-2. The List Box object allows a user to select an option from a list of choices.

3. Click the List Box object in Design View to select it, and in the Object palette, type **Which fla-vors do you prefer?** in the Caption box (see Figure 5-3).

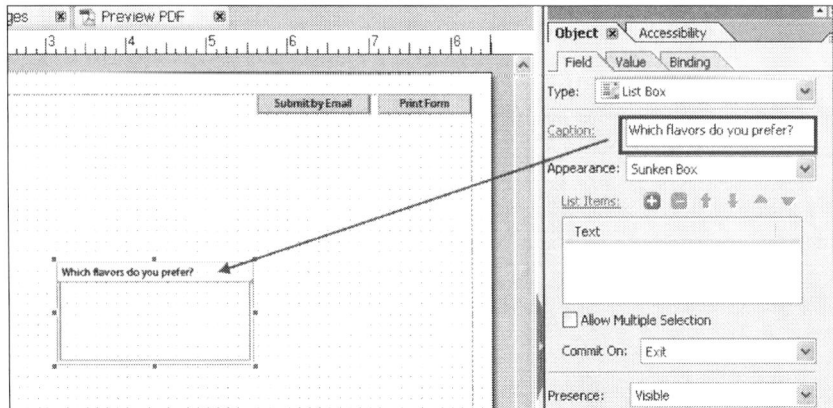

Figure 5-3. When you edit the Caption field in the Object palette, the field label updates automatically.

4. Enter the following options in the List Items box: **Chocolate**, **Strawberry**, **Vanilla**, **Caramel**, and **Coconut**.

5. Click the Custom category of the Object Library palette.

6. Click your object, and drag it into the Custom Category.

7. Assign the object title and description in the Add Library Object dialog box so that you can easily identify the object in the library when you want to use it in the future (see Figure 5-4), and click OK.

To use this in future forms, drag it from the Custom category onto Design View.

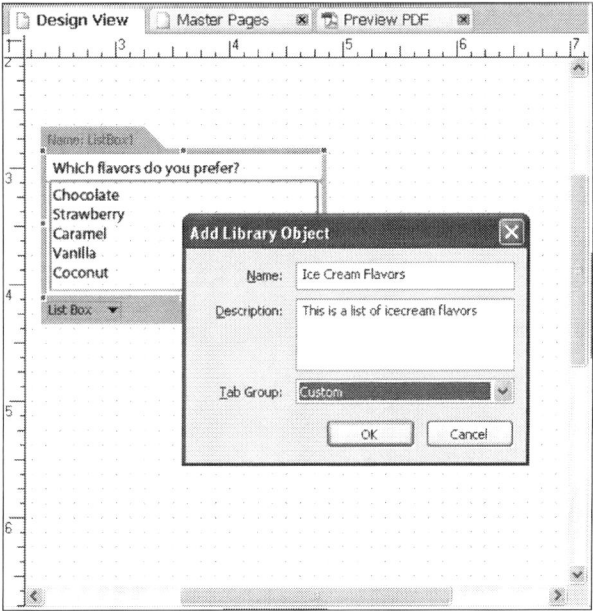

Figure 5-4. Creating a List Box library object

Adding calculations and scripts

Calculations and scripts enhance the user experience by extending the interactivity of form objects. Adobe LiveCycle Designer ES follows a standardized process to attach a script or calculation to an object.

To understand how calculations and scripts work in LiveCycle Designer, you must first understand the Script Editor and the two supported scripting languages, FormCalc and JavaScript. In the following sections, I'll show you each part of the Script Editor, define events, and give an overview of the FormCalc and JavaScript languages.

Working with the Script Editor

You will use the Script Editor to create and edit the calculations and scripts of your form. It has two views: a multiline view and a single-line view. The multiline allows you to view long scripts as you create them, and the single-line view maximizes your design layout area (see Figure 5-5).

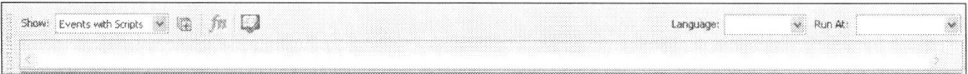

Figure 5-5. The single-line view of the Script Editor displays only one line of script.

The following are the components of the Script Editor:

Show: This drop-down box inventories all events that support user-defined scripting. If an event contains a calculation or script, it will have an asterisk (*) next to it.

Show Events for Child Object: This button, located next to the Show drop-down list, presents the currently selected event for an object and all its child objects.

Functions: Clicking the Functions button, directly to the left of the Show Events for Child Object button when you have an event selected in the Show drop-down list, displays a list of the functions available, as shown in Figure 5-6.

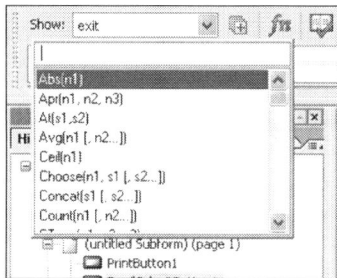

Figure 5-6. Clicking the Functions button displays the available functions that can be used to build scripts and calculations.

Check Script Syntax: The Check Script Syntax button authenticates the script for correct syntax. Any syntax errors are reported on the Log tab of the Report palette.

Language: The Language drop-down box is where you choose the scripting language you want to use for the calculation or script. You can choose FormCalc or JavaScript.

Run At: The Run At drop-down list enables you to select where you want the calculation or script to run: on the client, on the server, or on both the client and the server.

Child objects are related objects that are associated with each other in the database. You can view child objects in the Hierarchy *palette, as shown in Figure 5-7.*

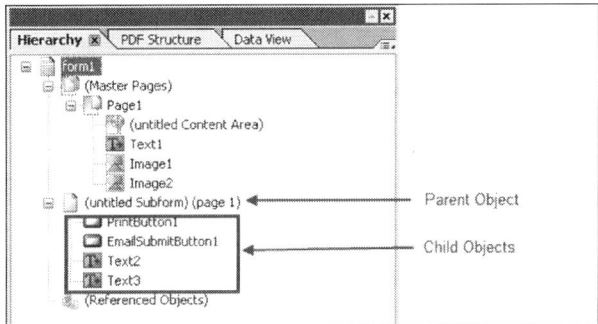

Figure 5-7. Child objects are directly related to parent objects.

Understanding events

When a form changes an automatic calculation or script, it changes the state of the form; this can be a call to add a dynamic line for data entry upon selection of an option or a form being populated with data from a database. **Form events** are the actions that change the state of a form. When you apply a calculation or a script to an event, you can then control every aspect of how your form objects are displayed and how data and objects respond to the user's interaction. You can apply more than one event to any given object, and a single change of form state can trigger multiple events.

For example, in a flowable dynamic form, if a particular answer to a question automatically makes a new form field appear, it is considered a form event. Likewise, clicking a button to submit data to the form builder is also considered a form event. Nearly every object can have either a calculation or a script applied to it, but not every object can support form events.

All bar codes, button types, check boxes, date/time fields, decimal fields, document signature fields, drop-down lists, image fields, list boxes, numeric fields, password fields, radio buttons, subforms, tables, and text fields support calculations and scripts. Circles, content areas, lines, rectangles, images, subform sets, sections of tables, and text do not support calculations and scripts.

In an interactive form, events are initiated as a result of the user completing form questions. You select the kind of event from the Script Editor. To view the Script Editor, select Window ➤ Script Editor (see Figure 5-8).

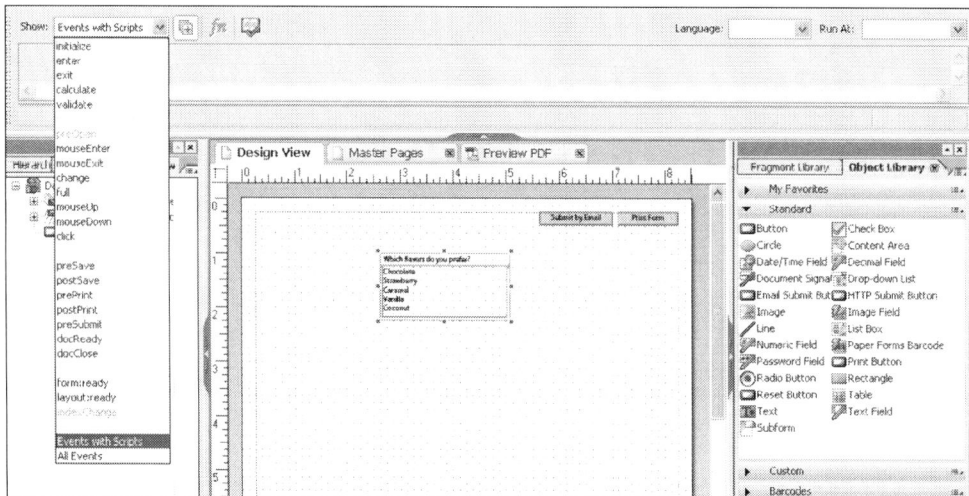

Figure 5-8. The Script Editor

Events are divided into three categories: application events, process events, and interactive events.

Application events are initialized because of actions that a server application or client application performs as a result of an automated process.

Process events are automatically initialized because of an action or internal process related to a form or objects on that form. They occur immediately after significant form changes. You will investigate process and application events further in Chapter 7.

Interactive events are initiated as a result of the form user interacting with the form. They are as follows:

Change event: This event initiates when a user changes the content of a field by typing a keystroke, selects an option from a list or drop-down box, selects or clears a check box, or chooses a radio button.

Click event: This event is initiated when a mouse click occurs on the object.

Enter event: This event is initiated when a user moves to a field on your form by tabbing into it or clicking it.

Exit event: This event is initiated when a user moves past the field on the form by tabbing off it or clicking another form object.

Full event: This event occurs when a user attempts to enter more than the allowed keystrokes into a field.

MouseDown event: This event occurs when the user presses the left mouse button at the same time the cursor is pointed over a field.

MouseEnter event: This occurs when the user moves the cursor into an area of the form field but doesn't press the mouse button.

MouseExit event: This event is initiated when the user moves the mouse cursor out of the field.

MouseUp event: This event occurs when the cursor is in a field and the user releases the mouse button.

PreOpen event: This event is used in conjunction with the drop-down list form object. It is initiated when the user clicks the arrow that causes the drop-down list to display.

Understanding calculations

Implementing calculations and scripts in your form design gives you the ability to enhance your forms and make them truly interactive. Calculations enhance the functionality of your form.

Using FormCalc in calculations

FormCalc is an intuitive calculation language that is derived from common spreadsheet functionality such as Microsoft Excel or Microsoft Access. It can be a timesaver because it incorporates a number of built-in functions. You do not need to know sophisticated programming languages such as JavaScript to use FormCalc. If you are familiar with basic spreadsheet operations, you will be able to commence working with FormCalc immediately.

FormCalc allows form developers to create forms quickly and allows you to conduct calculations as the form is being filled out, saving users from having to perform any cumbersome calculations that may be required to reach answers within the form.

The built-in functions that make up FormCalc cover a wide range of areas, including mathematics, dates and times, strings, finance, logic, and the Web. The simplest calculation requires only one FormCalc function. A more complicated calculation could see a single FormCalc function utilizing other FormCalc functions.

Attach a FormCalc function to a form

As an example, I will now show how to attach a FormCalc function to a form that will enable it to automatically calculate the sum of numeric fields that the user enters:

1. Open a new blank form in Adobe LiveCycle Designer ES.

2. Drag four Numeric Field objects from the Object Library palette onto Design View. Arrange them in a neat column (see Figure 5-9).

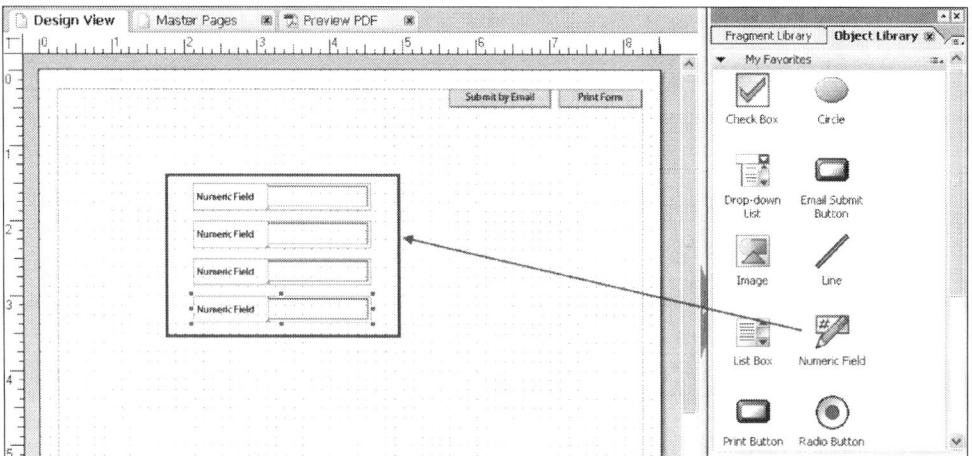

Figure 5-9. Assembling Numeric Field objects in Design View

3. Select the top Numeric Field object, and in the Object palette, change its caption to **Chocolate** on the Field tab, as shown in Figure 5-10.

4. With the top Numeric Field object still selected, click the Binding tab, and change its name to **Chocolate**, as shown in Figure 5-11.

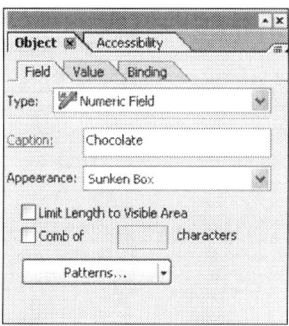

Figure 5-10. Renaming a Numeric Field object in the Object palette

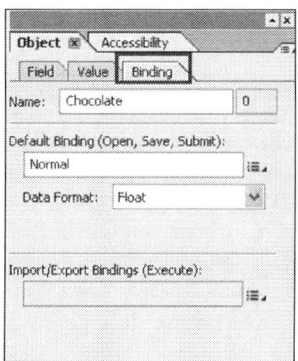

Figure 5-11. Changing the name on the Binding tab

5. Repeat this with the second and third fields, calling them **Vanilla** and **Caramel**, respectively.

6. Select the fourth field, and rename its caption to **Total** in the Object palette.

   You have now set up the design environment to enable a FormCalc calculation to be applied to the form. You will now apply the FormCalc calculation.

7. If the Script Editor is not visible, select Window ➤ Script Editor to open it.

118

8. Ensure the Numeric Field object with the Total caption is selected, and choose Calculate from the Show drop-down list.

If you have changed the settings or resized your Script Editor before, you may need to drag the Script Editor handle downward toward the middle of the screen to view it.

9. Click the Functions button in the Script Editor, and scroll down until you see Sum(n1 [, n2...]). Click it. The script will appear in the Script Editor.

10. Replace the default values in the script with **Chocolate+Vanilla+Caramel**, as demonstrated in Figure 5-12.

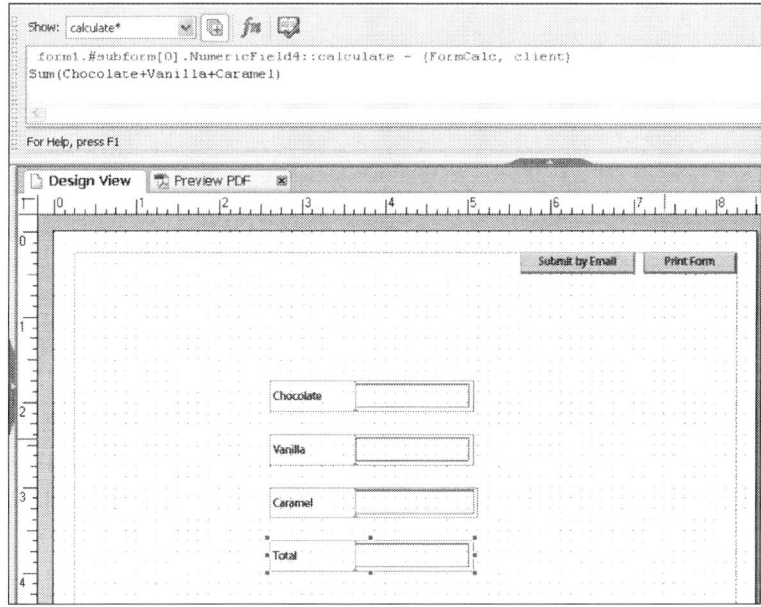

Figure 5-12. The FormCalc Sum calculation with values added

11. Click the Preview PDF tab, and enter numeric values in the topmost three numeric fields. You will notice the total sum of the numbers appear in the Total field, as shown in Figure 5-13.

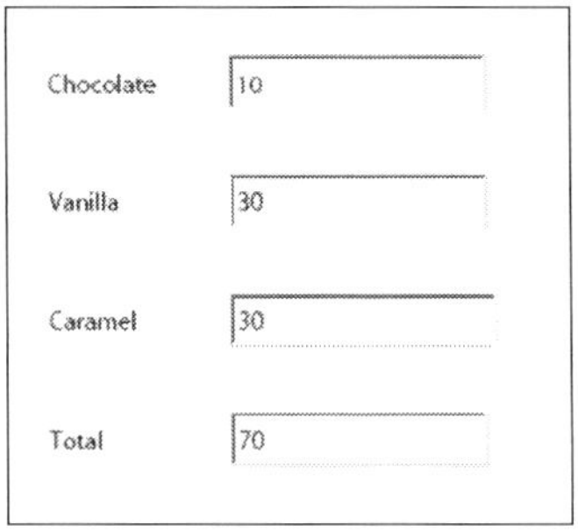

Figure 5-13. The completed FormCalc function

Using JavaScript in calculations

JavaScript is the second scripting language supported by Adobe LiveCycle Designer ES. It is more powerful and flexible than FormCalc and enables you to build more sophisticated and dynamic interactive forms. Form designers who already know JavaScript will be able to begin using JavaScript with LiveCycle Designer immediately. Adobe LiveCycle Designer ES supports JavaScript version 1.6 (or prior) in all scripting scenarios.

LiveCycle Designer has included a number of properties and methods that allow you to access the value of fields and objects via JavaScript. It allows you to easily manipulate form values and data.

To use JavaScript within your form design, you must also be familiar with constructing LiveCycle Designer reference syntax and using the XML Form Object Model reference, which organizes the objects within your form into a logical tree structure.

You will be using JavaScript in Chapter 8.

Using field objects in your form design

In Adobe LiveCycle Designer ES, objects fall into two categories: fields and boilerplate objects.

Form fields, like the ones you worked with earlier in the chapter, are interactive objects. They can both capture and display data and consist of buttons, drop-down lists, alpha and numeric entry, check boxes, radio buttons, date/time fields, list boxes, password fields, signature fields, bar codes, buttons image fields, and text fields.

Boilerplate objects are static and have no data capture or display capabilities. They can be used on all kinds of forms, whether they are interactive, dynamic, or print-and-fill forms, and they can be text, images, graphics, rectangles, circles, and lines.

Using a Date/Time object

The Date/Time object allows you to add the ability to record the date on your form, either by selecting it from a pop-up calendar on the field or by typing the date manually (see Figure 5-14).

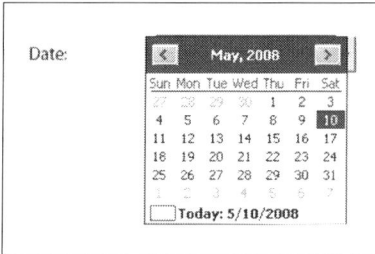

Figure 5-14. The date can be selected from a calendar or entered manually.

After you've added the Date/Time object to your form design, you are able to edit it in the Object palette. Date/Time objects support scripts and calculations, and you can validate data entered via scripting.

When you drag and drop a Date/Time object onto the design layout, three tabs appear in the Object palette: the Field tab, the Value tab, and the Binding tab.

Investigating the Value tab

The Value tab of the Object palette is where you set the values for the Date/Time object, as shown in Figure 5-15. To set values for a Date/Time field, you must first understand the Type options.

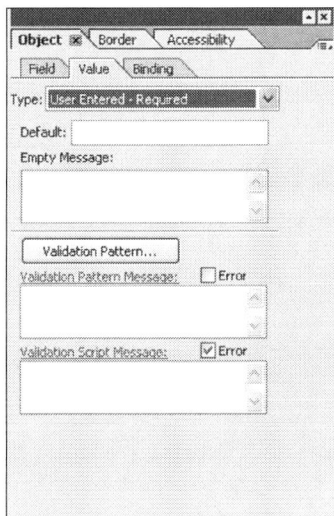

Figure 5-15. The Value tab sets the values for the Date/Time object.

The Type options allow you to choose how the user can interact with the Date/Time field. User Entered – Optional allows users to decide to enter data, User Entered – Recommended allows you to enter a custom message and causes a dialog box to appear to prompt users to enter a date, User Entered – Required ensures that the field is mandatory, Calculated – Read Only renders the field read-only and disallows users from interacting with it, Calculated – User Can Override allows the user to override the calculated field, and Read Only displays data that is calculated or merged from a data source.

Define a Date/Time field's behavior

To define a Date/Time field's behavior, follow these steps:

1. From the Object Library palette, drag and drop a Date/Time field onto the Design View area.
2. Ensure the Date/Time field is selected, and click the Value tab in the Object palette.
3. In the Type section, choose from the drop-down list User Entered – Required.
4. Type a message to prompt field completion into the Empty Message field.

If you choose User Entered – Recommended or User Entered – Required, you are able to prompt the user to complete the field by entering a message into the Empty Message field.

If you choose User Entered – Calculated, you use the Script Editor to attach the script to the field.

Creating interactive buttons

Buttons are used on forms to allow users to initiate actions, such as executing web services operations, performing database queries, and submitting data. Utilizing LiveCycle Designer's support for client-server communications, forms can complete a myriad of actions via buttons, including submitting data, using scripts to process data, signing the data, opening a host's connection, and invoking web service operations. When a user clicks a button object, the actions assigned to the button are executed.

LiveCycle Designer includes four preconfigured buttons designed to fulfill common and standard form actions. They are the e-mail submit button, the HTTP submit button, the print button, and a reset button.

By default, LiveCycle Designer launches new forms with the e-mail submit button and the print button. You will now examine each of these four buttons in depth.

Submitting data via an email submit button

The Email Submit Button object has properties already set to enable the user to submit the form data via e-mail.

It appears as a default on all new form designs. It is a good idea to include e-mail submit buttons on all forms that are not going to be printed and filled out because Adobe Reader doesn't save changes to PDF files. You manipulate the Email Submit Button object properties in the Object palette, as shown in Figure 5-16.

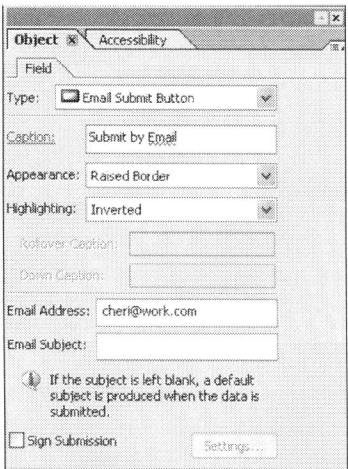

Figure 5-16. The Email Submit Button object in the Object palette

Understanding an HTTP submit button

The HTTP Submit Button object is preconfigured to allow users to submit their form data via an HTTP post. To implement an HTTP submit button, simply drag and drop the HTTP Submit Button form object onto your form. You set the destination URL for the HTTP Submit Button object in the Object palette, as shown in Figure 5-17.

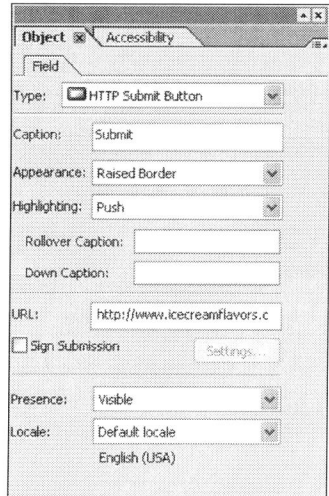

Figure 5-17. Set the destination URL for the HTTP Submit Button object in the Object palette.

Understanding a print button

The Print Button object is preconfigured to open the Print dialog box when the user clicks it. The print button has a script in the button's click event that prints the form when the button is clicked, as shown in Figure 5-18. You will be looking closer at buttons and scripting in Chapter 8.

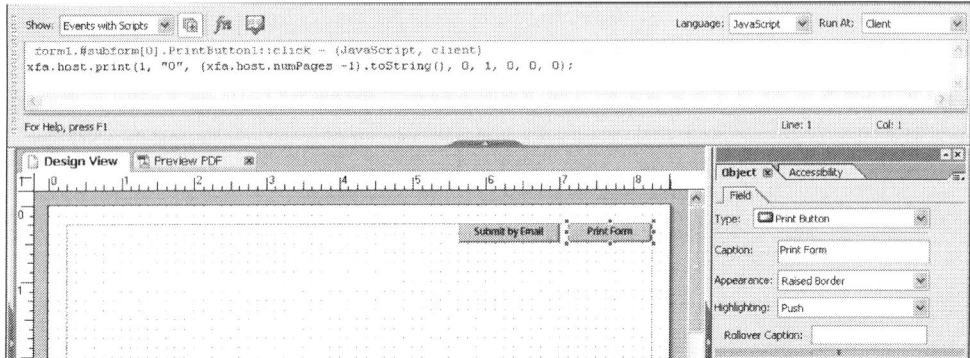

Figure 5-18. The Print Button object contains a script in its click event.

Understanding a reset button

The Reset Button object is preconfigured to reset all the fields on the form to their default values. This means the data entered into text fields will be cleared, and the user will need to reenter all field values.

Editing buttons in your form design

Once you've added a button to your form design, like all other form objects, you manipulate the settings in the Object palette. You can define the following properties in the button's Object palette:

- Specify the country of the form (the default is U.S. English)
- Change the button's caption
- Include a data signature
- Set the border and highlight styles of the button
- Set the destination URL
- Specify the button to be invisible, hidden, or visible

Understanding image objects and image fields

Adobe LiveCycle Designer ES contains two kinds of image objects. The first is a read-only Image object that users cannot affect on the form. This object enhances the aesthetics of a form. LiveCycle Designer supports the following kinds of image formats: Windows Bitmap (.bmp), Encapsulated PostScript (.eps), Joint Photographic Experts Group (.jpg), Graphics Interchange Format (.gif), Portable Networks Graphics (.png), and Tagged Image File (.tif).

The second kind of image object is the Image Field object, which will be discussed in the "Using image fields" section. Image Field objects allow an image to be added to an interactive form that can be changed.

Using image objects

The following exercise demonstrates how to implement an image on your form. Ensure that you have downloaded the image from the home page of this book on the Friends of ED website.

1. Open a new blank form in LiveCycle Designer.

2. From the My Favorites category in the Object Library palette, drag and drop an Image object onto Design View, as shown in Figure 5-19.

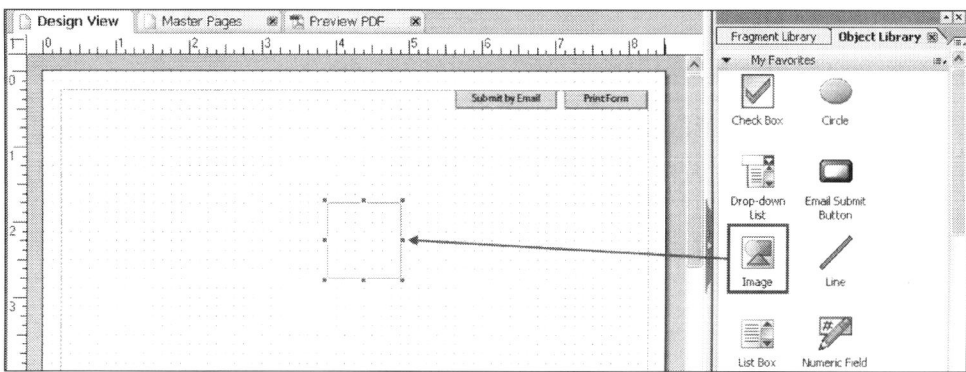

Figure 5-19. Dragging an Image object onto Design View

3. Double-click the Image object on Design View to open the Browse for Image File dialog box, as shown in Figure 5-20.

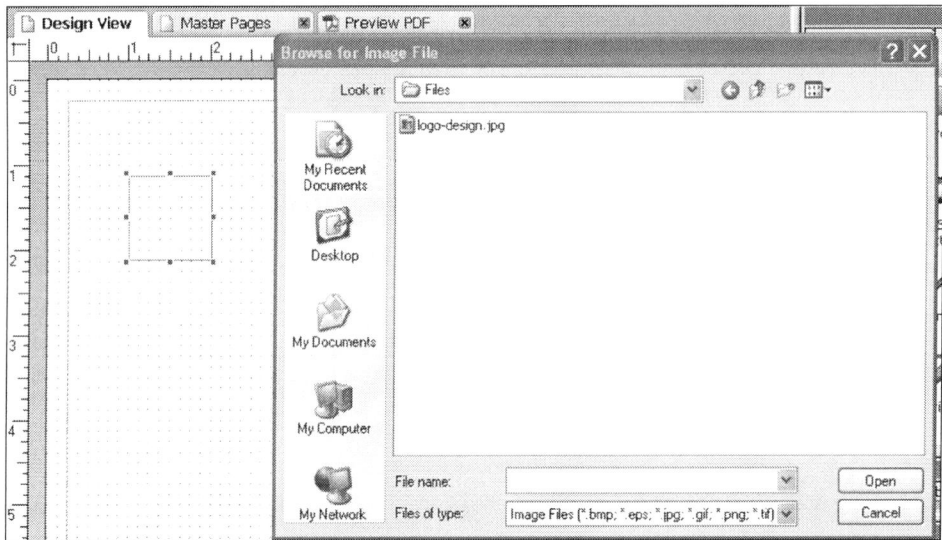

Figure 5-20. Double-clicking the Image object in Design View launches the Browse for Image File dialog box.

4. Browse to where you have saved your image file, and click Open. The image will appear in Design View, as shown in Figure 5-21.

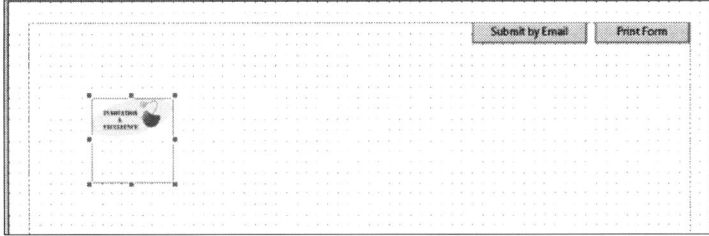

Figure 5-21. Selecting the image to populate your Image object

5. Click the image to select it.

In the Object palette of the image, you are presented with three options in the Sizing drop-down box. By default, the sizing of any image you import into Adobe LiveCycle Designer ES is set to Scale Image Proportionally. You will now investigate what happens when you choose each of the other two options.

6. In the Sizing drop-down box of the Object palette, select Scale Image to Fit Rectangle.

The image you have imported into Design View will change to fill the image rectangle, as shown in Figure 5-22.

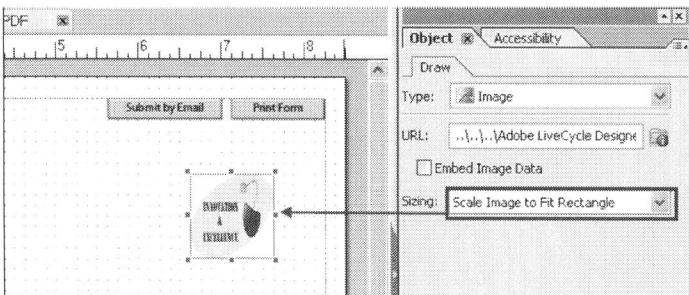

Figure 5-22. Scaling the image to fit the image rectangle

7. In the Sizing drop-down box of the Object palette, select Use Original Size.

The image you have imported into Design View will expand or contract to the size of the original image, as shown in Figure 5-23.

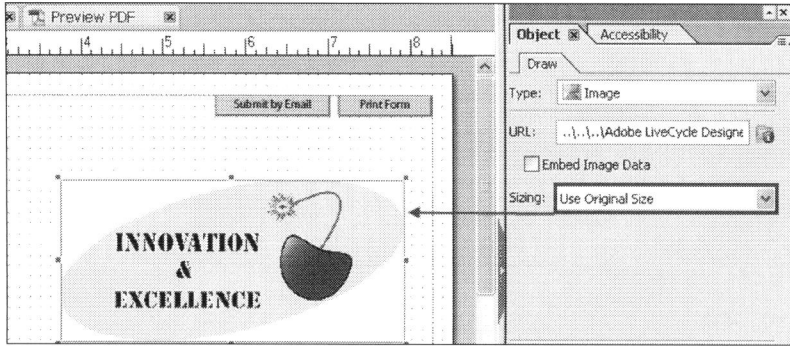

Figure 5-23. Setting your image to be the original size

After an image is added to a form, the object's properties are manipulated in the Object palette. Here you can decide whether to embed the image in the form, scale the image, and define the image as hidden, visible, or invisible.

Using image fields

Image Field objects allow you to add an image to the form via an external data source or scripting and through data binding, which allows the merging of external image data. For example, this is useful when you want to make an online catalog, where you can dynamically load images into a database and have the form automatically call each image in the database. This makes this field object very powerful because it allows images to be selected and loaded dynamically.

When you drag an Image Field object onto Design View, the Binding tab in the Object palette offers data binding choices for the object.

1. Open a new blank form in LiveCycle Designer.
2. From the Standard category of the Object Library palette, drag and drop an Image Field object onto Design View, as shown in Figure 5-24.

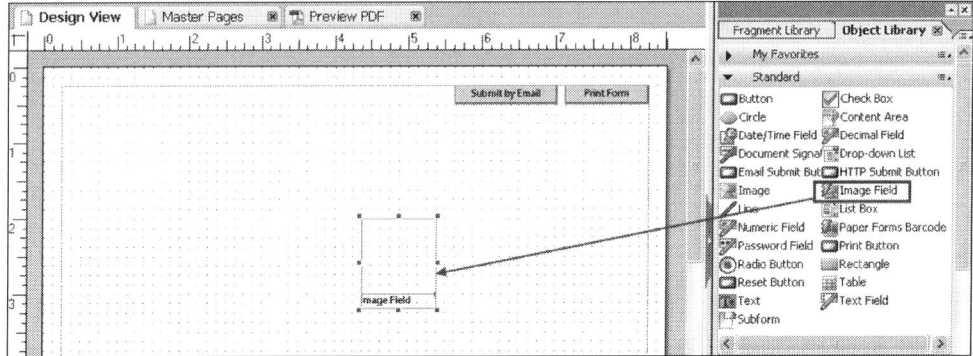

Figure 5-24. Dragging an image field object onto Design View

3. Double-click the Image Field object on Design View. The Browse for Image File dialog box will appear.
4. Type a URL of an image into the File Name box:
5. Click Open.

The image will appear on your form as shown in Figure 5-25.

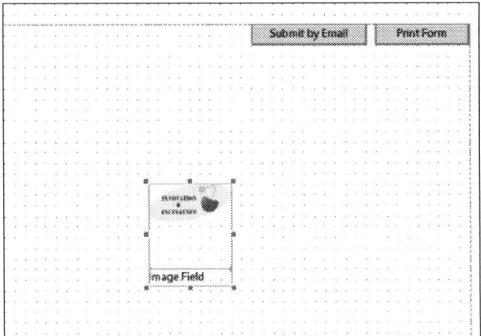

Figure 5-25. Populating the image field

Image Field objects are also immensely useful when designing interactive forms because you can create them to change images depending on selections made by the user filling in the form.

Summary

In this chapter, you saw the advantages of interactive forms over paper-based, print-and-fill forms. You will further expand on this knowledge in Chapter 6, where you'll learn how to control and guide user input and data display and investigate validation on different kinds of fields and edit patterns. You will also learn about applying conditional breaks within forms and much more.

Chapter 6

GETTING INTO ADVANCED FORM DESIGN

You now have a firm grasp on the capabilities of interactive forms and how they provide benefits both for the business processes and for the user. In this chapter, you will delve into the benefits provided by LiveCycle Designer when you build intuitive and dynamic forms. You will further investigate user input, data display, and sophisticated forms of validation, and you'll learn how these contribute to the success of the form. You will also learn how to customize forms for the language and standards of the country of form origin.

You will then learn about how scripts enable you to tailor your forms depending on the kind of information you are asking of your user and how to use conditional breaks to ensure that the form flow remains intact when you are requesting unknown quantities of data from the user.

Finally, you will spend some time understanding how subforms and tables enable you to expand the form with user-entered data, and you will learn about creating reusable form fragments that will streamline your form-building processes.

To complete some of the exercises in this chapter, it is recommended that you download the cheque.pdf document from the homepage of this book.

Controlling user input and data display

Client-side validation and data display control assists users in knowing the format in which you want them to submit their information. By providing comprehensive guides and instant feedback, you are ensuring that the user enters the data correctly the first time, which helps streamline business processes.

In the following sections, you will undertake some exercises on how to validate data on commonly used form fields, learn about applying patterns to fields, and learn how to specify locales.

Formatting and validating user input

Data validation is the process of checking the data the user has entered in the form to ensure it is correct. Data validation is one of the largest advantages of interactive forms over print-and-fill forms, because the data is validated at runtime, as the user is completing it.

You can apply three validations to every field. They are executed in the following order:

1. The field is tested to ensure it contains data.

2. The data is tested to ensure it meets specific pattern criteria.

3. A validation script is invoked.

Specifying validation on a Text Field object

The following exercise will take you step-by-step through validating a Text Field object that you have set as a mandatory field:

1. Open a new blank form. Drag a Text Field object onto Design View. Change the caption to **Name**.

2. Drag and drop a Numeric Text field object onto Design View below the Text Field object. Change the caption name to **Phone**. You will work with this form, shown in Figure 6-1, in the following exercise.

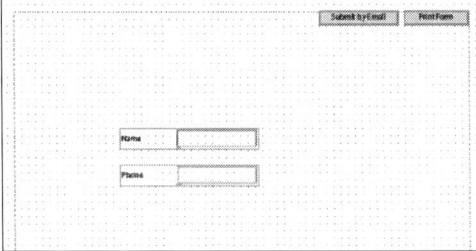

Figure 6-1. The form so far

3. Click the Name field to select it. Select the Value tab of the Object palette.

4. Select User Entered – Recommended from the Type drop-down list, as shown in Figure 6-2.

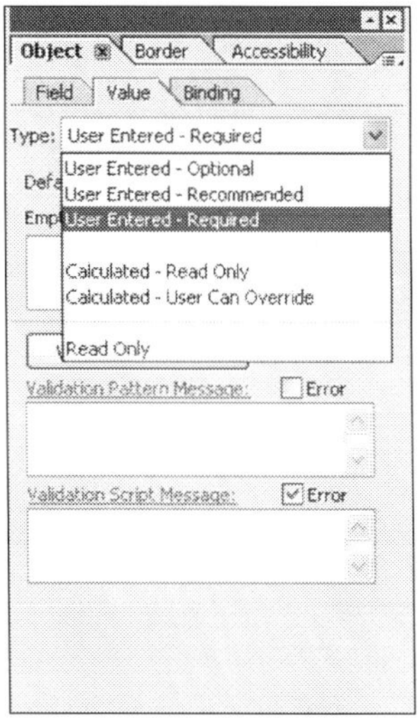

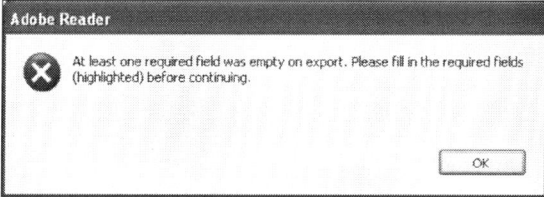

Figure 6-2. Selecting User Entered – Recommended

5. Enter **Please tell us your name.** in the Empty Message box.

6. Save this form as validation.pdf.

7. Click the Preview PDF tab to test your form. Click the Submit by Email Button object.

By default, Adobe Reader warns form users if the form they have completed is trying to submit the data via e-mail. Simply close this dialog box to continue, and the dialog box in Figure 6-3 will appear.

Figure 6-3. The LiveCycle Designer standard warning

You will note that the error message displayed is different from the one you entered in the Empty Message box, and the field object is highlighted. This is because the validation message you entered is executed only when a field has been entered and then the user has removed the data.

8. On the Preview PDF tab, type your name in the Name field, and then press the Tab key to tab to the Phone field. Click the Name field again, and delete your name.

9. Click the Submit to Email Button object. The message you entered appears, as shown in Figure 6-4.

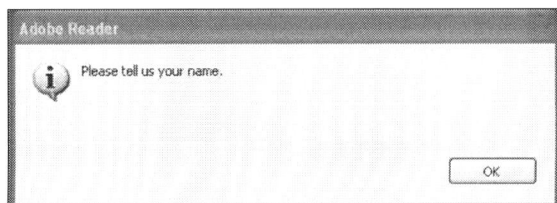

Figure 6-4. The form is validated.

Specifying validation and formatting on a Numeric Field object

Using the same form, you'll now set validation and data formatting on a Numeric Field object to ensure that users enter the correct format (111-111-1111) for telephone numbers:

1. Click the Numeric Field object to select it.

2. Click the Patterns button, as shown in Figure 6-5. The Patterns – Numeric Field dialog box will appear.

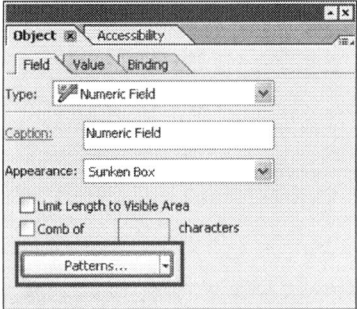

Figure 6-5. Click the Patterns button on a Numeric Field object's Object palette to display the Patterns – Numeric Field dialog box.

3. Click the Validation tab of the Patterns – Numeric Field dialog box.

4. Select 1234 from the Select Type list box.

You will see in the Pattern field there is a default entry of num{zzzzzzzzzzzz9}. You'll now replace this with a value that will dictate the telephone number's format.

5. In the Pattern field, enter **num{zzz-zzz-zzzz}**. This is the script that dictates the format of the telephone number, as shown in Figure 6-6.

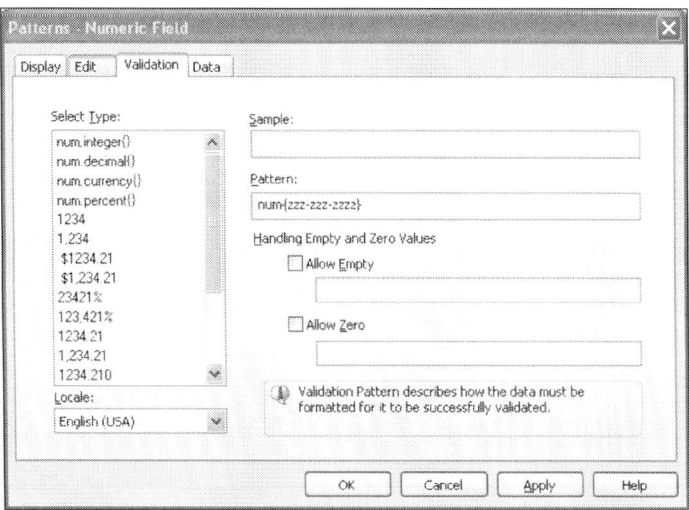

Figure 6-6. Dictating the data format for entry in the Patterns – Numeric Field dialog box

6. Click Apply and then OK.

7. Click the Preview PDF tab to test the form.

8. In the Name field, type **1234567890** in the Phone field, and click the Submit as Email Button object.

9. The alert box shown in Figure 6-7 will appear.

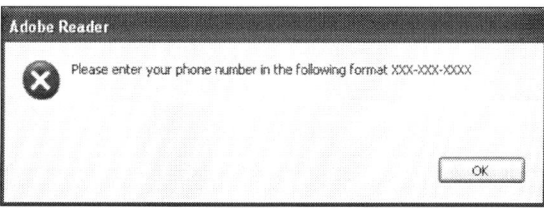

Figure 6-7. Validating a numeric field

Applying display and edit patterns

Display patterns determine how data will be displayed and formatted in the form design.

Adobe LiveCycle Designer ES enables you to specify patterns to control the way field values including text, numeric fields, and date/time fields are formatted when the user completes them.

135

Exploring types of patterns

Implementing patterns on your form objects enables you to control how field values are formatted when the user interacts with the form. The patterns you use to define your fields rely on your form's purpose. If your form is interactive, you need to specify validation patterns to ensure that the data the user submits is able to be processed.

You can edit patterns via the Patterns dialog box, as shown in Figure 6-8. To view the Patterns dialog box, click the Patterns button in the Object palette of an object.

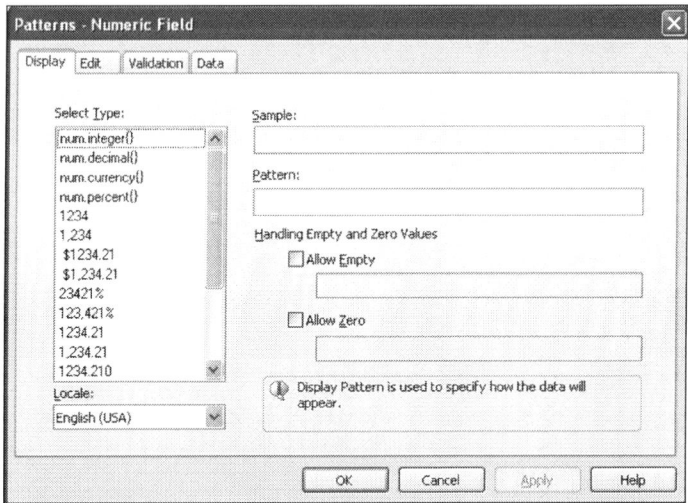

Figure 6-8. Patterns are edited in the Patterns dialog box.

The Patterns dialog box has four tabs, each fulfilling a function as follows:

Display: The Display tab describes how data is displayed in the form. It also formats user information and displays bound values when the user interacts with the form.

Edit: The Edit tab is chiefly concerned with defining date/time fields, text fields, numeric fields, and password fields.

Validation: The Validation tab validates the data a user enters into the form at the time they enter it. It ensures the data is correct before the data is submitted to you by the user.

Data: The Data tab defines the format of saved and bound data.

Setting and using locale information

Locale is the term used to identify a nation when developing international standards. Each one is comprised of the **local identifier**, a string of unique characters. The International Organization for Standardization (ISO) and the Internet Engineering Task Force (IETF) are responsible for standardizing local identifiers globally.

A local identifier is comprised of letters from the specific nation and letters from the language. In FormCalc, the locale defines the format for fields such as date/time fields, numeric fields, and currency values of a specific nation.

Table 6-1 displays the local identifiers for Adobe LiveCycle Designer ES 8.1.

Table 6-1. Local Identifier Strings

Local Identifier Code	Nation/Region	Language
ar_AE	United Arabian Emirates	Arabic
ar_BH	Bahrain	Arabic
ar_DZ	Algeria	Arabic
ar_EG	Egypt	Arabic
ar_IQ	Iraq	Arabic
ar_JO	Jordan	Arabic
ar_KW	Kuwait	Arabic
ar_LB	Lebanon	Arabic
ar_LY	Libya	Arabic
ar_MA	Morocco	Arabic
ar_OM	Oman	Arabic
ar_QA	Qatar	Arabic
ar_SA	Saudi Arabia	Arabic
ar_SD	Sudan	Arabic
ar_SY	Syria	Arabic
ar_TN	Tunisia	Arabic
ar_YE	Yemen	Arabic
bg_BG	Bulgaria	Bulgarian
zh_HK	Hong Kong	Chinese
zh_CN	People's Republic of China (Simplified)	Chinese

Continued

Table 6-1. Local Identifier Strings

Local Identifier Code	Nation/Region	Language
zh_TW	Taiwan (Traditional)	Chinese
hr_HR	Croatia	Croatian
cs_CAZ	Czech Republic	Czech
da_DK	Denmark	Danish
nl_BE	Belgium	Dutch
nl_NL	Netherlands	Dutch
en_AU	Australia	English
en_CA	Canada	English
en_IN	India	English
en_IE	Ireland	English
en_NZ	New Zealand	English
en_ZA	South Africa	English
en_GB	United Kingdom	English
en_GB_EURO	United Kingdom Euro	English
en_US	United States of America	English
et_EE	Estonia	Estonian
fi_FI	Finland	Finnish
fr_BE	Belgium	French
fr_CA	Canada	French
fr_FR	France	French
fr_LU	Luxembourg	French
fr_CH	Switzerland	French
de_AT	Austria	German
de_DE	Germany	German
de_LU	Luxembourg	German

Local Identifier Code	Nation/Region	Language
de_CH	Switzerland	German
el_GR	Greece	Greek
he_IL	Israel	Hebrew
hu_HU	Hungary	Hungarian
id_ID	Indonesia	Indonesian
it_IT	Italy	Italian
it_CH	Switzerland	Italian
ja_JP	Japan	Japanese
ko_KR	Republic of Korea	Korean
ko_KR_HANI	Korea Hanja	Korean
lv_LV	Latvia	Latvian
lt_LT	Lithuania	Lithuanian
ms_MY	Malaysia	Malay
nb_NO	Norway	Norwegian – Bokmal
nn_NO	Norway	Norwegian – Nynorsk
pl_PL	Poland	Polish
pt_BR	Brazil	Portuguese
pt_PT	Portugal	Portuguese
ro_RO	Romania	Romanian
ru_RU	Russia	Russian
sh_BA	Bosnia and Herzegovina	Serbo-Croatian
sh_HR	Croatia	Serbo-Croatian
sh_CS	Serbia and Montenegro	Serbo-Croatian
sk_SK	Slovakia	Slovak
sl_SI	Slovenia	Slovenian

Continued

139

Table 6-1. Local Identifier Strings

Local Identifier Code	Nation/Region	Language
es_EC	Ecuador	Spanish
es_SV	El Salvador	Spanish
es_GT	Guatemala	Spanish
es_HN	Honduras	Spanish
es_NI	Nicaragua	Spanish
es_PA	Panama	Spanish
es_PY	Paraguay	Spanish
es_PR	Puerto Rico	Spanish
es_UY	Uruguay	Spanish
es_AR	Argentina	Spanish
es_BO	Bolivia	Spanish
es_CL	Chile	Spanish
es_CO	Columbia	Spanish
es_CR	Costa Rica	Spanish
es_DO	Dominican Republic	Spanish
es_MX	Mexico	Spanish
es_PE	Peru	Spanish
es_ES	Spain	Spanish
es_VE	Venezuela	Spanish
sv_SE	Sweden	Swedish
th_TH	Thailand	Thai
th_TH_TH	Thailand Traditional	Thai
tr_TR	Turkey	Turkish
uk_UA	Ukraine	Ukrainian
vi_VN	Vietnam	Vietnamese

Specifying a locale for an object

For the purposes of this exercise, create a new blank form, and drag a Date/Time object onto it. Then follow these steps:

1. Click the Field tab of the Object palette.

2. Select the locale for your form from the locale list, as shown in Figure 6-9.

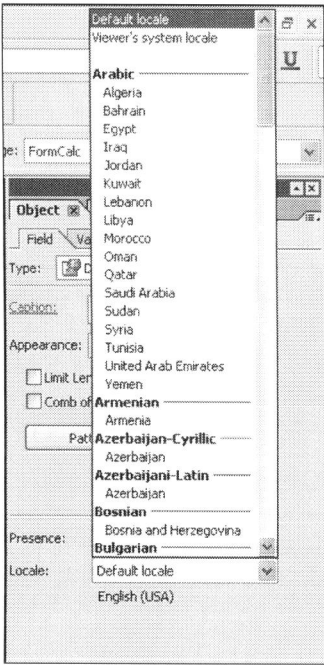

Figure 6-9. Specifying a locale for an object

Scripting form interactions

Scripting provides you with a way to enhance the user experience with the form design. It enables you to automatically calculate form values to prompt users to conduct certain actions. In the following sections, you will learn how to apply conditional form interactions to your forms and how to run calculations in JavaScript.

Creating conditional form interactions

Conditional form interactions in LiveCycle Designer ES allow you to verify data for a field in a subform that repeats against previous field instances. Conditional formatting enables you to set conditions that determine where page breaks should be based on data that is imported.

An example of this is a bank statement, where the repeating subform can be broken by the fields that contain the transaction date for each entry. The bank statement can then be broken down into transaction dates, making it more intuitive to read and understand.

See a conditional break in action

You'll now open ConditionalPageBreak.xpd from the form snippets that are installed along with LiveCycle Designer to investigate conditional breaks. LiveCycle Designer's form snippets have functions that range from calculations to date validations and that also import and export data.

1. Select File ➤ Open.
2. Browse to where ConditionalPageBreak.xpd is saved. By default, it is located in your LiveCycle Designer directory: \EN\Samples\Form Snippets\ConditionalPageBreak.xpd. Open the XPD form, as shown in Figure 6-10.

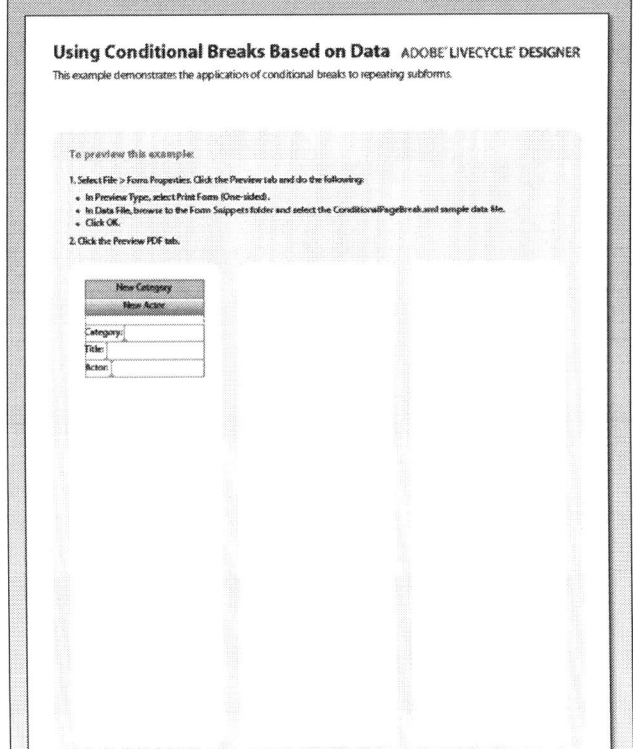

Figure 6-10. Design View of ConditionalPageBreak.xpd

3. Select File ➤ Form Properties. The Form Properties dialog box will appear.

4. Click the Preview tab. Set the Preview Type field to Print Form One-sided. The Data File field is automatically populated with a reference to ConditionalPageBreak.xml, as shown in Figure 6-11.

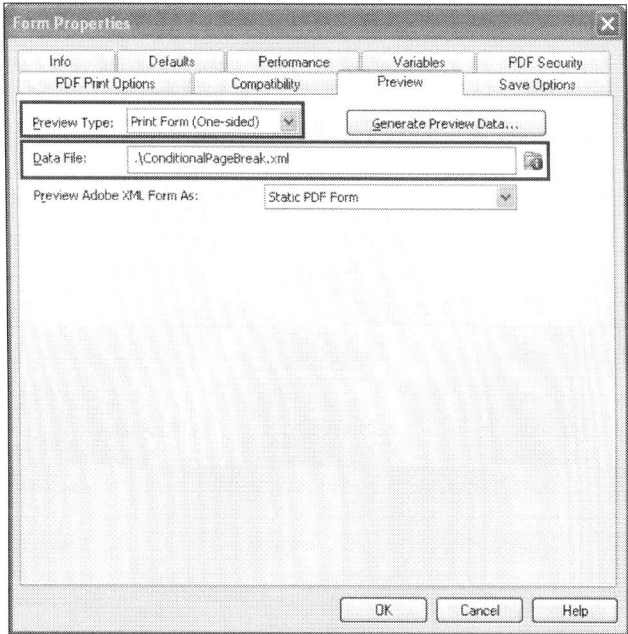

Figure 6-11. The Data File field is automatically populated with a reference to ConditionalPageBreak.xml.

5. Click OK to close the Form Properties dialog box.

6. Click the Preview PDF tab to view the form.

You will notice that when you preview the PDF, it has been populated with data from the XML file, as shown in Figure 6-12. You will also note that there has been two breaks placed in the data to contain it all on one page.

Figure 6-12. The PDF preview of the document shows the data from the associated XML file.

Conditional breaks are specified in your form in the Edit Conditional Breaks dialog box, as shown in Figure 6-13. You will now investigate this.

Figure 6-13. Click Edit on the Pagination tab to launch the Edit Conditional Breaks dialog box.

To open the Edit Conditional Breaks dialog box, select a subform or object from your dynamic form design, and click Edit on the Pagination Page on the Object palette.

You are able to work with conditional breaks only when the form is dynamic and flowable.

Understanding conditional breaks

Conditional breaks offer a flexibility that traditional static breaks do not: they allow for multiple breaks of an object. Instead of data overflow controlling where the form is paginated via conditional statements, conditional breaks enable you to manually control where a subform breaks. In the previous example of the bank statement, the subform could be broken to paginate the form and ensure the transactions are neatly listed on multiple pages.

When you launch the Edit Conditional Breaks dialog box on a dynamic form that has had no previous conditional breaks inserted, it is initially blank, as shown in Figure 6-14.

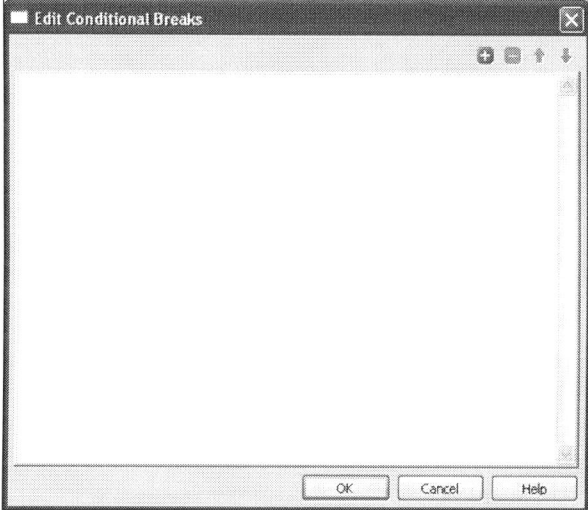

Figure 6-14. The Edit Conditional Breaks dialog box launches as a blank box.

145

I will now define each section of the Edit Conditional Breaks dialog box:

Add: Clicking the Add button adds a conditional break to your form, as shown in Figure 6-15. If the object you are applying the conditional break on already has conditional breaks inserted previously, the new break is listed following the existing ones.

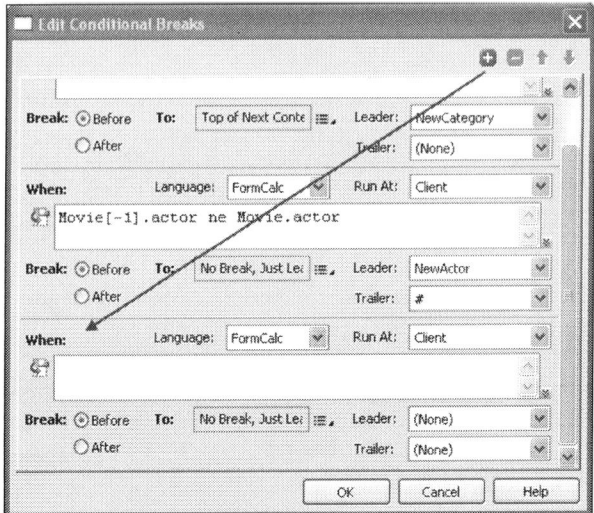

Figure 6-15. Adding a conditional break

Delete: Clicking the Delete button removes a conditional break from the object.

Move Up: Clicking this button enables you to reorder the conditional breaks in the Edit Conditional Breaks dialog box by moving the selected break up.

Move Down: Clicking this button enables you to reorder the conditional breaks in the Edit Conditional Breaks dialog box by moving the selected break down.

When: The When section allows you to define when a conditional break is required.

Language: The drop-down Language list allows you to specify which scripting language you want to use, FormCalc or JavaScript.

Run At: The Run At drop-down determines where the script will run at—on the client side, the server side, or both the client and server. Remember that to run scripts on the server side, they must be implemented in conjunction with Adobe LiveCycle Forms ES.

Break: The Break radio buttons enable you to specify where the conditional break should occur—before the current object or after.

To: This section determines where the remaining fields and data will be placed after the conditional break.

Trailer: This section enables you to specify the trailer subform for the conditional break.

Working with flowed form layouts

Flowed form layouts differ from static forms in that they do not have a fixed layout. Depending on the data entered by the user, they can expand and contract as required.

Adobe LiveCycle Designer contains a number of features that allow you to create these versatile forms. In the following sections, you will investigate subforms and tables, which allow you to accomplish this.

Understanding subforms

As mentioned in earlier chapters, a **subform** is a component of form design that is used to create a dynamic form that has a flowable layout. It is a container object that is responsible for the layout and the anchoring of objects. These objects can be arranged in tables, rows, and columns within the subform. Subforms offer your form great flexibility because they can be nested inside each other, and you can add multiple subforms to your form. If your form has a fixed layout, you will probably not need to use more than one subform in the form design.

Every form contains a root subform. In the Hierarchy palette, the root subform is called Form1 and appears as the parent node. Below this parent node, the default page subform ((untitled subform) (page 1)) appears as a child node. If you add a new subform (Subform 1), it appears below the default page subform, as shown in Figure 6-16.

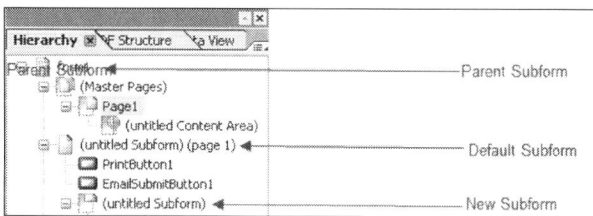

Figure 6-16. Identifying subforms in the Hierarchy palette

You can add a subform to a form design in two ways, via the Library palette or via the main menu.

Using subforms in dynamic forms

Subforms are used in dynamic forms to create sections that expand and contract to accommodate the data being merged into them. This is done via nesting subforms into the form hierarchy to match the XML data file that will be merged with it.

A flowable form usually includes subforms that have been nested together. Each subform contains one or more objects.

Each subform can be configured so that when you render the form to a PDF document, only the subforms containing the objects that are necessary when representing data are placed. You can also use a subform to draw a border around another group of subforms.

Using tables

Tables provide a logical way of structuring form content in a coherent and rational fashion. A **table** is a list of information that is arranged in a grid of rows and columns. Each section of the grid is called a **table cell**. In Adobe LiveCycle Designer, you can store different objects in table cells to create an ordered and intuitive form structure.

Creating nested tables

In Chapter 2, you investigated how to create tables via the Table Assistant and the Insert Table dialog box. You will now create a formatted table, and then you will nest a new table within it.

1. Create a new, blank form in LiveCycle Designer.
2. Create a basic table by dragging the Table object from the Standard palette onto Design View. The Insert Table dialog box will appear.
3. Using the Insert Table dialog box, create a table that has five rows and four columns. Ensure the Include Header Row in Table check box is selected, as shown in Figure 6-17.

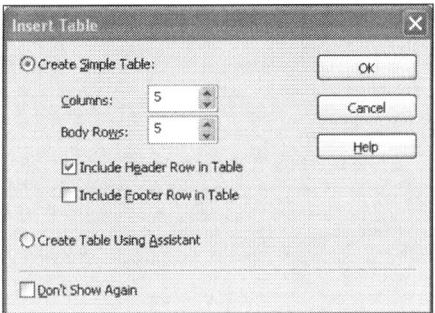

Figure 6-17. Creating a table with the Insert Table dialog box

4. Double-click the top-left header row to select the text. Rename each of the headings from left to right: Date, First Name, Last Name, and Order, as shown in Figure 6-18.

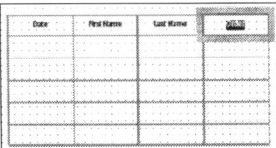

Figure 6-18. Renaming headings in a table

5. Double-click a header cell to select it. From the menu, select Table ➤ Select ➤ Row Cells to select all the cells from the header row.

6. From the menu, select Window ➤ Border to display the Border palette.

7. With the header row still selected, choose Solid from the Background Fill section's drop-down list, and choose the color lemon from the color picker, as shown in Figure 6-19.

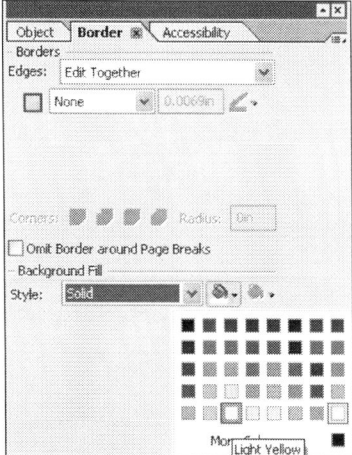

Figure 6-19. The Border palette

If you click the PDF Preview tab, your table displays, as illustrated in Figure 6-20. This is the basic table. You will now nest a new table for the order details in the Order column.

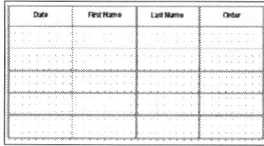

Figure 6-20. A basic table with header defined

8. From the Standard section of the Object Library palette, drag and drop a Table object into the topmost body cell under the Order column. This is a nested table.

9. Resize the table by dragging the right side until all the nested table's headings are visible.

10. Using steps 4–7, change the headings of the new table to **Date**, **Quantity**, and **Flavor**, and change the background color of the heading row to pink, as shown in Figure 6-21.

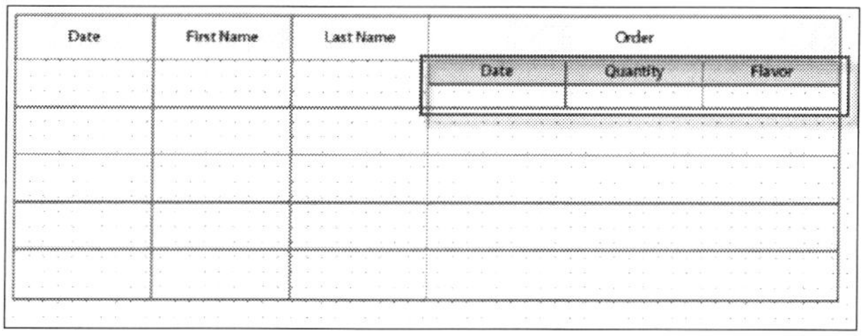

Figure 6-21. A nested table is indicated by the red border.

149

Creating dynamic tables

You can use both tables and subforms to create dynamic forms. In fact, you can speedily create tables that adjust to accommodate form data and flow over multiple form pages.

Create a Table

In the next exercise, you will create a table that expands when a button is clicked, using the New Form Assistant in the predesigned cheque.pdf form:

1. In LiveCycle Designer, open the cheque.pdf file you downloaded from the friends of ED website, as shown in Figure 6-22.

Figure 6-22. The cheque.pdf form prior to adding a table to it

2. From the Standard section of the Object Library palette, drag and drop a Table object onto Design View, as shown in Figure 6-23.

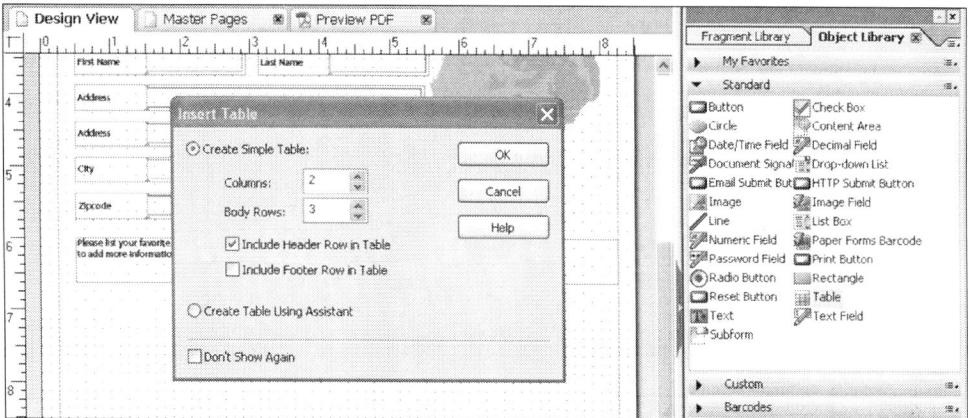

Figure 6-23. The Insert Table dialog box appears upon dragging a Table object onto Design View.

3. In the Insert Table dialog box, select the radio button Create Table Using Assistant, as shown in Figure 6-24.

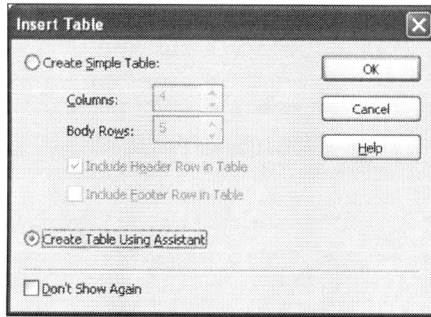

Figure 6-24. Initiating the Create Table Assistant via the Table object

4. Select the Body Rows Vary Depending on Data button in the Table Assistant.

5. At the Number of Columns section, enter **2**, and click Next, as shown in Figure 6-25.

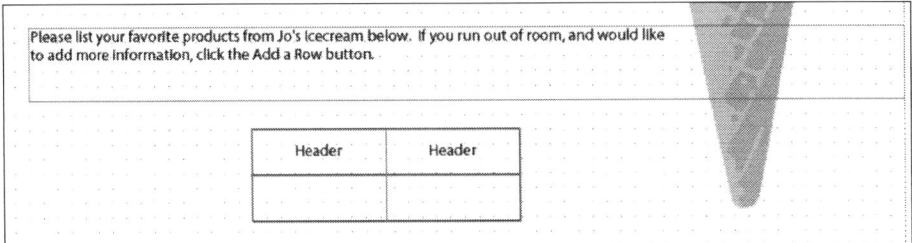

Figure 6-25. Creating a table with two columns via the Table Assistant

6. Accept the defaults on the Header and Footer screens.

7. For the 4. Sections section, select Has Body Row and No Sections. Click Next.

8. Accept the default for the 5. Row Shading section, and click Finish.

The table will appear in your form, as shown in Figure 6-26.

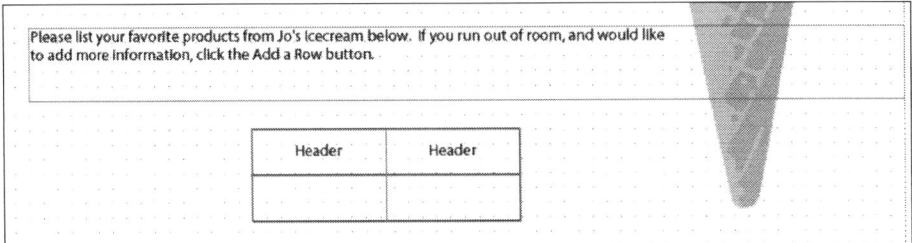

Figure 6-26. The default table inserted into your form

9. Save the form as a dynamic XML form (.pdf) document.

Make tables productive

In the next exercise, you will make the headings intuitive and change the product body cell into a text field that can capture data:

1. Click the leftmost heading.

2. Select Table ➤ Row Cells to select the row.

3. Select Window ➤ Border to display the Border palette.

4. In the Border palette, choose Solid from the Background Fill section's Style drop-down list. From the color picker, choose the color pink, as shown in Figure 6-27.

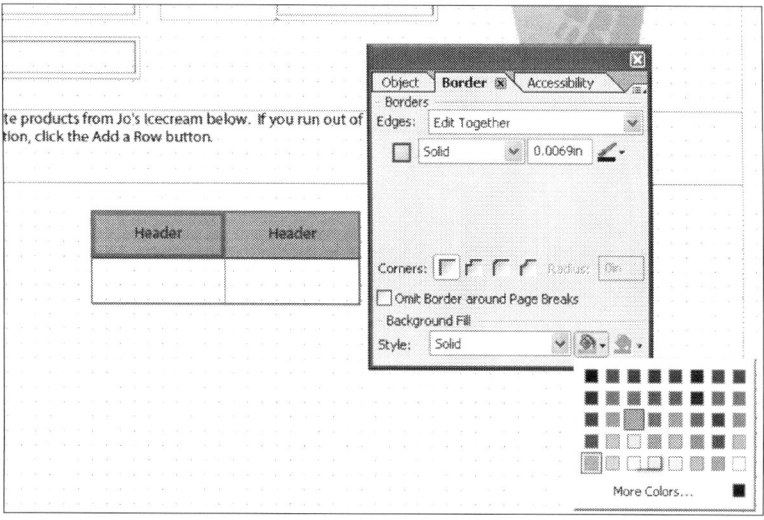

Figure 6-27. Using the Border palette to define your table formatting

5. Double-click the left header to select it. Change the header to **Command**.

6. Double-click the right header to select it. Change it to **Favorite Product**.

7. Select the entire table, and use the handles to drag it to be approximately 60 percent of the screen width, as shown in Figure 6-28.

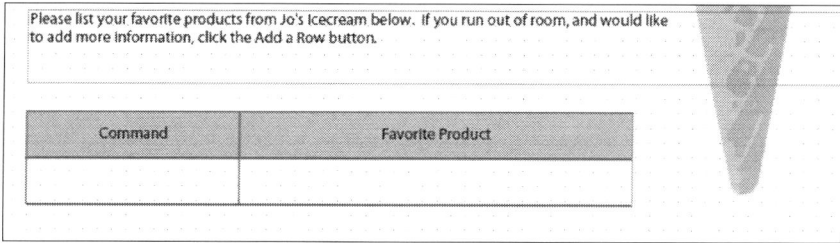

Figure 6-28. Resizing the table and editing the table header

153

8. Click the body cell under the Favorite Product heading to select it.

9. In the Object palette, change the Type drop-down list to Text Field, as shown in Figure 6-29.

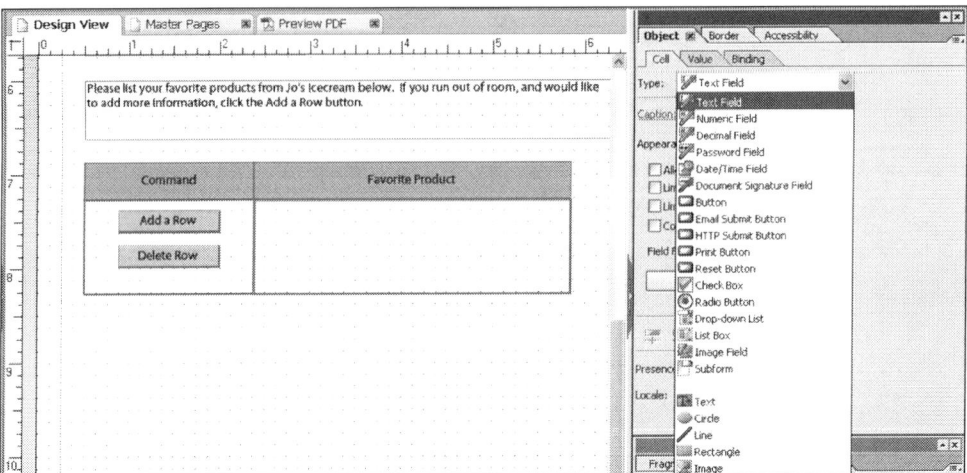

Figure 6-29. Changing a table cell to a Text Field object in the Object palette

Click the Preview PDF tab to view the form. If you click in the body cell under the Favorite Product heading, you will now be able to enter text in it, as shown in Figure 6-30.

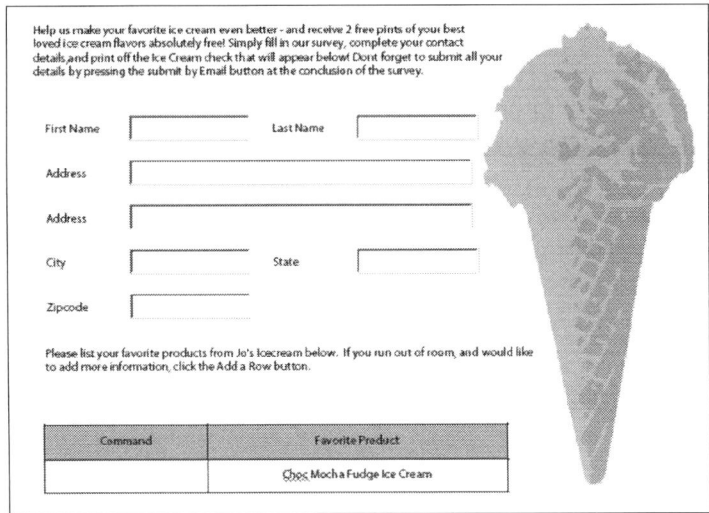

Figure 6-30. The table cell is now a text field and is editable.

Your form is now ready to become an interactive form. You will now transform the static table into a subform and add buttons that will allow the user to add or delete lines depending upon the number of products they want to enter into the form.

10. Click the first cell in the first body row to select it.

11. Select Subform from the Type drop-down list in the Object palette, as shown in Figure 6-31.

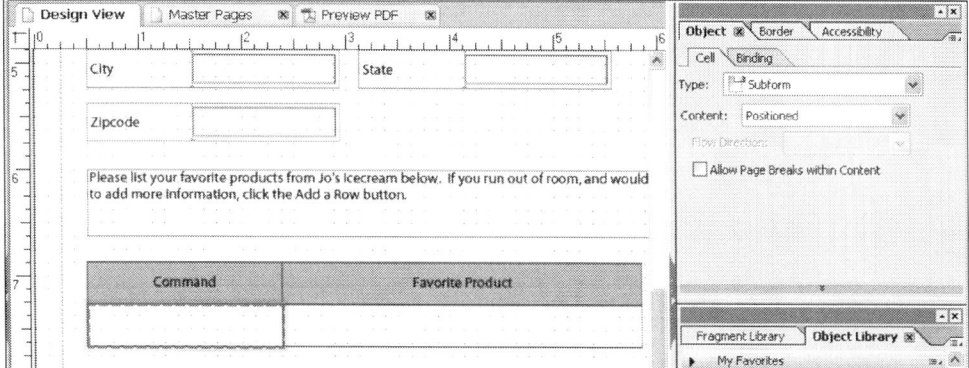

Figure 6-31. Changing a table cell into a subform

You need the cell to be transformed into a subform so you can add two buttons to it. You can also accomplish this by dragging the Subform object into the cell from the Object Library palette.

12. From the Standard category in the Object Library palette, drag the Button object into the first cell of the topmost body row, as shown in Figure 6-32.

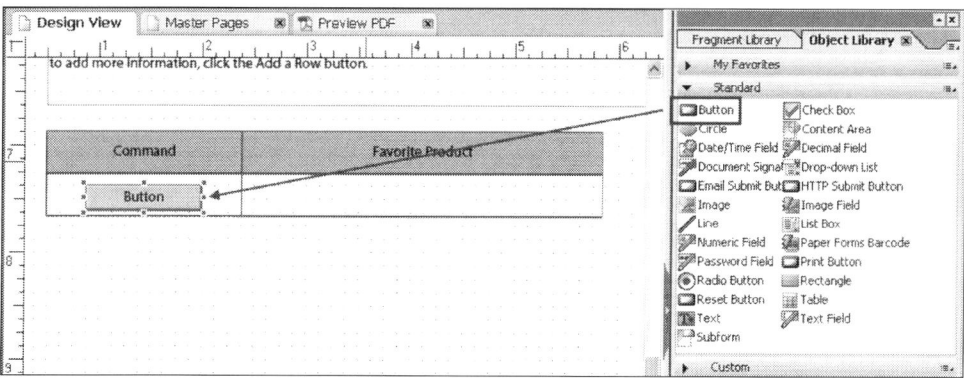

Figure 6-32. Dragging a Button object onto Design View

13. Click the Field tab of the Object palette, and change the caption to **Add a Row**, as shown in Figure 6-33.

Figure 6-33. Changing a button's caption in the Object palette

You will need to change the cell dimensions to enable the button to sit comfortably within the field. You are about to add a button for deleting a row to the same cell, so also ensure there is enough room for a second button to sit under the Add button, as shown in Figure 6-34.

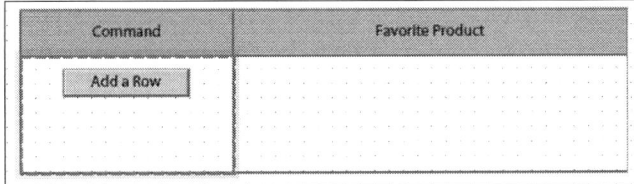

Figure 6-34. Making the table area larger by dragging

14. Drag the Button object from the Object Library palette into the same table cell where the Add a Row button is.

15. Click the Field tab of the Object palette, and change the button caption to **Delete Row**, as shown in Figure 6-35.

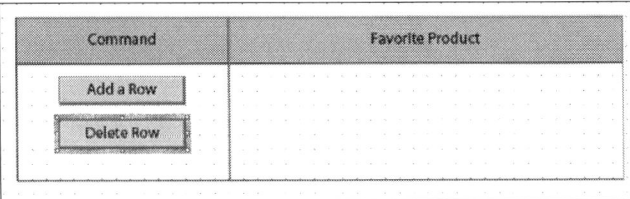

Figure 6-35. Adding a Delete Row button to the table cell

You'll now apply JavaScript to the Add a Row button to assign it the behavior of adding a row to the table when it is clicked.

16. Click the Add a Row button to select it.

17. Display the Script Editor if it is hidden by selecting Window ➤ Script Editor.

18. Select Click from the Show list, and select JavaScript from the Language drop-down list.

19. Enter the following script into the Script Editor (see Figure 6-36):

```
Table.Row1.instanceManager.addInstance(1);
```

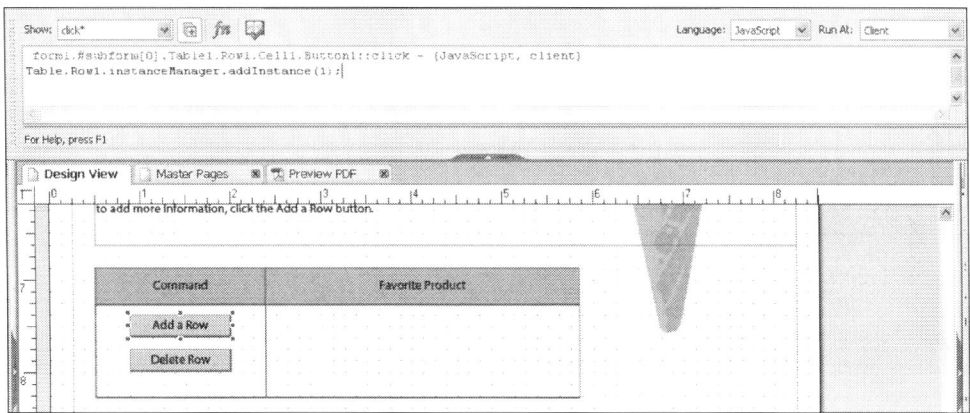

Figure 6-36. Adding a script to a button

20. Click the Delete Row button to select it.

21. In the Script Editor, select Click in the Show list, and select JavaScript in the Language drop-down list.

22. Enter the following script into the Script Editor:

```
Table.Row1.instanceManager.removeInstance(1);
```

You have now successfully created a table that can expand upon user interaction. If a user wanted to enter two or more items into the table, they need only click the Add a Row button. If they decide they want to remove an entry, they simply click the Delete Row button.

Creating shared and reusable form content

Creating reusable content such as form fragments and custom objects enables you to streamline your form creation process, because it means you can build form objects that can be used multiple times on a single form or share the reusable content between forms. This helps you standardize form fields across similar forms.

Creating and using custom objects

In Chapter 3, I touched briefly upon custom objects. In this exercise, you'll create and save a custom object:

1. Open a new blank form in LiveCycle Designer.
2. Drag a Text Field object onto Design View.
3. Change the caption to **FirstName**.
4. Click the Custom section of the Object Library palette.
5. Drag the object that's on Design View to the Custom Object library.
6. Complete the Add Library Object dialog box (as shown in Figure 6-37) by entering **First Name** in the Name field and by entering a description in the Description field. Click OK.

Figure 6-37. Labeling a custom object in the Add Library Object dialog box

The FirstName custom object will appear in the Custom Object library palette and can be implemented as a regular object, as shown in Figure 6-38.

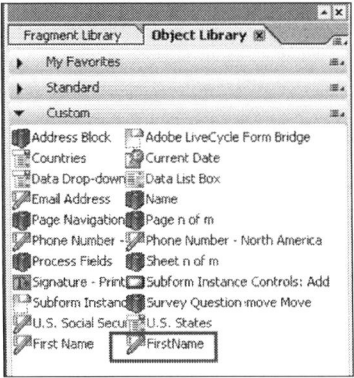

Figure 6-38. The custom Object Library palette with the new custom object

Using form fragments

Form fragments are parts of a form that can be reused and inserted into many different form designs. When you are creating a new form, you simply insert a reference to the fragment you want to use, and it will be displayed in the form. Fragments are saved in the file system and the Fragment Library as separate XDP files. Fragments are timesavers because they speed up the creation and maintenance of forms that require the same information in them, and they are all created in the same way. If you need to update the form objects in a fragment, you need only to edit the fragment, and the changes will be updated throughout all the forms that contain the fragment.

Fragments can be created in the current form design, or you can open a new form and create them there. When a fragment is saved, it is saved in the file system, and it can be implemented not just in multiple forms but by more than one form designer, provided the form is being created in Adobe LiveCycle Designer ES.

Creating a fragment from a Text Field object

I will use a basic text field to demonstrate how to create a fragment. This fragment will be saved into the Fragment Library palette. Follow these steps:

1. Open a new blank form in LiveCycle Designer.

2. Drag and drop a Text object onto Design View, as shown in Figure 6-39.

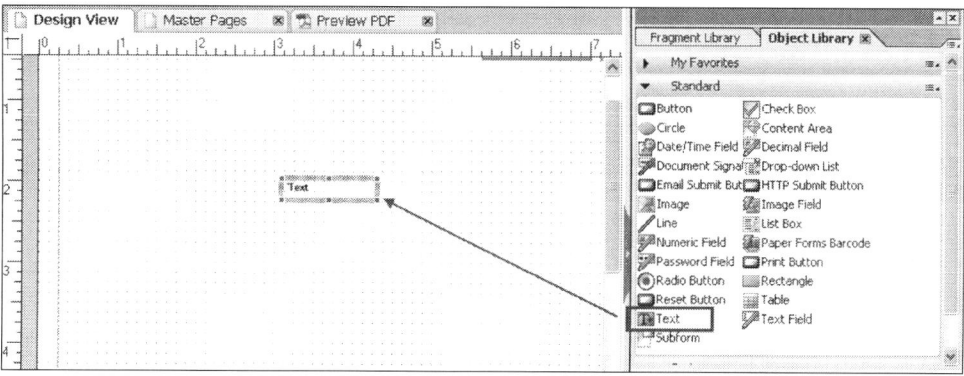

Figure 6-39. Dragging a Text object onto Design View in preparation of transforming it into a form fragment

You'll next create a fragment you can use in the cheque.pdf document.

3. In the Font palette, change the font to Copperplate Gothic Light and the size to 26.

> To display the Font palette, select Window ➤ Font.

4. Double-click the object to enable editing. Change the text to **Ice Cream Voucher**, as shown in Figure 6-40.

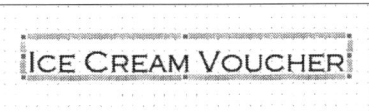

Figure 6-40. Editing the Text object

Now that you have formatted the Text object to suit the cheque.pdf document, you will turn it into a fragment.

5. From the menu, select Edit ➤ Fragment ➤ Create Fragment.

6. In the Create Fragment dialog box, enter **Ice Cream Voucher** in the Name field and the text **This is the heading for the Ice Cream voucher** in the Description field, as shown in Figure 6-41.

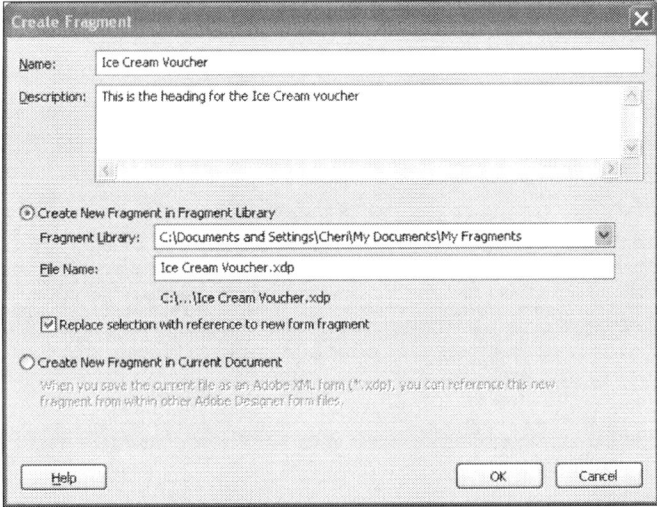

Figure 6-41. The Create Fragment dialog box

7. Ensure the Create Fragment in Fragment Library radio button is selected.

Notice how the string for the Fragment Library and File Name fields are automatically updated based upon your entry in step 2.

8. Click OK to save your new fragment.

When a fragment is saved into the Fragment Library, a new tab, Fragment Library, appears next to the Object Library tab. In this new palette, you can insert and edit fragments as required.

Inserting a fragment into a form design

To insert a predesigned fragment into a form design, follow these steps:

1. Open the cheque.pdf document you worked on previously in this chapter.

2. Scroll down until you see the second page, as shown in Figure 6-42.

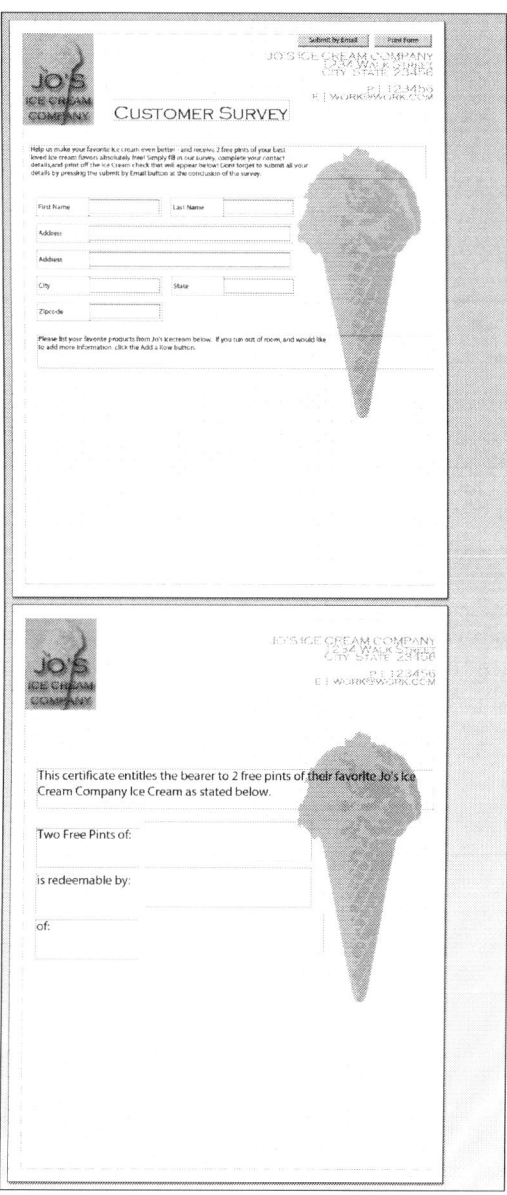

Figure 6-42. The second page of the cheque.pdf document

3. From the menu, select Insert ➤ Fragment, as shown in Figure 6-43.

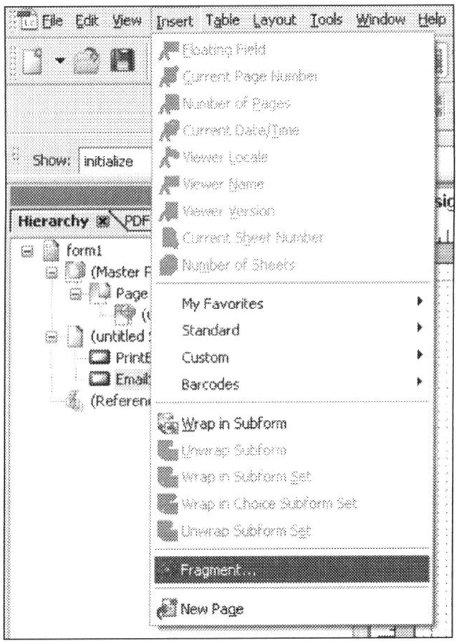

Figure 6-43. Inserting a fragment via the menu

4. Select Ice Cream Voucher.xpd in the Insert Fragment dialog box, as shown in Figure 6-44. Click OK.

Ice Cream Voucher.xpd is inserted into your form, as shown in Figure 6-45. If the program does not automatically browse to your Fragment Library, you can find it manually. As a default, you can find the Fragment Library at C:\Documents and Settings\YourUserName\My Documents\ My Fragments.

5. Save your form as an Adobe dynamic XML form, and close it. You will return to it shortly.

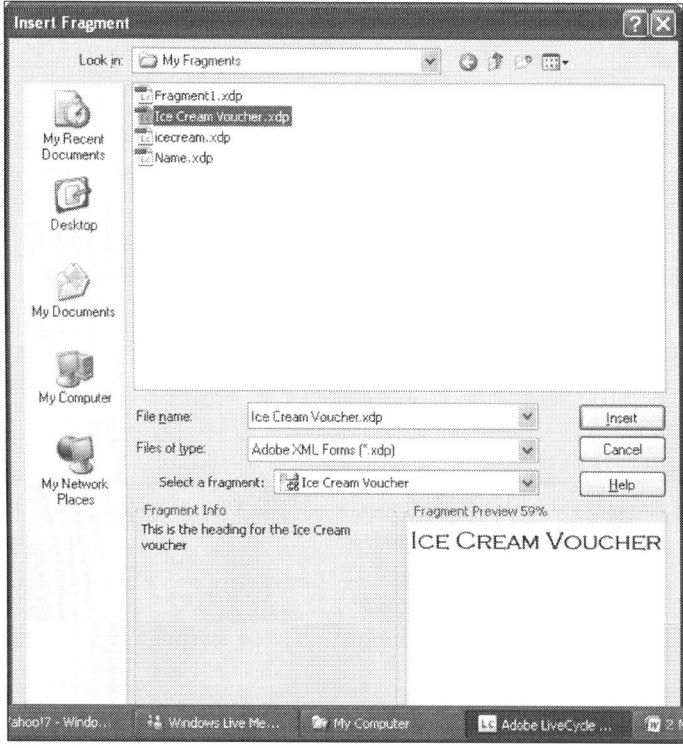

Figure 6-44. Inserting Ice Cream Voucher.xpd into a form

Figure 6-45. Inserting the Ice Cream Voucher.xpd fragment into your form

Editing a form fragment

When you edit a form fragment, it automatically updates all the forms in which that fragment appears.

Edit a Fragment

To edit a fragment, you do not have to have a form open; just follow these steps:

1. Launch Adobe LiveCycle Designer ES.

When you create a fragment, a tab automatically appears next to the Object Library tab, as shown in Figure 6-46.

Figure 6-46. The Fragment tab appears next to the Object Library tab.

2. Click the Fragment Library tab. A list of all form fragments that have been saved into the Fragment Library palette will appear.

3. Right-click Ice Cream Voucher in the Fragment Library palette, and select Edit Fragment, as shown in Figure 6-47.

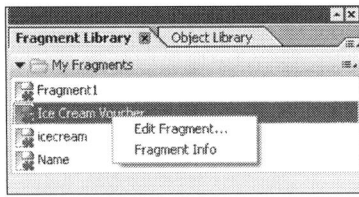

Figure 6-47. Editing your fragment via the Fragment tab

The fragment will open in Design View.

4. Double-click the object on the palette to select it.

5. Rename the object from Ice Cream Voucher to **Free Ice Cream Certificate**.

6. Close Ice Cream Voucher.xpd, saving the change when prompted.

7. Open the cheque.pdf form. Note how the caption has changed from Ice Cream Voucher to Free Ice Cream Certificate, as shown in Figure 6-48.

Figure 6-48. The updated fragment in the cheque.pdf form

Using global field bindings

Global fields are fields that contain information appearing more than one time on your form. An example of this is a telephone bill that contains your telephone number, invoice number, and account number in more than one place on the document. In this example, the invoice number, telephone number, and account number could all be set as global fields, which allows you to implement them wherever they are needed in the form. All interactive fields can have global field bindings applied to them.

You'll now use the cheque.pdf form to add a number of global bindings that will complete the free ice cream certificate. If you open the form and fill it out, you will notice that State and Favorite product fields in the first and second pages have been completed for you. You'll now finish the certificate by creating a global binding on the first name.

Apply a global field binding to a form design

To apply a global field binding to a form design, follow these steps:

1. Open the cheque.pdf form in Adobe LiveCycle Designer.

2. Click the First Name field to select it. Select the Binding tab of the Object palette.

3. In the Name section of the Binding tab, change the name of the Text Field object from TextField1 to **FirstName**, as shown in Figure 6-49.

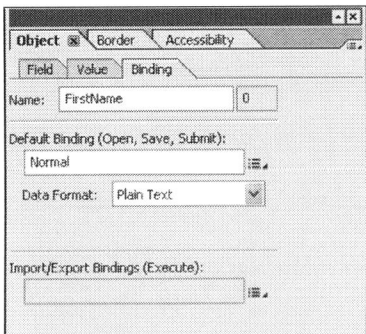

Figure 6-49. Changing the object name on the Binding tab of the Object palette

4. Click the option button for the Default Binding (Open, Save, Submit) setting, as shown in Figure 6-50. Select Global Binding in the list.

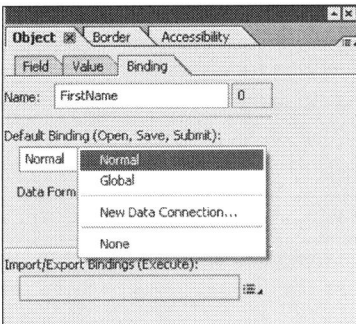

Figure 6-50. Clicking the option button for the Default Binding (Open, Save, Submit) setting

A dialog box will appear to warn that global binding will be set for all fields with similar names, as shown in Figure 6-51.

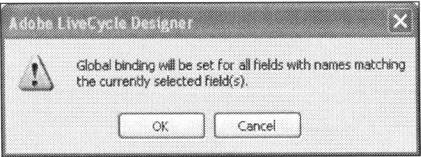

Figure 6-51. A dialog box warns when global binding is being applied.

You will now begin to populate the second page of the form with information that is globally bound from the information the user inputs on the first page.

5. On the second page of the form, click the text field next to the copy Is redeemable by to select it, as shown in Figure 6-52.

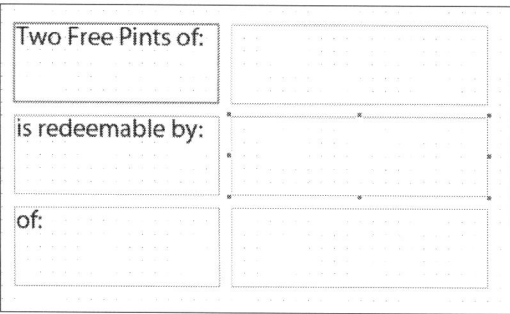

Figure 6-52. Selecting the appropriate text field

6. Click the Binding tab of the Object palette.

7. Again, replace the default name with **FirstName**.

Click the Preview PDF tab to test the form. In the First Name field on the first page of the form, type the name **Jerry**. Scroll down to the second page. The name Jerry has automatically appeared in the text field next to the Is redeemable by copy, as shown in Figure 6-53.

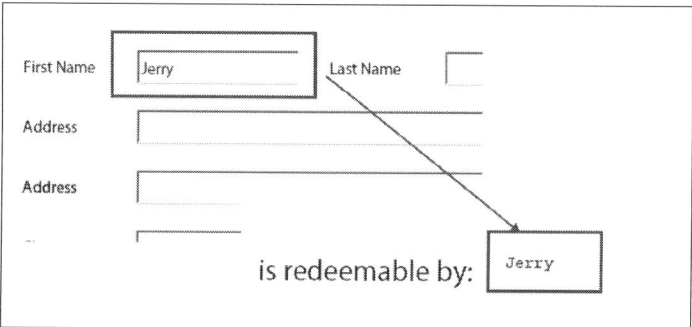

Figure 6-53. Fields displaying global binding properties

Summary

In this chapter, you learned how various form components and scripts help shape the data that the user is submitting and how features in LiveCycle Designer help the form creator streamline and standardize form-building processes.

In Chapter 7, you'll learn how XML relationships work in LiveCycle Designer and how to design forms using data connections.

Chapter 7

USING EXTERNAL FILES IN YOUR FORM

In previous chapters, you saw the flexibility that Adobe LiveCycle Designer ES offers you when creating stand-alone interactive forms. In this chapter, you will learn how to populate your forms using XML schemas and WSDL data connections. Data connections enable you to take your form beyond the standard fill-and-submit functionality to more fully integrated and compelling form offerings.

When you integrate your form design with web services and databases, you can build forms that can display database information to the user, validate data that the user has entered, and enter that data directly into a corporate data source. This flexibility and sophistication is enabled by connecting one or more data sources to your form design and then binding the data to fields on your form. In Chapter 5, you learned how to connect a Microsoft Access database to a form design. In this chapter, you'll learn how to connect a form to an XML schema and a WSDL connection.

Designing XML relationships in LiveCycle Designer

To begin to understand the XML relationships in LiveCycle Designer, you must first understand the purpose of electronic forms. They provide the accessibility of a traditional document while allowing users to interact with business processes.

An XML **schema** defines the data the form generates; in other words, it contains the data that will populate your form. As illustrated in Figure 7-1, the process of designing XML relationships in LiveCycle Designer commences when you establish a data connection between LiveCycle Designer and a schema definition. To create this connection, you use the New Data Connection dialog box, where you specify the location of your XML file and import it into the form. The information in the XML document then appears on the Data View palette of the form. Then, you can design the form based on the fields in the Data View palette. The final step of this process is rendering the form into a PDF document.

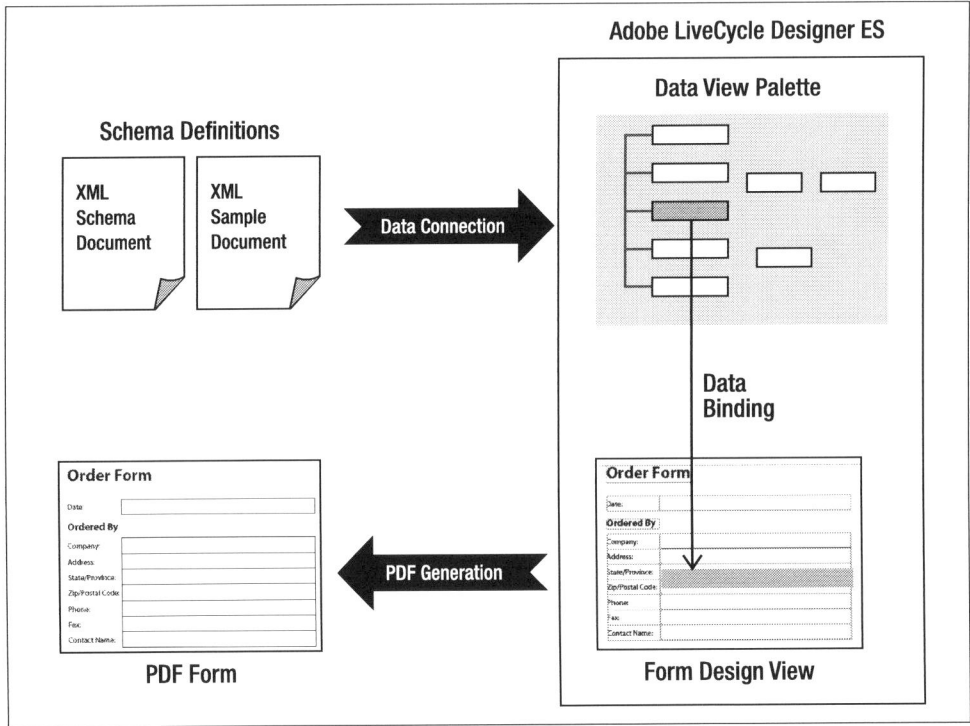

Figure 7-1. The XML schema relationship with LiveCycle Designer. The three-step process begins when you connect an XML schema to a form. Then the form is designed based on the information supplied by the schema, and finally it is rendered into a PDF document.

In LiveCycle Designer, XML schemas can be bound to form fields and subforms, which enables them to procure the XML schema characteristics such as validations and categories of data. Form developers also manipulate XML schema elements to customize information in interactive PDF forms.

Connecting to an XML schema

As discussed in Chapter 6, forms are composed of subforms, and each subform is responsible for controlling a section of the presentation, behavior, and structure of the form. Subforms can contain interactive objects such as fields and noninteractive objects such as images, as well as contain other subforms that define the final way the form will be displayed when it is opened.

XML schemas define elements in an XML document. In Adobe LiveCycle Designer, you are able to connect one XML schema to a form and then bind elements and attributes defined by the schema to fields in your form. This allows you to map data to and from form fields in a way that is dictated by the schema, which enables you to quickly implement forms from existing schemas and database collection tools.

In XML schemas, the element declaration is an important piece of the XML schema document, because it specifies the type, occurrence, structure, and value constraints of an elements. Furthermore, XML schema element declarations can have either simple or complex types.

Implementing XML Schemas in LiveCycle

By now you might be wondering how subforms and XML element declarations are related. In LiveCycle Designer, XML elements that have simple types are mapped directly to fields, but elements with complex types, which define element contents, are mapped to subforms.

In LiveCycle Designer fields and subforms are named after the XML schema definition elements that are mapped to them. By default, the caption for a subform or field is also the name of the XML schema element that maps to it.

As mentioned earlier, you can connect XML schemas to a form using the New Data Connection dialog box. You first encountered the New Data Connection dialog box in Chapter 6 when you used it to connect a Microsoft Access database to a drop-down field.

Connect a form to a schema

You will now use the New Data Connection dialog box to connect a form to an XML schema:

1. Ensure that you have downloaded the .zip file for this book and have extracted the sample.xsd and OrderForm.pdf files. (You can download the .zip file from http://www.friendsofed.com.)
2. Open OrderForm.pdf in LiveCycle Designer.
3. Select File ➤ New Data Connection.
4. In the Name New Connection field, name the new data connection **XMLTest**.
5. Select the XML Schema radio button under Get Data Description from (see Figure 7-2).
6. Click Next.

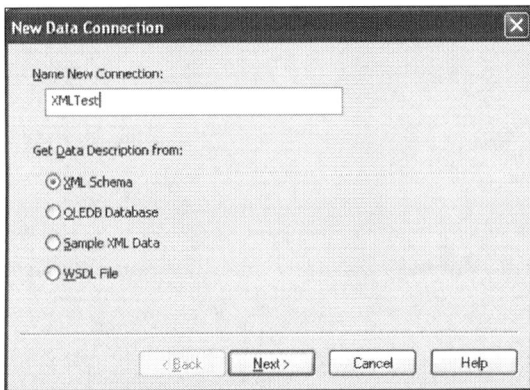

Figure 7-2. Creating an XML schema connection via the
New Data Connection dialog box

7. Click the button next to the Select XML Schema File field, and browse to where you have saved
the `sample.xsd` file, as illustrated in Figure 7-3.

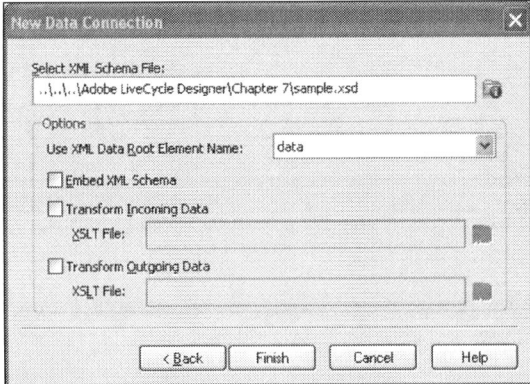

Figure 7-3. Browse to where the `sample.xpd` file is saved on
your system.

8. Ensure that Use XML Data Route Element Name is set to IceCreamOrder.

9. Select the Embed XML Schema check box, as shown in Figure 7-4. Click Finish.

10. Save your form.

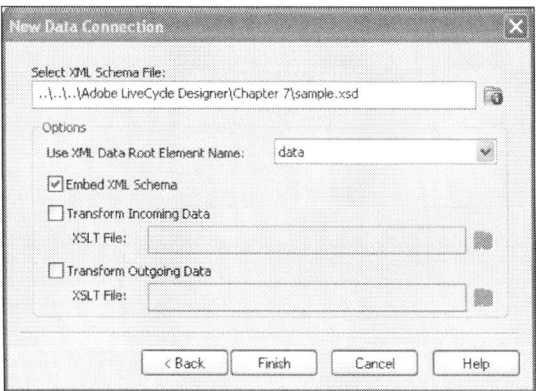

Figure 7-4. Specifying the XML data root element type and embedding an XML schema

Creating data binding with an XML data file

The first step in binding fields to a form design is connecting the form design to a data source. Before we launch into bringing the `sample.xsd` file into Adobe LiveCycle Designer, let's review exactly what an XML schema does.

An XML schema defines the fundamental building blocks of an XML document. It defines elements and attributes that appear in the document as well as defines which elements are child elements and the order that those child elements should appear. It also defines the data types of attributes and elements, whether they may be empty or not, and provides default and fixed values.

When one or more data sources are connected to the form design, the Data View palette displays a hierarchy view of each data source. Figure 7-5 shows the Data View palette of the sample file you have opened.

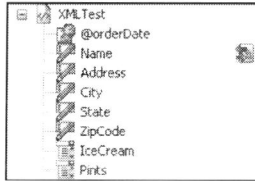

Figure 7-5. The `sample.xsd` file populated in the Data View palette with nodes and fields ready to be dragged and dropped into your form

Once a data form is established, you can create subforms and fields that correspond with the data you want to display. Creating subforms and fields is a good option to utilize when displaying data from your XML schema, because often you want to display only specific data in a schema, not the entire database, or you can design the form and then bind data from the schema to your form fields.

Use a schema

In this exercise, you'll use the XML schema. It's here you will see the value of using XML schemas, because they are so easy to translate into your PDF form.

1. Open the form OrderForm.pdf you used in the previous exercise. This is essentially a blank form (see Figure 7-6).

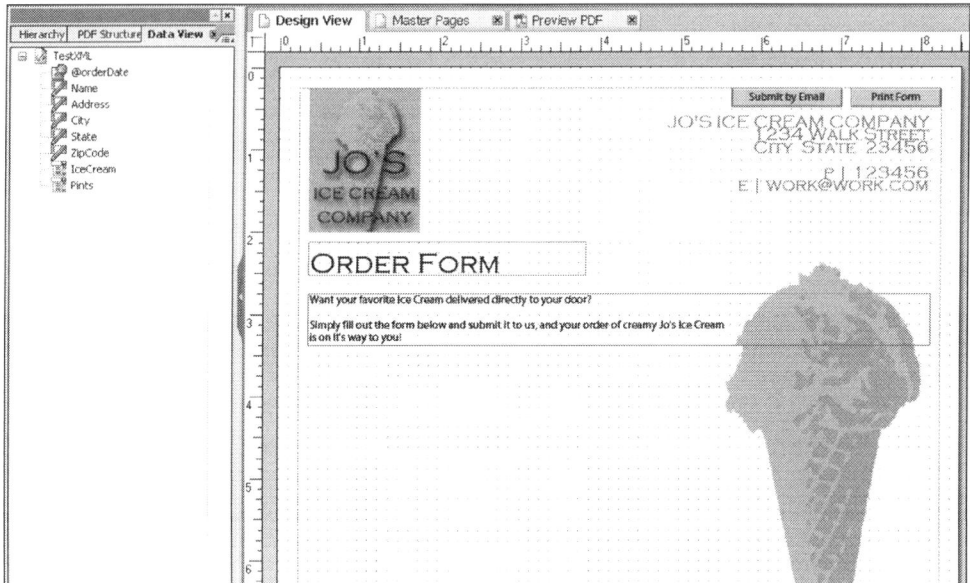

Figure 7-6. The OrderForm.pdf file with an XML schema attached displays the information from the XML form in the Data View palette.

2. Drag the XMLTest node from Data View to Design View, as shown in Figure 7-7.

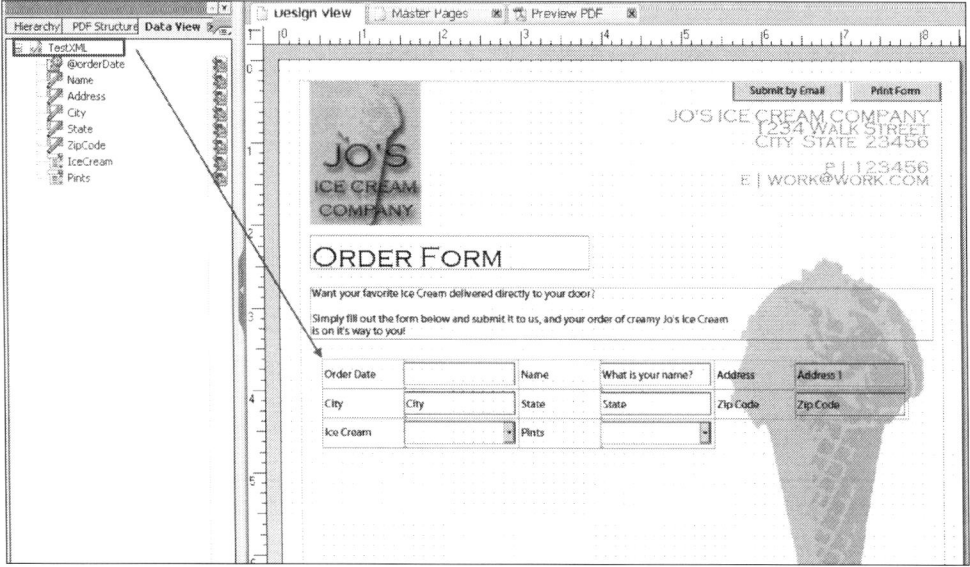

Figure 7-7. The XML schema dragged as a complete node onto Design View

Notice the way that the entire form has been created by the XML schema! You will now switch to the Preview PDF view to see what your PDF form will look like when it is published.

3. Click the Preview PDF tab. Your PDF form will display, as shown in Figure 7-8.

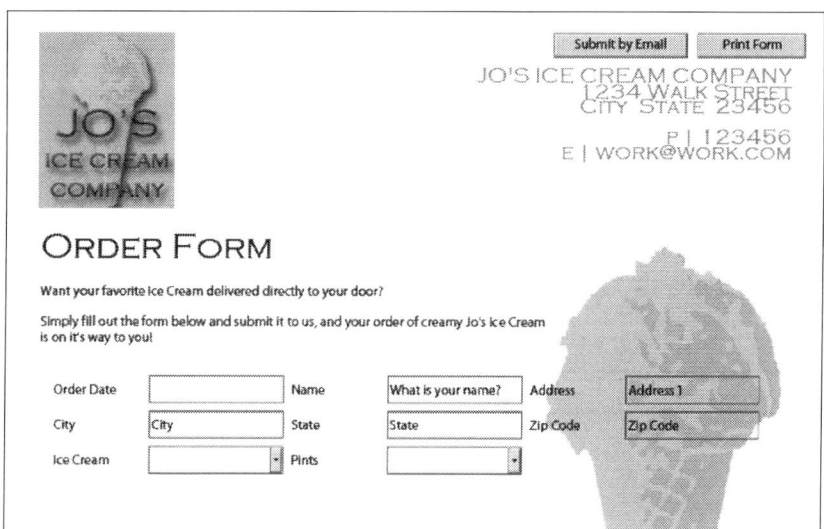

Figure 7-8. A PDF form built by dragging an XML schema onto Design View

4. Click the Ice Cream drop-down list. What do you see? It's populated with a number of options! Of course, they have come from the XML schema file. It's the same with the Pints drop-down list. LiveCycle Designer makes this even easier for you because it automatically assigns object properties such as the drop-down lists.

5. Save this form as OrderForm2.pdf, and close it.

Assign XML schema values individually

You will now investigate assigning XML schema values individually to a form design:

1. Open the form FormOrder.pdf file you used in the previous exercise, as shown in Figure 7-9.

Figure 7-9. The Form Order.pdf file prior to implementing an XML schema

In the previous exercise, you saved it as OrderForm2.pdf, so the form you open should not have any data connections or fields on it.

2. Create the data connection to sample.xsd by selecting File ➤ New Data Connection.

3. Select the XML Schema radio button under Get Data Description from (see Figure 7-2).

4. In the Name New Connection field, name the new data connection **XMLTest**.

5. Select the XML Schema radio button under Get Data Description from (see Figure 7-2).

6. Click the button next to the Select XML Schema File field, and browse to where you have saved the sample.xsd file, as illustrated in Figure 7-3.

7. Ensure that Use XML Data Route Element Name is set to IceCreamOrder.

8. Select the Embed XML Schema check box. Click Finish.

9. From the Data View palette, drag the @orderDate node to Design View (see Figure 7-10).

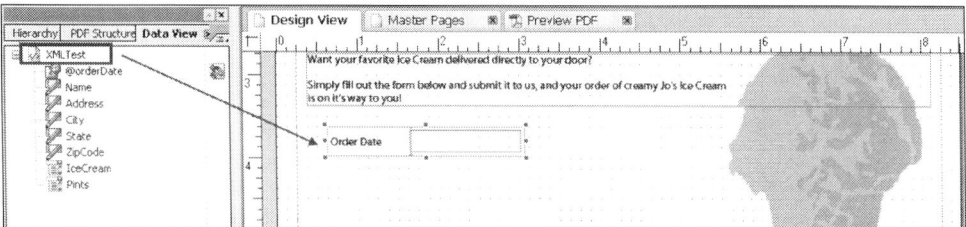

Figure 7-10. Dragging nodes across to Design View to build the form

10. Repeat this process with the Name, Address, City, State, ZipCode, IceCream, and Pints nodes. Your form should resemble Figure 7-11.

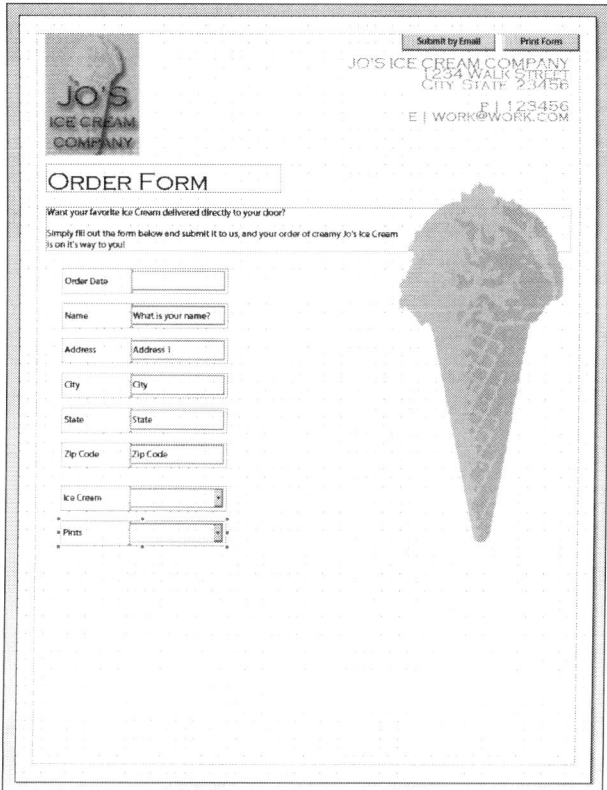

Figure 7-11. The form composed the nodes dragged onto Design View

Notice the symbols that appear each time you drag a data node to Design View, as shown in Figure 7-12. This is an easy way to see which data nodes are bound in the form on forms that have multiple pages.

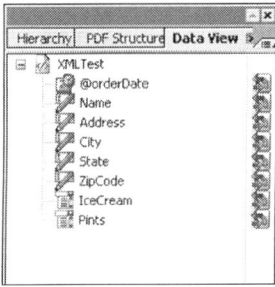

Figure 7-12. The symbols on the right of the XML node indicate the field has been deployed in your form.

11. Save your form, and click the Preview PDF tab to view it, as shown in Figure 7-13.

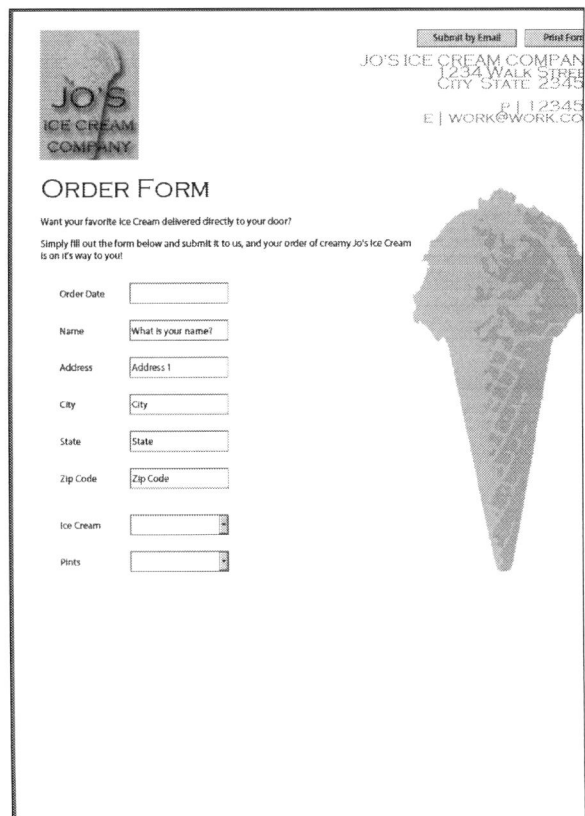

Figure 7-13. The form was created instantly by dragging all the fields from the Data View palette together.

Using WSDL files in your form design

A Web Service Definition Language (WSDL) file is a language that is based on XML and provides a template for describing web services. It describes four essential pieces of data: location information for being able to find the specified service, binding information that dictates the transport protocol, data type information for message requests and responses, and interface information that describes all the functions that are publically available.

In LiveCycle Designer, a WSDL file defines an input or output message for each operation it is bound to in your form. The server replies to these operations with an output message. When you bind objects in your form to a WSDL data connection, specific fields can be both the source of the input message and the output message destination.

Implementing a WSDL connection within your Adobe LiveCycle Designer ES form allows you to perform operations such as using Acrobat SOAP JavaScript objects to write client-side scripts, exchanging data with a web service, enabling SOAP 1.1–style communication, enabling access to all returned script elements regardless of whether they are bound to fields, executing web service operations, and bringing multiple operations.

Simple Object Access Protocol (SOAP) enables programs that run in one type of operating system to communicate with a program that runs on the same or different operating system by using an HTTP protocol and XML to transfer information.

Services and features that are not enabled in LiveCycle Designer WSDL data connections include some XML schema features, the ability to use sMTP and FTP protocols as the transport for SOAP, secure web services (HTTPS), and the ability to use GET WSDL and HTTP POST bindings.

Connecting your form to a WSDL file

To connect to a WSDL file, follow these steps:

1. Open a new, blank form in Adobe LiveCycle Designer ES.
2. Select File ➤ New Data Connection. The New Data Connection dialog box appears.
3. In the Name New Connection field of the New Data Connection dialog box, type **WSDLConnection**.
4. In the Get Data Description from section, select the WSDL File radio button (see Figure 7-14).

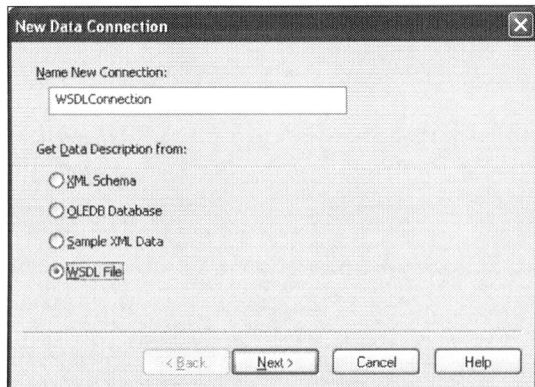

Figure 7-14. Creating a WSDL connection in the New Data Connection dialog box

> *For the purposes of this exercise, the URL that we will use is courtesy of WebserviceX.NET (www.webservicex.net), which provides free U.S. address verification. There are many free WSDL providers such as XMethods (www.xmethods.com). The particular web service that we are going to implement offers two services to find geographical information for cities in the United States and to retrieve weather forecast information. In this exercise, we will produce a form that will give us the geographical information for U.S. cities.*

5. In the New Data Connection dialog box, type **http://www.webservicex.net/globalweather. asmx?wsdl** in the WSDL File field, and then click Next (see Figure 7-15).

Figure 7-15. Entering the web service URL into the New Data Connection dialog box to create an interactive form

6. You now need to determine which operation you want to call. This particular web service offers two options: looking up weather in specific cities and finding a city by country. Choose the topmost GetWeather option, as shown in Figure 7-16.

Figure 7-16. Selecting the web service in the New Data Connection dialog box

When you select the topmost GetWeather item on the left side, the right side populates with a definition of the GetWeatherByZipCode web service:

```
GetWeatherByZipCode
Input Message: GetWeatherByZipCodeRequest
Message Part: parameters
Output Message: GetWeatherByZipCodeResponse
Message Part: parameters
Port Type: WeatherForecastSoap
This operation has a binding_operation element
This operation has an SOAP:BINDING element
This operation has an SOAP:OPERATION element
This operation has an SOAP:ACTION of :
http://www.webservicex.net/GetWeatherByZipCode
This operation has an SOAP:ADDRESS of :
http://www.webservicex.net/WeatherForecast.asmx
```

7. Click Finish.

8. Save your form as a dynamic PDF form called WSDLTest.pdf.

You will notice something has happened. Click the Data View tab if the palette is not already in view. Via the WSDL data connection, it is now populated with data nodes the same way your XML form was in the previous section. See Figure 7-17.

Figure 7-17. The WSDL connection populates the Data View palette with data nodes relating to the service you have chosen to use.

Using WSDL files to create forms that dynamically return information

In this exercise, you will drag and drop these nodes onto the Data View palette to create an interactive form that will tell you the geographical information for a ZIP code that is entered by the user. Follow these steps:

1. Click the plus (+) button to expand each node to its fullest.

2. Drag and drop the ZipCode node onto the Design View area, as shown in Figure 7-18.

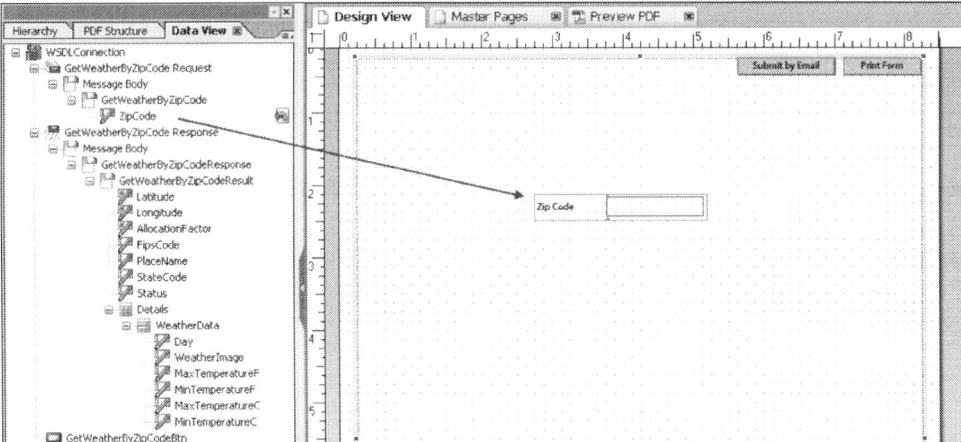

Figure 7-18. Dragging the ZipCode node onto Design View to make the entry field for the form

3. Drag and drop the following nodes onto Design View: Latitude, Longitude, AllocationFactor, FipsCode, PlaceName, StateCode, and Status. Arrange them well below the ZipCode field, as shown in Figure 7-19.

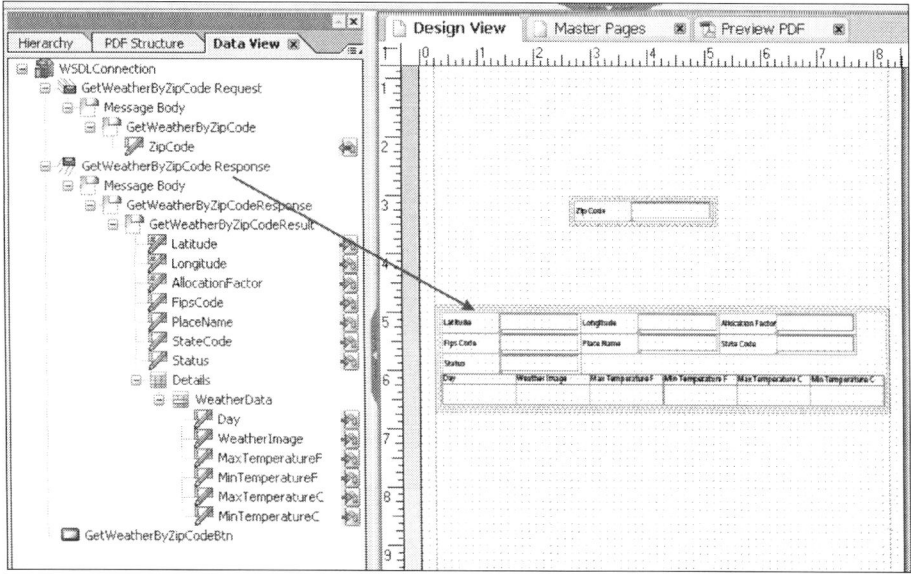

Figure 7-19. Dragging the geographical information from the WSDL connection onto Design View sets the fields for the WSDL connection to return data from the form query.

4. Drag and drop the GetWeatherByZipCode node onto Design View. Position it in the center of the page between the Zip Code field and the geographical details, as shown in Figure 7-20.

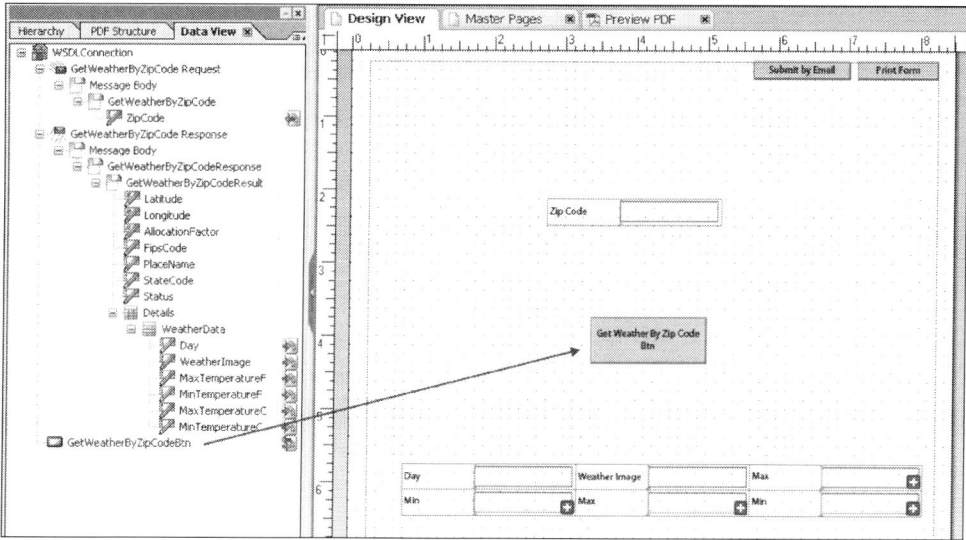

Figure 7-20. Adding a button to the WSDL connection form

5. Save your form as a dynamic XML form (.pdf). Click the Preview PDF tab to view your completed form.

You will now test your form in the Preview PDF tab. In the Zip Code field, enter the ZIP code **90210**, and click the GetWeatherByZipCode button. In most cases, you will receive an Adobe Acrobat warning (see Figure 7-21).

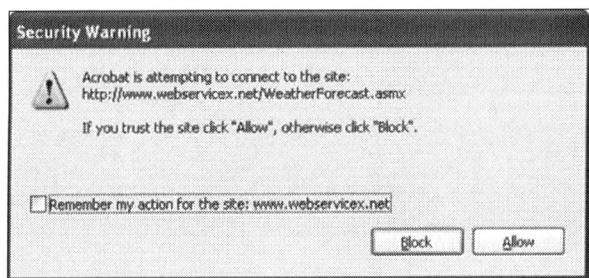

Figure 7-21. Adobe Acrobat Security Warning dialog box

6. Click Allow in the Adobe Acrobat Security Warning dialog box. Your form will populate automatically with the geographical information for the ZIP code 90210, as illustrated in Figure 7-22.

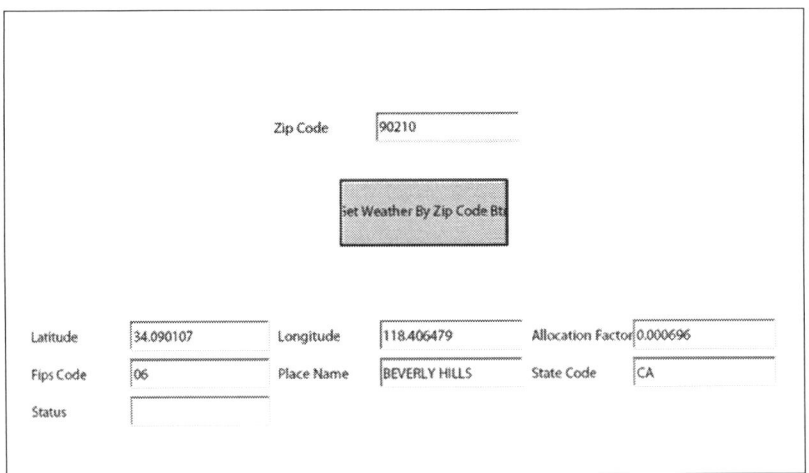

Figure 7-22. Your form populated with data from the WSDL connection

Differentiating kinds of data binding

Mapping form objects to data file elements creates a data binding. There are two forms of data bindings, and each is useful in different ways:

- *Implicit data binding*: You now know that forms created using XML and WSDL data connections contain automatic binding. This kind of binding is called **implicit data binding**. It simply means the names of form design objects match the names in the data node on the Data View palette.

- *Explicit data binding*: You are able to override implicit binding by using a specified data reference instead of an object name to map the nodes in the data source in the form design. This is called **explicit data binding**.

You can create explicit bindings by using absolute or relative binding expressions:

- *Absolute binding expressions*: Absolute binding expressions are expressions that start with $record or $data, which you can view in the Object palette. They are qualified Scripting Object Model (SOM) expressions. To create an explicit binding with an absolute binding expression, simply drag an individual node onto the form from the Data View palette, as shown in Figure 7-23. You have already learned how do to absolute binding in this chapter.

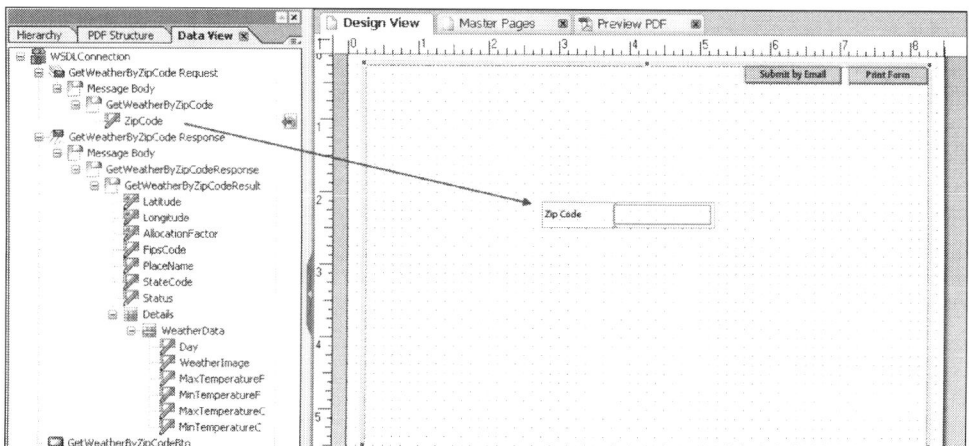

Figure 7-23. Dragging an individual data node from the Data View palette onto Design View is an absolute binding expression.

- *Relative binding expressions*: A relative binding expression is relative to the data node that is bound to the parent object. To create an explicit binding with a relative binding expression, drag a parent node from the Data View palette onto the form design, as shown in Figure 7-24. You will notice that the children nodes accompany the parent. You created an explicit binding with a relative binding expression when you dragged the geographical information onto Design View in the previous WSDL exercise.

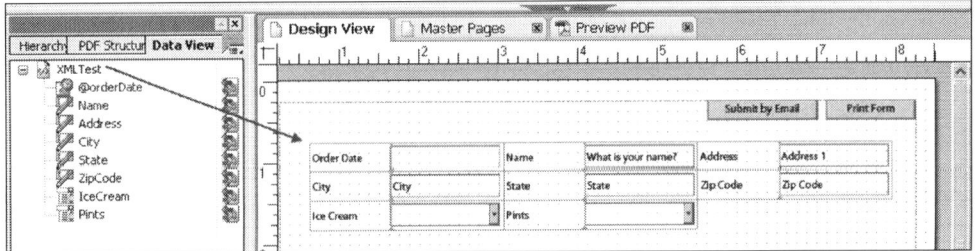

Figure 7-24. Dragging a parent data node from the Data View palette onto Design View is a relative binding expression.

Importing forms from other programs

LiveCycle Designer allows you to import forms that have been created in third-party form-authoring and XForm XML applications as well as forms created in spreadsheet applications such as Microsoft Excel. LiveCycle Designer preserves the layout of the original document when importing to the maximum extent that it can and automatically converts elements into form objects.

Importing PDFs

To import a form via the New Form Assistant, follow these steps:

1. Select File ➤ New.

2. Select the Import a PDF Document radio button, as shown in Figure 7-25.

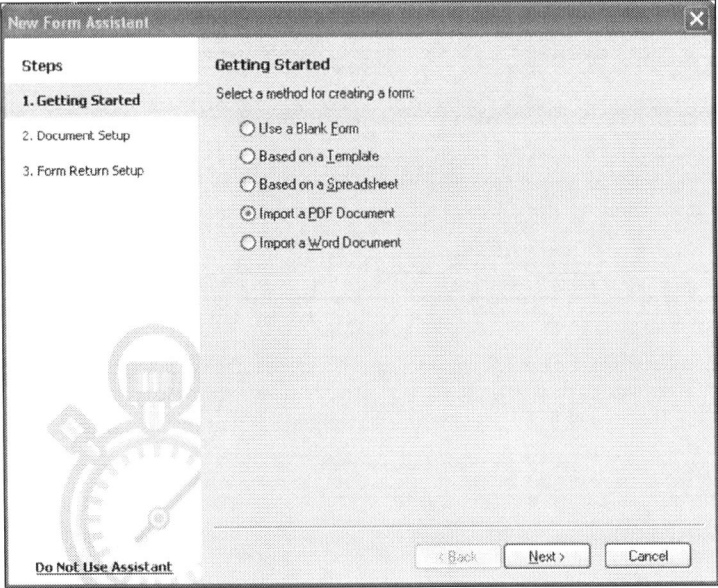

Figure 7-25. Selecting Import a PDF Document

3. Browse to where the PDF document you want to import is.

4. Select Finish. The static form will open in LiveCycle Designer, as shown in Figure 7-26.

> *You are also able to import a form by choosing* File ➤ Open *and browsing to the PDF document you want to import.*

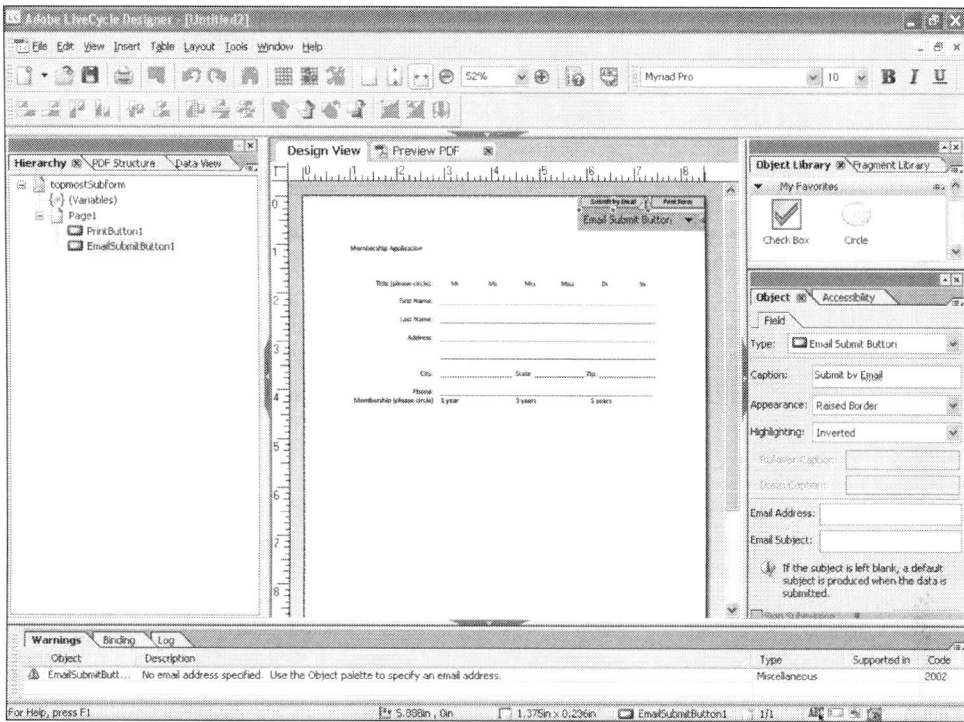

Figure 7-26. Importing a static PDF form into LiveCycle Designer

Working with Word files

Adobe LiveCycle Designer ES is able to import Microsoft Word 2003 and later as well as Microsoft Word XP files. When a Microsoft Word file is imported into LiveCycle Designer, the file's layout is preserved, but you may need to do some manual reformatting to ensure that the final document displays correctly.

For example, file properties, scripts, and page borders are imported exactly, but you will need to check paragraph formatting; in addition, you may need to adjust some table borders and form fields.

Importing a Word file

To import a Word file, ensure that you have downloaded the file `IceCream Order Form.doc` (see Figure 7-27) from `www.friendsofed.com` along with the rest of the exercise sample files. Save this on your local drive.

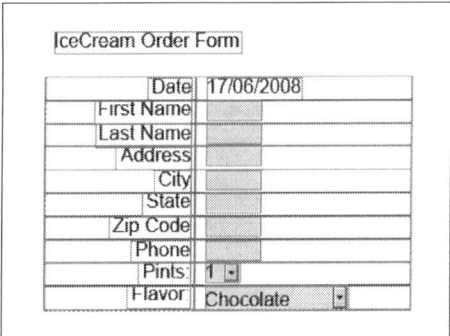

Figure 7-27. The `IceCream Order Form.doc` file you will import into LiveCycle Designer

1. Open a new blank form in LiveCycle Designer.
2. Select File ➤ New. The New Form Assistant opens.
3. Select Import a Word Document, and click Next.
4. Browse to where the Word document you want to import is located on your computer. Click Next.
5. Complete the Form Return Setup screen, and click Next.
6. Click Finish.

The File Import Options dialog box appears, and you are presented with a number of options (see Figure 7-28):

Password to open file: This option allows you to set a password on the Adobe LiveCycle Designer ES PDF form that you will create from the imported Word document.

Password to unprotect file: This option allows you to use a password that lets users remove the protection set on the form.

Ignore missing Fonts: Checking this check box allows LiveCycle Designer to substitute fonts for any fonts that are contained in the Word document but that LiveCycle Designer does have. We will explore font-mapping options in the "Mapping fonts and characters" section of this chapter.

Convert Images: This check box must be selected if you want LiveCycle Designer to convert the images in a Word document and import them into your form. If you do not check this, LiveCycle Designer will not convert the images and instead inserts placeholder images into your form.

Maintain flow layout: This check box should be selected to ensure the text will flow instead of being positioned.

Generate log file: Selecting any other option than the default, Do Not Log, will create a log file that contains information about the conversion process and stores it in a log in a location of your choice.

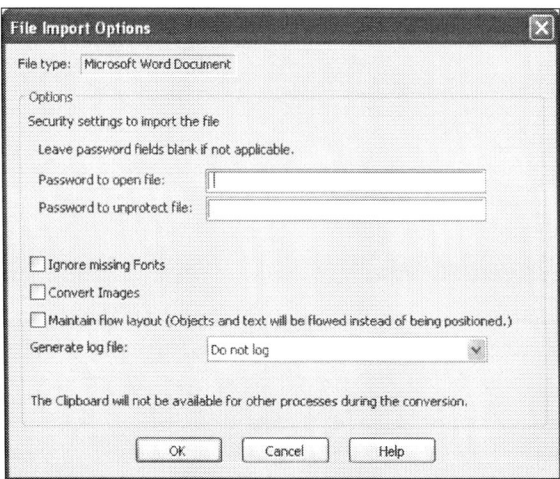

Figure 7-28. The File Import Options dialog box

The Word document will open in LiveCycle Designer, as shown in Figure 7-29.

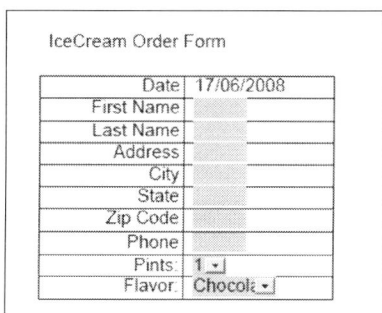

Figure 7-29. A Word document imported into LiveCycle Designer

Click the Preview PDF tab to preview the form. You will notice that the fields look different, although they will display the same kind of data connection behavior when you attach them to an e-mail address or database.

Importing Adobe Output Server files

Adobe Output Designer is design software that enables you to create electronic document templates. These templates are used in conjunction with the Output Server product family. To be able to import Adobe Output Designer files, you must have Adobe Output Designer version 5.4 or later installed on the same computer as Adobe LiveCycle Designer ES.

To import an Adobe Output Designer file, follow these steps:

1. Select File ➤ Open in the menu bar.

2. Select Adobe Output Designer Form (.IFD) in the Files of Type section.

3. Browse to where the Output Designer form is located on your computer or network.

4. Select the appropriate options in the File Import Options dialog box.

Mapping fonts and characters

When a PDF or Word document is imported into Designer, font replacement options are offered in the Import Options dialog box. This means LiveCycle Designer suggests fonts that best match the unavailable font in the Missing Fonts dialog box, and you can choose to accept the replacement font or choose another font altogether. To make this font replacement permanent, you need to map the font.

Font mapping

To map a font permanently in LiveCycle Designer for PDF forms, you will need to make changes to the ConvertPDF_FontMap.txt file that is in the installation directory. This file is empty by default. Upon mapping a font to replace an unavailable font in the ConvertPDF_FontMap.txt file, all substitutions of the unavailable font become permanent and will happen with subsequent forms automatically, even if the unavailable font is installed on your computer later.

Summary

In this chapter, you learned how to utilize external files to both build your forms and improve their interactivity. Doing this can greatly streamline your business processes immediately because you do not have to spend a lot of time on form design. Using XML schemas and WSDL databases, you discovered how to vastly improve user experience in interactive forms and populate form fields with data from the data sources, which enables you to offer a whole new level of information to users of your forms.

You also learned how to further extend the interactivity of forms that you have created in other software programs such as Microsoft Word and Adobe Output Designer by importing them into Adobe LiveCycle Designer ES.

In the next chapter, you will learn how to move beyond basic scripting. Using JavaScript and FormCalc, you will utilize all that you've learned already and apply it to creating powerful and interactive forms.

Chapter 8

PERFORMING ADVANCED FORM SCRIPTING

In Chapter 5, I touched briefly on the richness that implementing JavaScript and FormCalc can add to your forms as an extra layer of interactivity and data capture. In this chapter, I'll expand on that knowledge and show you how to implement events and scripts.

Adding scripts to your forms brings a whole new level of interactivity for the user. For example, you can anticipate exactly what a user is going to do and ensure that they do what you want them to do. Or, also using scripts, you can adjust the form to respond to a user's response, thus customizing the form on the fly in response to user inputs.

Implementing scripting in a form in LiveCycle Designer is entirely optional. You saw in previous chapters how to build interactive forms using purely stand-alone objects and databases. You will now take that knowledge and learn how to implement scripts to make your forms truly interactive.

Please ensure that you have downloaded the files for Chapter 8 from the friends of ED website (www.friendsofed.com) before commencing with the exercises in this chapter.

About scripting in LiveCycle Designer

To begin to implement scripts, you must first understand what they do in a form. A form developer implements calculations and scripts to enhance the user experience by either guiding them through form completion or assisting them to complete tasks such as calculations. Among other things, eliminates the need for the user to manually work calculations out, as well as provides validation to ensure the data that the user enters is accurate and in the correct format. Nearly all form fields can have a calculation or a script added to them.

As I've mentioned in previous chapters, LiveCycle Designer supports two scripting languages: FormCalc, which is based on spreadsheet functionality, and JavaScript, which is the standard scripting language of the World Wide Web (though it can be used in many other ways). FormCalc allows form builders to script and build interactive forms that behave like spreadsheet programs, such as Microsoft Excel and Apple Numbers. JavaScript allows form users who are comfortable writing scripts to build even more sophisticated form functionality. In fact, an advanced scripter can create custom scripting functions in JavaScript that expand the possibilities for form automation well beyond the standard, in-the-box functionality.

LiveCycle Designer enables you to alter various form objects using an event-based model. Basically, you add scripts to various objects depending on when you want the script to be executed. You will learn more about events in the next section of this chapter.

Place a script in an event

For now, you'll learn how to place a script within an event; follow these steps:

1. Open the Chapter8.pdf file in Adobe LiveCycle Designer ES.

2. Ensure your Script Editor is visible. If it is hidden, select Windows ➤ Script Editor. If you have used the Script Editor previously, you may have to grab a handle and drag it down to display it, as shown in Figure 8-1.

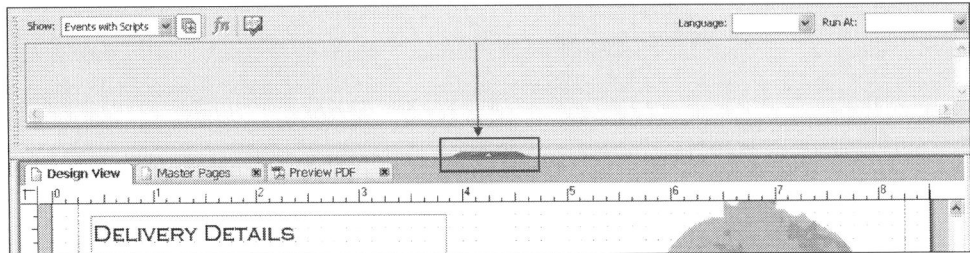

Figure 8-1. Displaying the Script Editor by dragging the handle at the top of the page

3. Drag a Button object from the Object palette onto Design View of the form (see Figure 8-2).

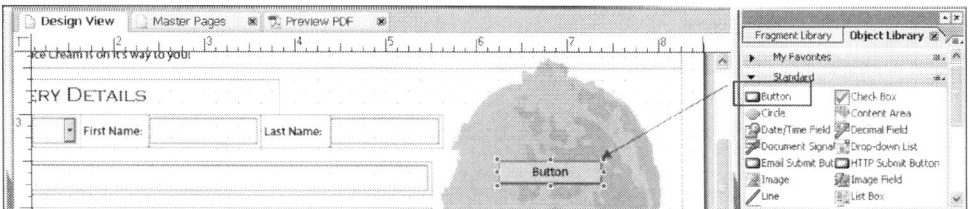

Figure 8-2. Dragging a Button object from the Object palette to Design View in preparation for the event script to be applied

4. Click the button on Design View to select it.

When you click the button, you will notice the reference appears in the Script Editor. The reference syntax in the Script Editor accurately reflects the hierarchy of the object. If you examine the Hierarchy palette (Figure 8-3) of your blank form, you can begin to see the scripting order. Figure 8-2 shows the hierarchy of the simple form you have created.

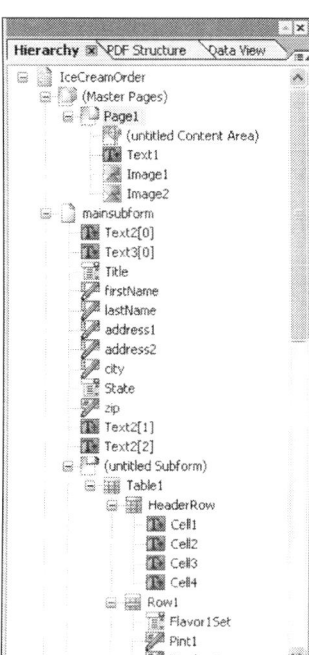

Figure 8-3. The Hierarchy palette displays an organized view of your form objects.

5. With the button still selected, ensure that JavaScript is the language selected in the Language drop-down list in the Script Editor.

6. Select Click from the Show drop-down list in the Script Editor.

Now let's pause for a minute to examine the reference syntax of the button so that you can see how it reflects the Hierarchy palette's structure.

195

7. In the Script Editor, add the following JavaScript after the reference syntax (see Figure 8-4):

```
xfa.host.messageBox("Thanks for ordering Jo's Ice Cream");
```

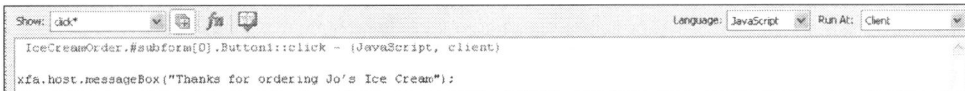

Figure 8-4. Using JavaScript in the Script Editor to create a pop-up message box

8. Select the Preview PDF tab, and click the button.

Your script now activates the pop-up message when you click the button (see Figure 8-5).

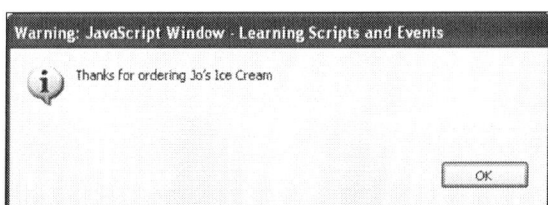

Figure 8-5. The pop-up box generated by the JavaScript

Events make things happen

Events are incredibly powerful additions to your form design because they give you control over every aspect of your form. They are there to guide the form user through the form completion process from the time the form design is merged with data to the time the user interacts with various form objects and submits the data to you. In the previous section, you placed a script upon the Button object that caused a message to pop up when it was clicked. This is an example of a **click event**. Now you'll see even more examples about how truly valuable events are.

Form events are simply actions that change the state of your form. Every script that is attached to a form object is associated with a specific event. When this stage change occurs, a calculation or script is automatically invoked. Form state change examples include clicking a button to submit form data or a field automatically appearing when a particular question is answered.

Types of events

In Chapter 5, I covered methods for implementing different kinds of events in your form. I will now expand on this to explain each kind of event and what each can accomplish in your form design. There are three kinds of events: process events, interactive events, and application events.

Process events automatically initiate internally within the form. An example of this is detailed in the "Process events" section, where you'll set up automatic calculations between a product cost, the total for the number of the product the user is purchasing, the sales tax, and the total.

Interactive events are initiated in response to an action by the form user. You'll also step through this process in this chapter by assigning an interactive event to a Drop-down List object to determine the price of the available options.

Application events are initiated as a direct response to actions performed by a client or server application, such as the preSave event that initializes when a user saves the form in Adobe Reader. The preSave event will initiate immediately before the save operation. You will create a preSave event later in this chapter that will scan the form and remind the user about any mandatory fields.

Process events

Process events automatically execute when an action that is related to form objects or an internal process is conducted on your form. In the following exercises, you'll conduct a number of calculations that fire a calculate process event that assigns a value when the user chooses an option from a dropdown list, and you'll see how selecting a radio button to reveal hidden fields actually executes a series of process events.

Process events that are available from the Show list in the Script Editor are calculate, form:ready, IndexChange, initialize, layout:ready, and validate (see Figure 8-6).

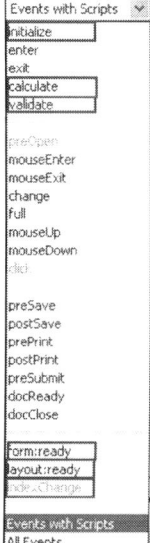

Figure 8-6. Identifying process events in the Show list of the Script Editor

Process events are driven by dependencies that are actions associated with a singular event that initiates further events.

Interactive events

Interactive events are executed as a result of user actions. Because of this, interactive events are useful for scripting and calculation tasks. An example of this is implementing a script on the mouseEnter event that will change the border of the object field to red; another example is a mouseExit event that reverts the border to its original color. In the following exercises, you will add mouseEnter and mouseExit events that will help guide the user through the form completion for the contact details area of the form, and you'll add a click event on the button that will help you validate the form.

Interactive events that are available from the Show list in the Script Editor are enter, exit, preOpen, mouseEnter, mouseExit, change, mouseUp, mouseDown, and click (see Figure 8-7).

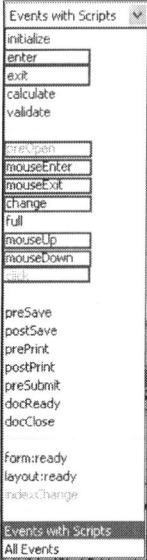

Figure 8-7. Identifying interactive events in the Show list of the Script Editor

In the later exercises of this chapter, you'll create interactive events that will change the color upon the cursor entering the field to help guide the user to fill out the form.

Application events

Actions performed by a client application or server application initiate application events. They perform in response to a user's action or to an automate process. In the following exercises, you will create a preSave event that will check that all mandatory fields have been completed by the user prior to submitting the data, and you'll add a docClose event that will display a message to the user indicating the form has been completed.

Application events that are available from the Show list in the Script Editor are preSave, postSave, prePrint, postPrint, preSubmit, docReady, and docClose (see Figure 8-8).

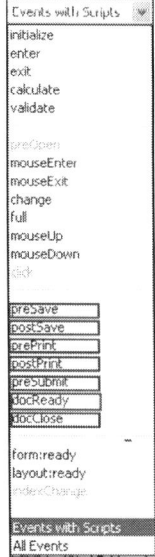

Figure 8-8. Identifying application events in the Show list of the Script Editor

Using statement completion in the Script Editor

The statement completion functionality in Script Editor assists you in building your scripts. When you are compiling your script, every time you type a period (.), the statement completion functionality appears and offers you a selection of available options (see Figure 8-9). This means you can save time and energy when debugging your scripts.

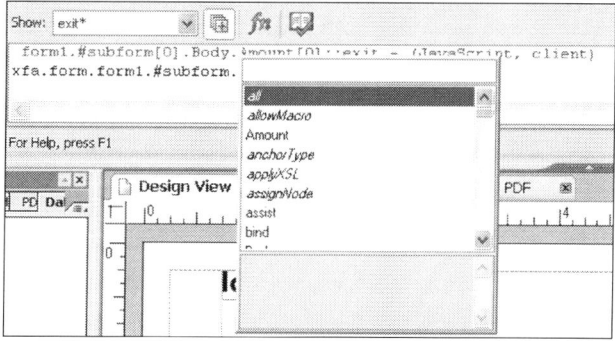

Figure 8-9. The statement completion functionality offers you a selection of available scripting options.

If you are compiling a script and the statement completion does not appear, it means you have typed the property name or reference incompletely.

Adding spreadsheets using FormCalc

You are already familiar with FormCalc from Chapter 5. You know it is a simple calculation language that is derived from spreadsheet software, and it contributes to faster, more efficient form design without requiring sophisticated scripting knowledge. It is the default language in all scripting locations in LiveCycle Designer, and the option to use it is displayed by default in the Script Editor (see Figure 8-10). If you decide to implement your form utilizing JavaScript, you need to change this drop-down list, as you did earlier in the chapter.

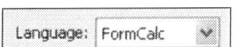

Figure 8-10. FormCalc is the default scripting language in the Script Editor.

FormCalc scripts are typically shorter than most scripts you will write in JavaScript, and they usually consist of one line only. FormCalc also offers support for international dates and time, currencies, and number formats, as well as built-in URL functions for Put, Post, and Get commands, which are methods that indicate the desired action you want to use.

Using the built-in FormCalc functions

FormCalc helps form builders without sophisticated scripting knowledge quickly and easily create calculations and scripts via built-in functions in LiveCycle Designer. These built-in functions are accessible via the Script Editor (see Figure 8-11).

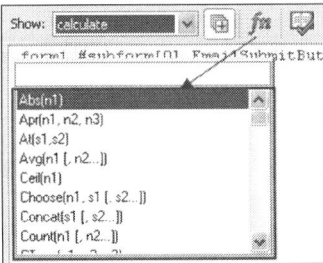

Figure 8-11. Pressing the Function key in the Script Editor displays the built-in FormCalc functions in LiveCycle Designer.

Built-in functions cover a wide range of calculation requirements including dates and times, scientific calculations, financial calculations, and mathematical calculations. Every built-in function contains a specific syntax notation that you need to know and enter in order for the function to be able to perform properly. Table 8-1 summarizes the FormCalc built-in calculations.

Table 8 1. Built in FormCalc Calculations

Syntax Notation	Value of Notation	Example
D	Date string	An example is 06/24/2008.
F	Date string format	An example is MM/DD/YYYY.
K	Locale identifier	An example is en_US.
N	Numeric value	Examples for this change from script to script.
S	Units of measurement	Any valid unit of measurement, such as cm for centimeters.
V	Reference syntax	For example, $event represents the current object event.

Creating custom calculations with FormCalc

You will use FormCalc for this example calculation. FormCalc is a simple yet powerful calculation language modeled on common spreadsheet software. Its purpose is to facilitate fast and efficient form design without requiring knowledge of traditional scripting techniques or languages.

Add a calculation with FormCalc

You use the Script Editor to enter calculations for the different objects on the form.

1. Open the Chapter8.pdf file you downloaded (see Figure 8-12).
2. Ensure the Script Editor is visible. If it is hidden, make it visible by selecting Window ➤ Script Editor. If you have used the Script Editor previously, you may need to drag the Script Editor handle down to be able to see the Script Editor.

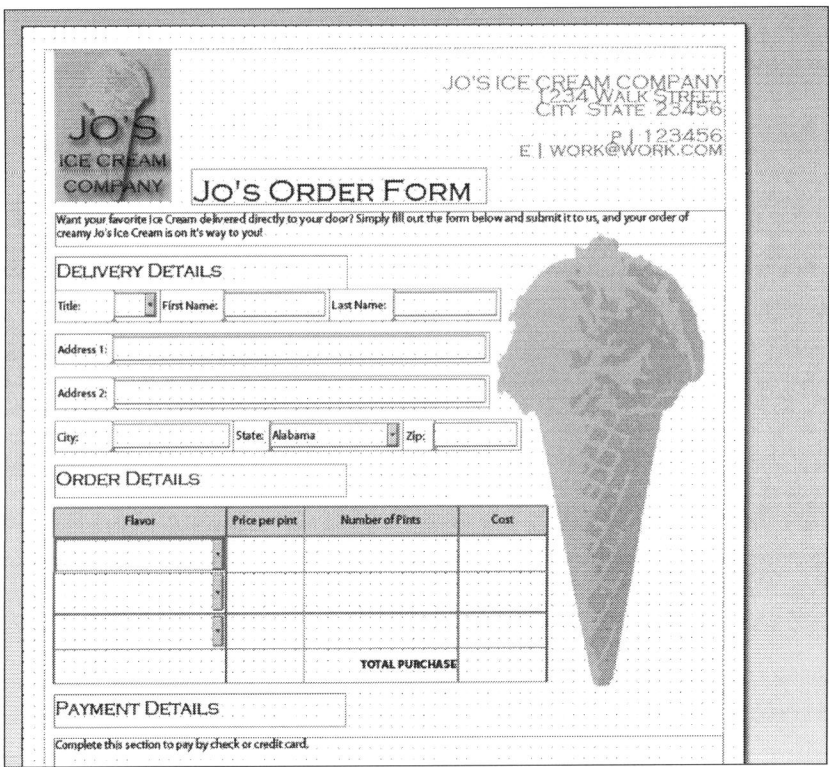

Figure 8-12. This form requires manual input without scripts.

3. Select the topmost cell under Cost (see Figure 8-13).

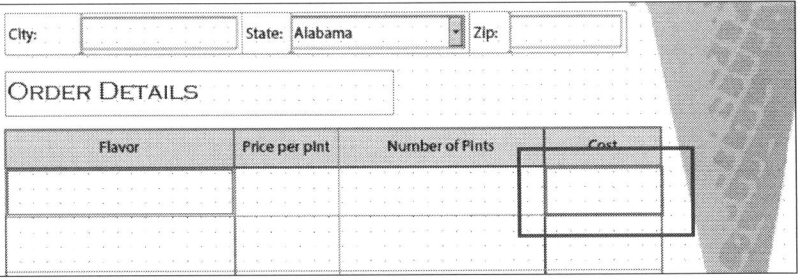

Figure 8-13. Selecting a cell to apply a calculation

You will now set up the Script Editor for the object by specifying the language of FormCalc and specifying the event for the script.

4. Select Calculate from the Show list in the Script Editor.

5. Select FormCalc from the Language drop-down list in the Script Editor.

6. Select Client from the Run At drop-down list in the Script Editor (see Figure 8-14).

Figure 8-14. Specifying the language and the calculation type in the Script Editor

7. Enter the following calculation into the Script Editor under the reference syntax (see Figure 8-15):

Pint1*Number1

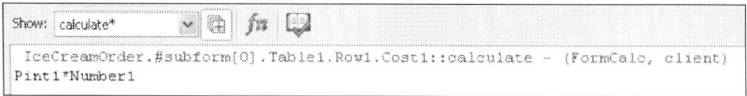

Figure 8-15. A view of the Pint1*Flavor1 calculation in the Script Editor

8. Click the Preview PDF tab to see your script in action.

9. Enter **1**, and press Tab. In the topmost Price per pint cell, enter **10**. Figure 8-16 shows what happens.

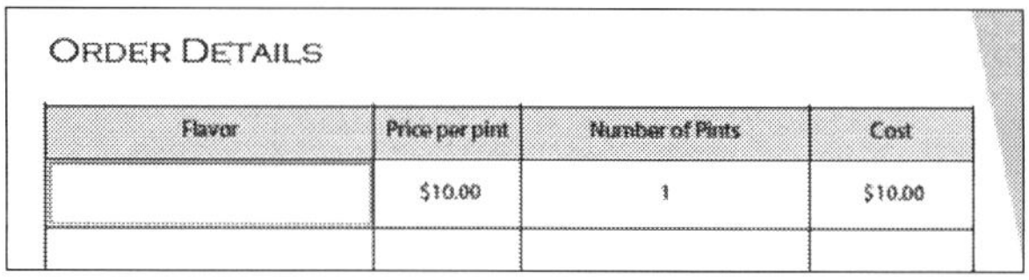

ORDER DETAILS

Flavor	Price per pint	Number of Pints	Cost
	$10.00	1	$10.00

Figure 8-16. The amount is calculated automatically via the FormCalc calculation applied to the cell.

When you type the figures in the cells, the amount is automatically calculated! Your Amount cell should read $10.00. FormCalc is calculating the number of products you entered in the Number of Pints cell and the dollar value you entered in the Price per pint cell. However, if you enter amounts in the cells under the cells you previously entered values into, they remain blank. You need to return to each Amount cell, enter the script in each cell, and then save your form (see Figure 8-17).

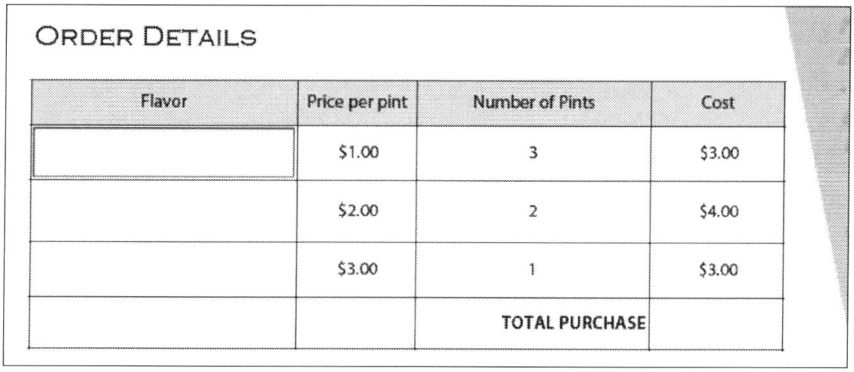

ORDER DETAILS

Flavor	Price per pint	Number of Pints	Cost
	$1.00	3	$3.00
	$2.00	2	$4.00
	$3.00	1	$3.00
		TOTAL PURCHASE	

Figure 8-17. Your form with the script implemented in each of the Cost cells

203

Add another a FormCalc calculation

To complete this section of the order form, you need to enter a FormCalc calculation into the Total Purchase field. Follow these steps:

1. Open the Chapter8.pdf document, and ensure it is in Design View.

2. Select the field next to Total Purchase (see Figure 8-18).

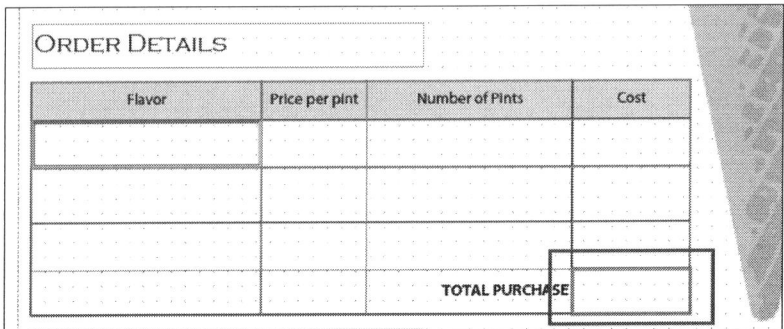

Figure 8-18. Selecting the cell to apply the calculation

3. Ensure the Script Editor is displaying. Type the following script into the Script Editor:

   sum(Table1.Row1[*].Cost1)+(Table1.Row2[*].Cost2)+(Table1.Row3[*].Cost3)

4. Click the Preview PDF tab, and populate the Number of Pints and Price per pint columns with values.

5. The Total Purchase field is automatically populated as you enter data into the form (see Figure 8-19).

ORDER DETAILS

Flavor	Price per pint	Number of Pints	Cost
	$1.00	1	$1.00
	$2.00	2	$4.00
	$3.00	3	$9.00
		TOTAL PURCHASE	$14.00

Figure 8-19. The final form with calculations applied in FormCalc

The FormCalc script that you used to obtain the final figure for the total purchases contains a path for each of the Cost cells. For example, Table1.Row1[*]Cost1 tells LiveCycle Designer to take the value of the first Cost cell, as illustrated in Figure 8-20.

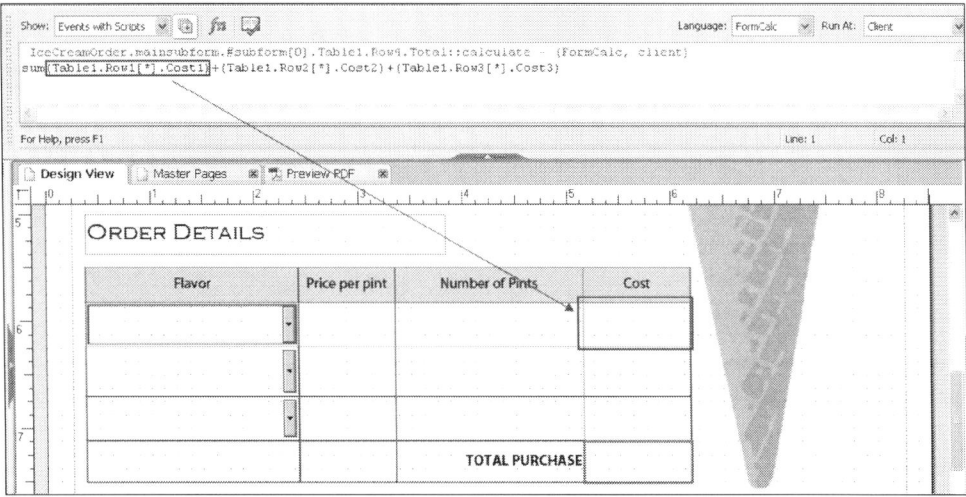

Figure 8-20. Table1.Row1[*]Cost1 tells LiveCycle Designer to take the value of the first Cost cell.

You will now move onto JavaScript where you will begin to apply a whole new level of interactivity to your order form, including automatically populating fields upon selecting a drop-down list option, hiding and revealing credit card details, and validating a credit card number.

Adding a world of automation using JavaScript

Coding JavaScript in Adobe LiveCycle Designer ES is similar in many aspects to coding JavaScript in other applications. Form developers who have previous JavaScript experience will be able to implement it in their LiveCycle forms immediately.

LiveCycle Designer enables form designers to easily integrate JavaScript with form fields and object values. This integration is combined with the LiveCycle Designer reference syntax, which enables you to easily edit and manipulate data within your form.

You should use JavaScript if you are designing your forms to be rendered into HTML. FormCalc scripts and calculations are invalid in HTML browsers and are automatically removed upon rendering the form. Therefore, you need to use JavaScript for any form automation that will be implemented in a web page.

Using JavaScript to automatically populate a value from a drop-down list

You'll now return to the Chapter8.pdf document to further build on its usability and functionality. Continuing to focus on the actual order content of the form, you'll use JavaScript to enable the user to select a product and have a numeric field automatically populated with the price of the product. This means the form user doesn't have to enter data that they are not aware of, such as the product price, which in turns removes a considerable margin of error.

This is also a kind of process event called a **change event**.

Add a script with JavaScript

To do this, you need to recognize some values on the existing drop-down lists to reference within the JavaScript. Follow these steps:

1. Open Chapter8.pdf if it is not already open.

2. Select the topmost Flavor drop-down list, as shown in Figure 8-21.

Flavor	Price per pint	Number of Pints	Cost
		TOTAL PURCHASE	

Figure 8-21. Selecting the Flavor drop-down list in order to apply a script to it using JavaScript

3. Click the Binding tab of the Object palette.

4. Select the Specify Item Values check box.

   When the Specify Item Values check box is selected, Adobe LiveCycle Designer automatically assigns each item in the drop-down list a value to represent that list item, as shown in Figure 8-22. For the purposes of this exercise, you'll use the default values. You will use these default values in your JavaScript.

   You are able to change these default values in the Specify Item Values setting by double-clicking the value you want to change and typing the new value that you want associated to the item value into the field.

   The final steps of this exercise will show you how to use these values to assign a price in the corresponding Price per pint cell.

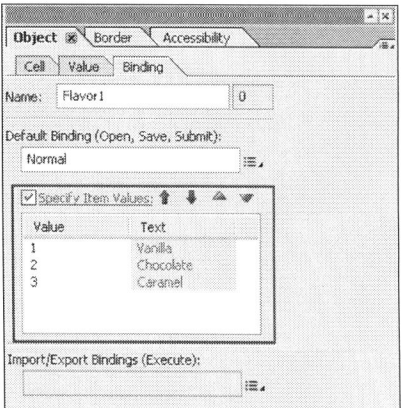

Figure 8-22. The Specify Item Values setting assigns a default value to each item in a drop-down list.

5. Open the Script Editor if it is not already open.

6. Set the language to JavaScript, and ensure Client is selected in the Run At drop-down list.

7. Select change from the Show drop-down in the Script Editor, as shown in Figure 8-23.

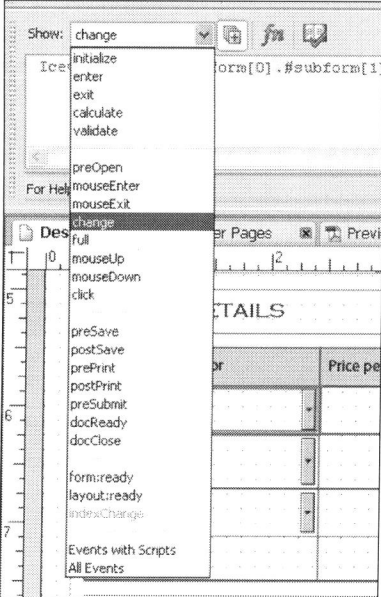

Figure 8-23. Selecting the change event in the Show drop-down list

Now you'll insert a piece of JavaScript that is going to change the whole interactivity of this form and give the user less to do, which is conducive to the form being correctly filled out and returned to you.

Figure 8-24 shows the JavaScript that you are going to insert. Before you insert it into your form, I'll briefly explain what it is telling the form to do.

```
IceCreamOrder.#subform[0].#subform[1].Table1.Row1.Flavor1Set::change - (JavaScript, client)


var sNewSel = this.boundItem(xfa.event.newText);
var bEnableTextField = true;

switch (sNewSel)
{
  case "1": // drop-down select Vanilla
    Pint1.rawValue = "3.50";
    break;

  case "2": // drop-down select Chocolate
    TextField1.rawValue = "4.00"
    break;

  case "3": // drop-down select Caramel
    TextField1.rawValue = "4.50"
    break;

}
```

Figure 8-24. Raw JavaScript ready to be entered into your form

In the first line of the script, this.boundItem refers to the value associated to an item in the drop-down list. (xfa.event.newText); is what is used to retrieve that selected item. In steps 1–5 previously, you recognized the value associated with each item in the drop-down list, as shown in Table 8-2.

Table 8-2. Assigned Values and Their Corresponding Items in the List

Value	Drop-Down List Item
1	Vanilla
2	Chocolate
3	Caramel

The remainder of the code checks the values, assigns their corresponding monetary values, and tells the form where these values should appear.

For example, Case "1" refers to the Vanilla selection. The next line of the code indicates how much the product is (rawValue = "3.50";) and where raw value should be displayed in the table (Pint1).

Apply JavaScript to a drop-down list

Let's return to the exercise and place the code into the form. First download the Drop-Down Javascript.txt file from the friends of ED website. You can then paste it into the Script Editor. Next, follow these steps:

1. Ensure the top Flavor drop-down object is selected and that steps 1–7 in the previous exercise have been completed.

2. Paste the code from the Drop-Down JavaScript.txt file into the Script Editor after the reference syntax, as shown in Figure 8-25.

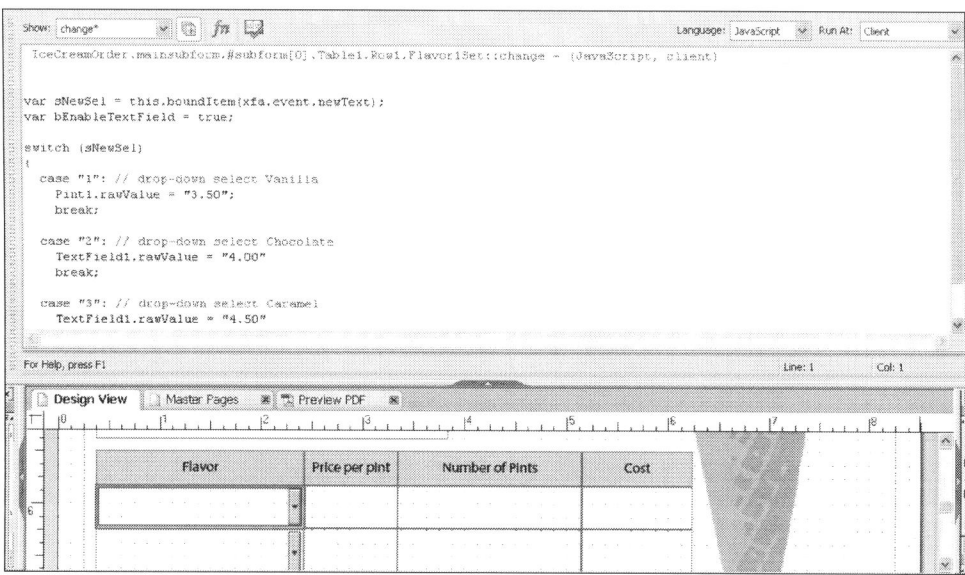

Figure 8-25. Entering code into the Script Editor to assign a monetary value to a product in a drop-down list

3. Save the form, and then click Preview PDF to test it.

This is where you can begin to see the layers of your form really come together! On the Preview PDF tab, select Vanilla from the top Flavor drop-down list. You will see that it is automatically populated with the Price per pint value of $3.50! Enter **4** under the Number of Pints column. You will also see that the FormCalc script you created earlier automatically tallies the value, as shown in Figure 8-26.

ORDER DETAILS

Flavor	Price per pint	Number of Pints	Cost
Vanilla	$3.50	4	$14.00
		TOTAL PURCHASE	$14.00

Figure 8-26. The JavaScript assigns a value to the drop-down list. The FormCalc script totals the value for each order.

You can repeat this exercise by selecting each of the remaining drop-down lists individually and pasting in the code with a minor change each time; specifically, swap Pint1 in the (Pint1.rawValue) code to Pint2 for the middle drop-down list and Pint3 for the bottom drop-down list.

Showing and hiding fields using JavaScript

Now that you have a working order form, you can enable users to choose how they would like to pay for their order—by credit card, which will enable them to submit their order electronically, or by check, which will enable them to print their completed order form and mail it along with their check for the order to be completed.

At the bottom of your form there are two subforms that are currently hidden called cc and checkSubform. The cc subform contains all the information that users need to be able to submit their credit card details along with the order information electronically via email, as shown in Figure 8-27.

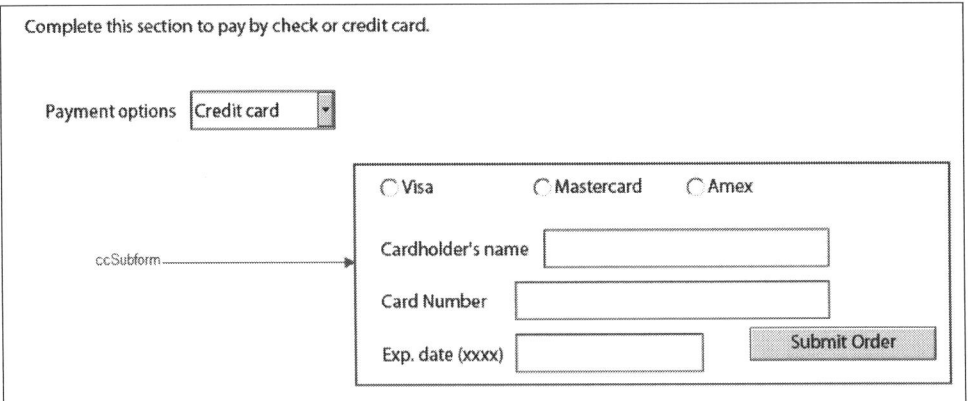

Figure 8-27. JavaScript enables the appropriate subform to display upon selection of Credit card in the Payment options drop-down list.

The checkSubform contains all the information that users need to be able to print the form and send a check to purchase the product, as shown in Figure 8-28.

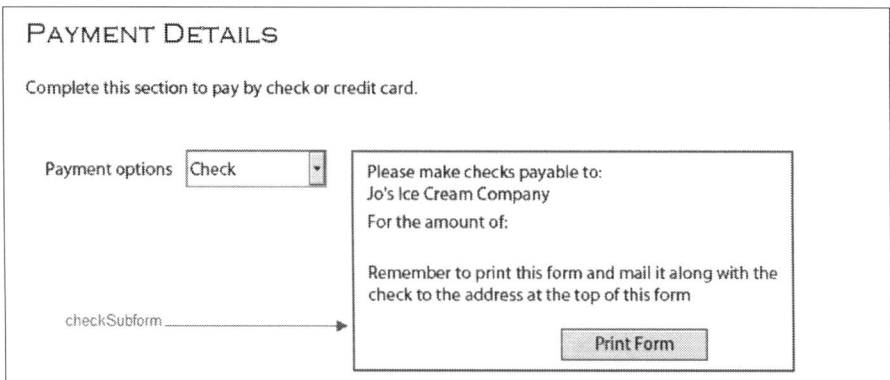

Figure 8-28. JavaScript enables the appropriate subform to display when the Check item is selected in the Payment options drop-down list.

Add a JavaScript to display subforms on selection of a drop-down list

To add the JavaScript to the drop-down list, follow these steps:

1. Drag and drop a Drop-down List object onto your form.

2. Rename the caption of the drop-down list to **Payment options**, as shown in Figure 8-29.

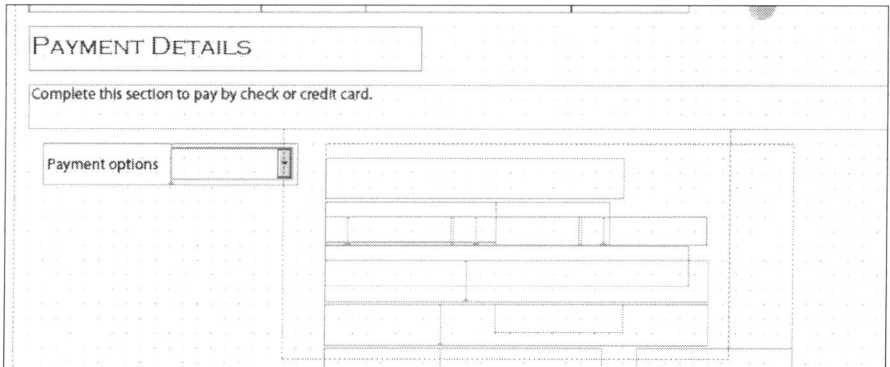

Figure 8-29. Setting up the Payment options drop-down list that will be linked to the payment option subforms via JavaScript

211

3. In the Object palette, add the **Credit card** and **Check** items to the drop-down list, as shown in Figure 8-30.

Figure 8-30. Adding the Credit card and Check items

In the next part of the exercise, you'll add a script to the drop-down box that will enable the two subforms that are at the bottom of Chapter8.pdf to display the appropriate information for users to enter credit card or check information depending upon their selection. Ensure you have downloaded the showing subforms with javascript.txt file because it contains the code you are going to insert into the form.

4. Click the Payment options drop-down list to select it.

5. Open the Script Editor if it isn't already displayed.

6. Select Change from the Show drop-down list in the Script Editor, and ensure the Language drop-down is set to JavaScript.

7. Paste the code into the Script Editor, and save the form.

8. Click the Preview PDF tab.

Let's test the form to show its new interactivity. Choose Vanilla from the topmost Flavor drop-down list, and choose to order one pint. As before, the Total cell is automatically populated. But now let's scroll down to the bottom of the page.

In the Payment options drop-down box, select Check. Figure 8-31 shows the result.

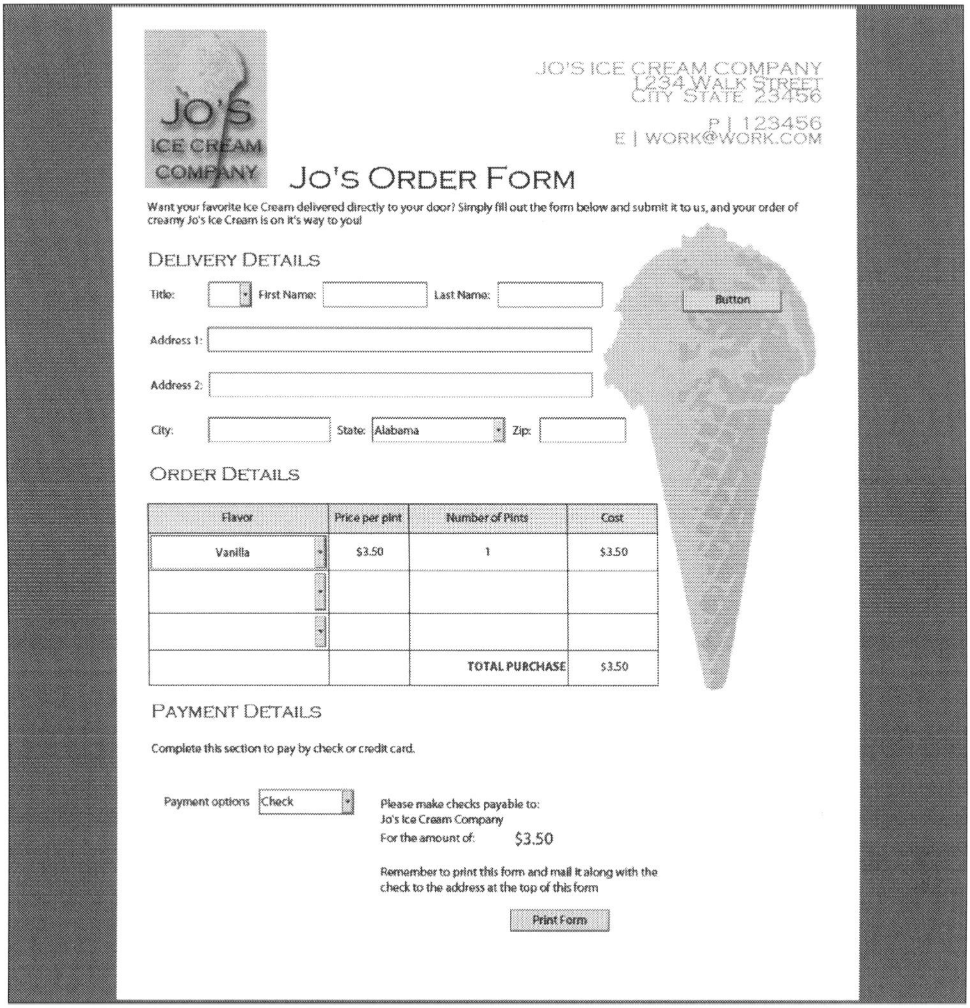

Figure 8-31. The check details along with the payment total are displayed in the check subform.

Now select Credit card from the Payment options drop-down box. You will see the check information disappear and the credit card payment details appear along with a Submit Order button, as shown in Figure 8-32.

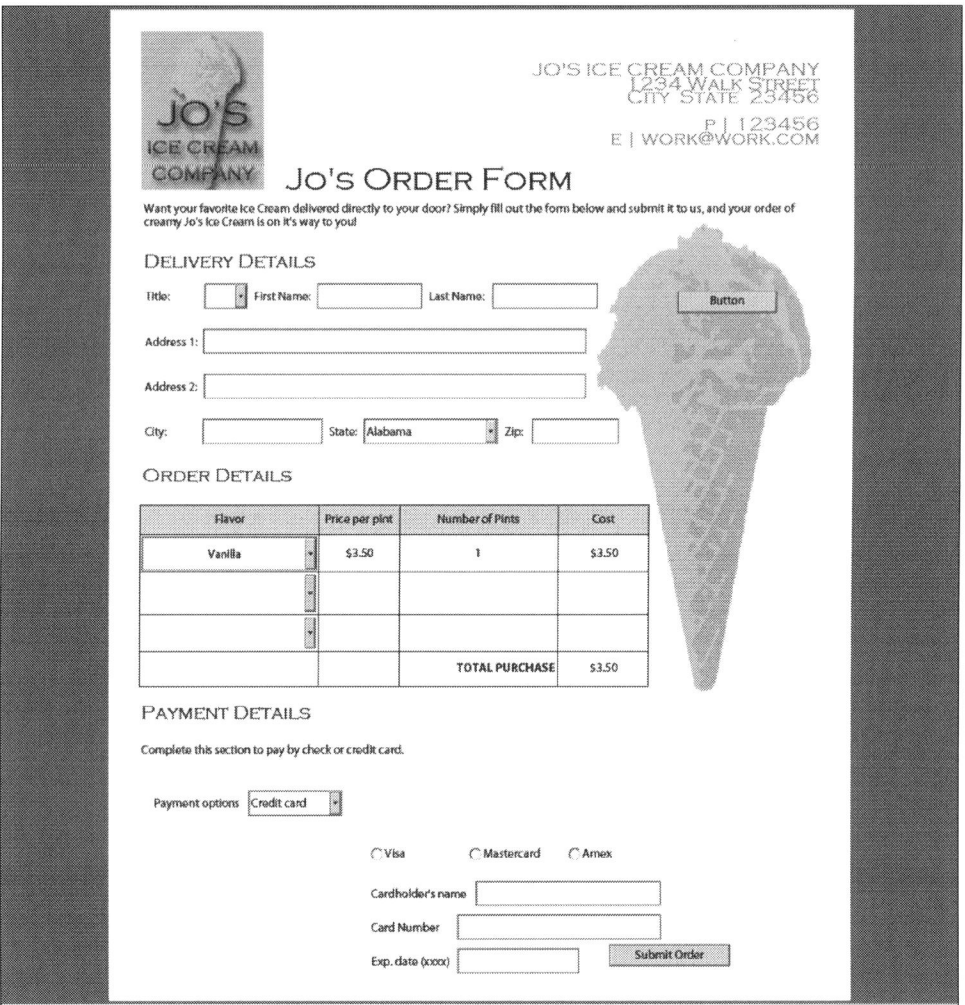

Figure 8-32. The credit card details are displayed in the credit card subform.

Highlighting contact information with JavaScript

You'll now apply JavaScript to the Chapter8.pdf form that will help you further guide your user through form completion by identifying mandatory fields via JavaScript:

1. Open the Chapter8.pdf form in LiveCycle Designer.

2. In Design View, click the Title field to select it.

3. Ensure the Script Editor is displaying. If it is not, select Window ➤ Script Editor to display it.

4. Change the language to JavaScript in the Language drop-down in the Script Editor (see Figure 8-33).

Figure 8-33. Selecting JavaScript from the Language drop-down enables you to now apply JavaScript to the form object.

5. Ensure that Client is selected in the Run At drop-down list.

6. From the Show list in the Script Editor, select mouseEnter (see Figure 8-34).

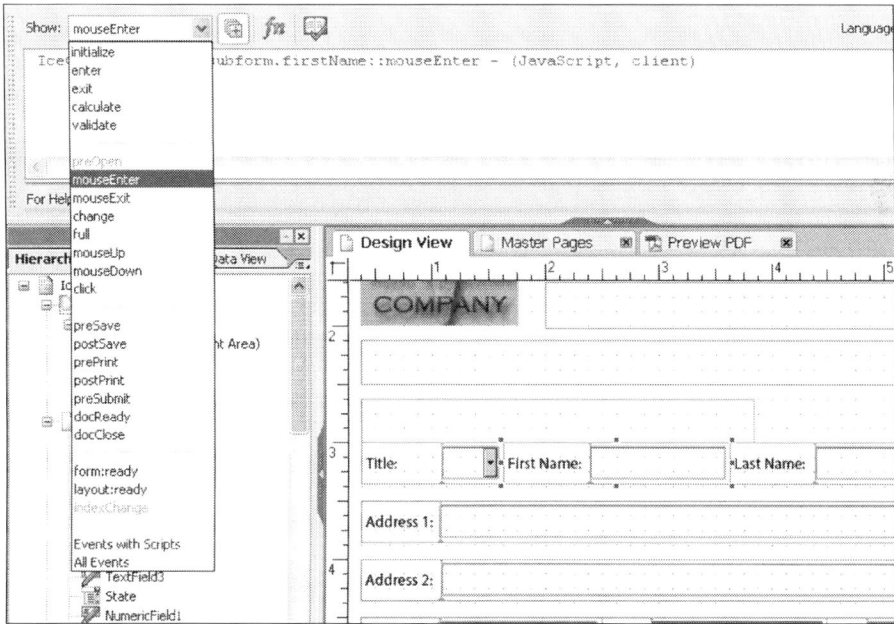

Figure 8-34. Selecting the mouseEnter event from the Show drop-down list

7. Type the following into the Script Editor (see Figure 8-35):

```
xfa.resolveNode("firstName.ui.#textEdit.border.edge").stroke = "solid";
xfa.resolveNode("firstName.ui.#textEdit.border.fill.color").value ➥
= "255,100,150";
```

```
Show: mouseEnter*

IceCreamOrder.mainsubform.firstName::mouseEnter  -  (JavaScript, client)

xfa.resolveNode("firstName.ui.#textEdit.border.edge").stroke = "solid";
xfa.resolveNode("firstName.ui.#textEdit.border.fill.color").value = "255,100,150";
```

Figure 8-35. Adding JavaScript to the form object

215

Now pause the exercise for a moment to see what impact adding the script has had on your form design. Click the Preview PDF tab. What happens when you click the Name field? Figure 8-36 shows the result.

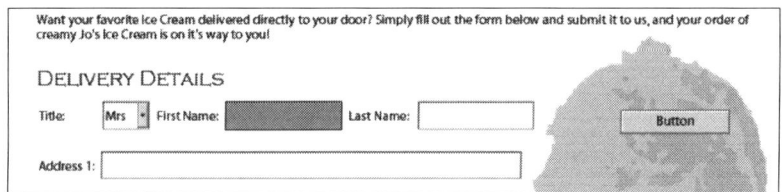

Figure 8-36. The JavaScript adds highlighting to the form field to guide the user through the form process.

Apply a mouseExit event

The fillable part of the Name field is highlighted in pink. Press Tab once. Your cursor moves to the address field, but the Name field remains highlighted in pink. In the remainder of this exercise, you will add a mouseExit event that will cause the highlight to disappear when the user tabs or clicks out of the field into the next one. Follow these steps:

1. In Design View, click the Name field once again to select it.

2. Select mouseExit from the Show list in the Script Editor, as shown in Figure 8-37.

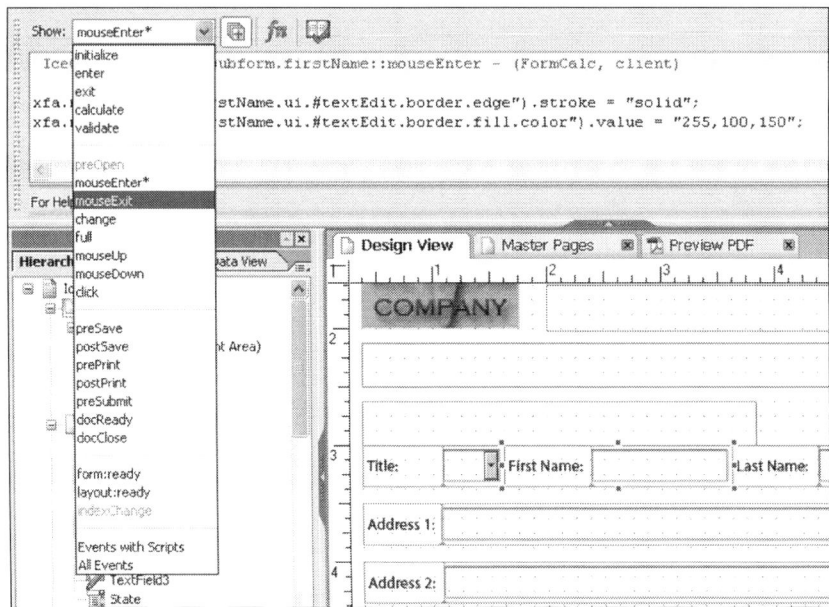

Figure 8-37. Amending the JavaScript to add to the Contact Name field

3. Enter the following code in the Script Editor (see Figure 8-38):

```
xfa.resolveNode("firstName.ui.#textEdit.border.edge").stroke = ➡
"lowered";
xfa.resolveNode("firstName.ui.#textEdit.border.fill.color").value ➡
= "255,255,255";
```

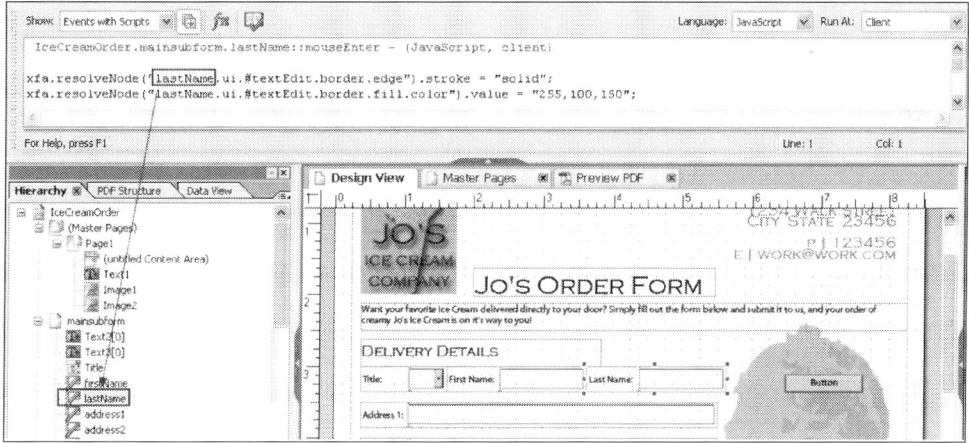

Figure 8-38. Referencing the Contact Name field in the JavaScript

Click the Preview PDF form, and click the Name field. As before, it is highlighted in pink. Now press Tab to move to the address field. What happens? Unlike before, the pink highlight disappears from the Name field.

You will now go through and apply the enter and exit JavaScript events to the remainder of the contact details section. To do this, you can simply individually copy the script from the Name field and paste it into the remainder of the fields, changing only the object name in the script.

To customize the script for the remainder of the contact details, you simply need to replace the object name with the current one.

For example, to update the script to have the highlight apply to the Last Name field, simply change firstName to lastName (see Figure 8-39), and step through the previous exercise again.

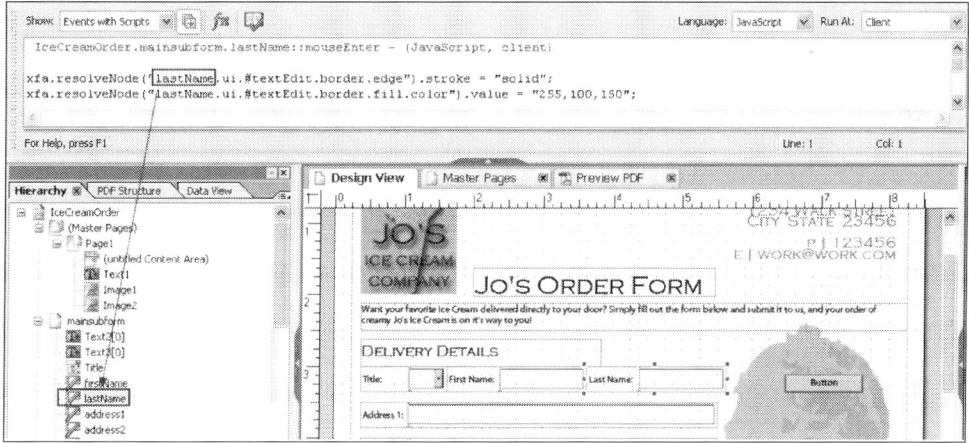

Figure 8-39. JavaScript references the object name from the Hierarchy palette.

Go ahead and apply the scripts to all the contact details fields. Figure 8-40 illustrates the final product as the user tabs through the contact details fields.

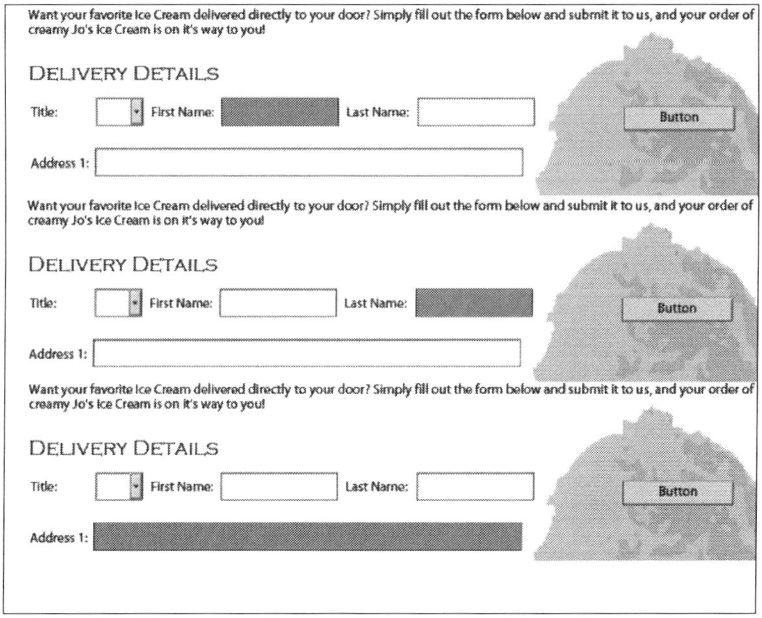

Figure 8-40. Tabbing through your form, you can see the effect of the JavaScript in your form.

Separating form and function: Creating a Script object

You can find the Script object in the Object Library palette; it enables you to save JavaScript functions unattached from any individual form object. You can use Script objects to create functions and methods that you want to use repeatedly in your form. The Script object streamlines your form and makes form building more efficient because it minimizes the amount of scripting required.

Create a Script object

To insert a Script object, follow these steps:

1. Open the Chapter8b.pdf form in Adobe LiveCycle Designer ES.
2. Right-click Subform1, and select Insert Script Object, as shown in Figure 8-41.

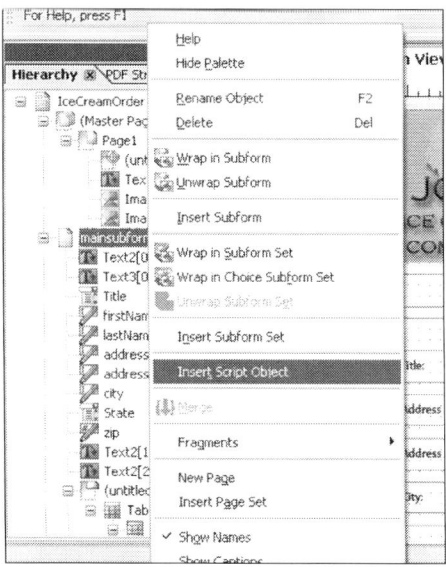

Figure 8-41. Inserting a Script object into the Hierarchy palette

The Script object will appear in the Hierarchy palette (see Figure 8-42).

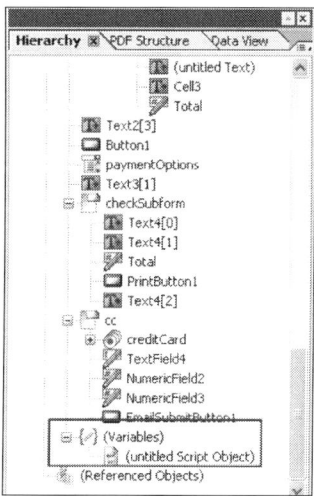

Figure 8-42. The Script object appears in the Hierarchy palette.

3. Ensure that the Script Editor is displaying. If it is hidden, select Window ➤ Script Editor to display it.

4. Enter the following code into the Script Editor (see Figure 8-43):

```
function emptyCheck(oField) {
 if ((oField.rawValue == null) || (oField.rawValue == "")) {
 xfa.host.messageBox("You must leave a comment.", "Error Message", 3);
 }
}
```

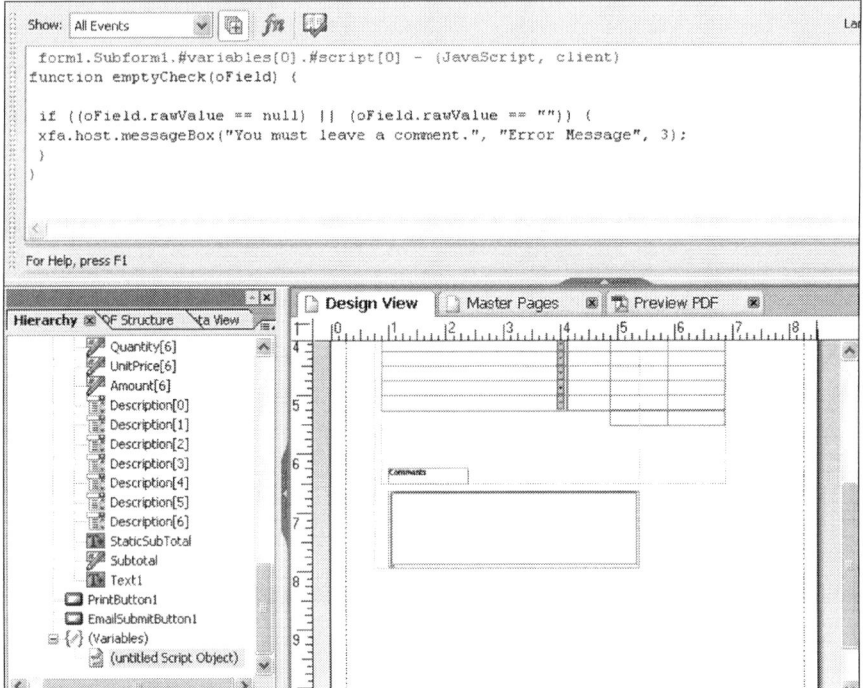

Figure 8-43. Adding the validation script to the Script object

5. Click the Form object to rename it. Call it **Validation**.

Now that you have assigned the JavaScript to the Script object, you can reference the Script object to a form object.

6. Select the Comments field in Chapter8b.pdf.

7. With the Comments field still selected, ensure that the Language drop-down is set to JavaScript, the Run At option is set to Client, and the Show drop-down list is set to Validate.

8. Type the following script after the reference syntax (see Figure 8-44):

```
Validation.emptyCheck(this);
```

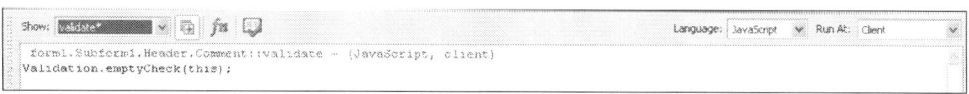

Figure 8-44. Adding the Validation script to the Script object

9. Click the Preview PDF tab, and without completing form fields, click the Submit by Email button. You will see the script that was inserted into the Validation Script object referenced by the Comments field (see Figure 8-45).

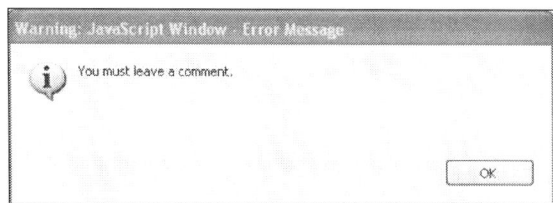

Figure 8-45. The script applied to the Comments field via the Script object warns the user to type an entry into the Comments field.

Debugging and troubleshooting calculations and scripts using the Report palette

In LiveCycle Designer ES, the Report palette provides information about your form design as you build your form. To view the Report palette, select Window ➤ Report. The Report palette will appear at the bottom of the screen (Figure 8-46). If you have presized the display area, the Report palette may not appear instantly, and you will have to drag the bottom of the screen handle up to reveal it.

Figure 8-46. The Report palette helps you troubleshoot issues in your form.

The Report palette in Adobe LiveCycle Designer enables you to debug the calculations and scripts that you have placed on your form. The Report palette contains information about your form design as you build it. It consists of three tabs: the Warnings tab lists errors in your forms as you build them, the Bindings tab lists objects on your form and information about the way you have applied bindings to them, and the Log tab lists actions that are reported by Adobe LiveCycle Designer ES.

Using the Warnings tab of the Report palette

The Warnings tab of the Report palette enables you to view errors or messages generated by Adobe LiveCycle Designer ES as you build your form. The Warnings tab logs error messages as LiveCycle Designer finds them during the form build process (see Figure 8-47).

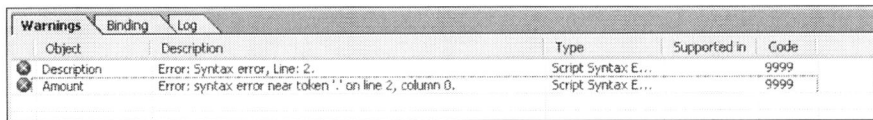

Figure 8-47. The Warnings tab lets you know of potential issues throughout your form.

To clear the Warnings tab, you need to address the issues as they arise. If you do not address them, they will continue to be listed. The Adobe LiveCycle Designer Help has an extensive list of codes and helpers that you can use to assist you clear the log.

Using the Binding tab of the Report palette

The Binding tab of the Report palette lists the fields defined by the method in which you bound them to data (see Figure 8-48).

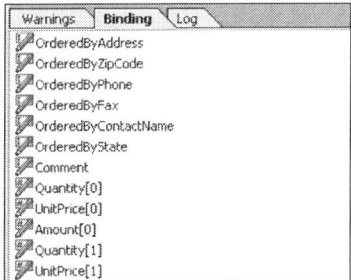

Figure 8-48. The Binding tab of the Report palette lists the bound fields that exist within your form.

Using the Log tab of the Report palette

The Log tab of the Report palette enables you to view a log of actions reported by LiveCycle Designer (see Figure 8-49). When you click the Preview PDF tab to test your form, this log is automatically updated with associated events when the form is publishing.

Figure 8-49. The Log tab of the Report palette reports on events that occur upon publishing your form.

Summary

In this chapter, you have learned about adding calculations and scripts to your form in LiveCycle Designer by applying either JavaScript or FormCalc to your objects. You also learned how to create a scripting object that you can apply to multiple form fields within your form to make your form creation more efficient as well as how to use the Script Editor to write your scripts and calculations. You now know how to use the Report palette to troubleshoot and debug scripts, which helps ensure that when you distribute forms, they work the way you intended them to work.

In the final chapter of this book, you will learn about the functionality of data submission buttons on your forms, how to submit data via email, and how to submit form data to databases.

Chapter 9

COMPLETING YOUR FORMS WITH DATA SUBMISSION

In the chapters leading up to this one, you learned about the form design process, about how to group information so that your forms are intuitive for users, and about choosing objects and scripts to make it easier for the form user to fill out data. You'll now delve into the different interactive ways that users can send their data to you and then at the ways you can collect this data. After all, the success of a form is best measured by the quantity and quality of the data collected.

LiveCycle Designer utilizes buttons to specify the format in which your data is sent. The format for data submission is defined in two ways: by placing a generic button on your form design and choosing the data submission format or by placing a pre-defined Email Submit Button object or HTTP Submit Button object onto your form design.

The overwhelming importance of security

Before you launch any kind of interactive form that collects people's data, you need to be able to assure your users that their data is completely secure. The first step to do this is to draw up a **security policy** that you make available to your users before they submit their data to you. Security policies detail many things, including who has access to the information, why they have access, who has authorized their access, why the data needs to be protected, and from whom it needs to be protected.

As a form host, you have a duty to protect your user's data and to ensure that it is protected at all times. Aside from implementing LiveCycle Designer's built-in security devices such as digital signatures, which are discussed later in this chapter, you also have a responsibility to your users to ensure that the storage devices where the users' data is captured, saved, and stored are secure and that data integrity is guaranteed.

The all-important submission button

Your users know when they've finished filling out your interactive form because they click the submit button. This is the defining moment when data entry becomes data collection. It's satisfying to be able to define this point so precisely with just the click of a button.

Lots of things can happen when your user hits that submit button, though. Who knows what hidden functions are linked to that single click event? Well, you do, because you did the programming! LiveCycle Designer recognizes the importance of data collection and does a wonderful job of simplifying the implementation of this complex point on many forms. So, let's start this discussion of the submit button with a detailed look at the Object palette, as shown in Figure 9-1.

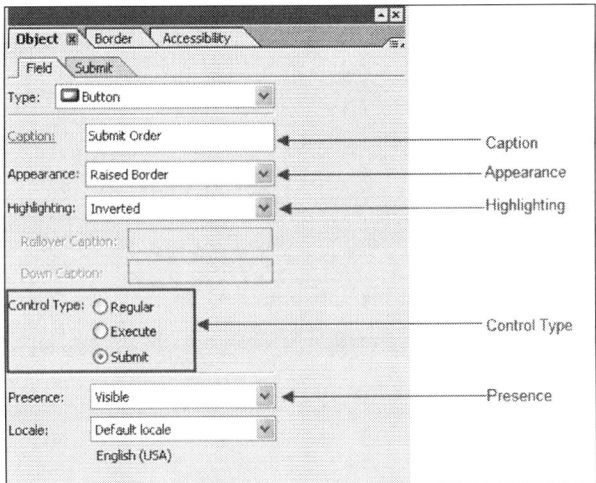

Figure 9-1. The Button type has a number of properties, and they are all defined and identified within the Object palette. Think of it as a repository for button intelligence and functionality.

Customizing generic buttons

Button objects can perform many actions. For example, you can use a Button object as a submit button. Via scripting, you can use a Button object to send the user a message after a button click, as you saw in Chapter 8. In Chapter 5, you saw how you can use a Button object to return information from a WSDL connection. As you can see, Button objects have the ability to fulfil many functions on your form and to make every part of the experience truly interactive.

Add a button to your form

To begin, you'll place a Button object on a form to examine it. Follow these steps:

1. Open a new blank form in LiveCycle Designer.

2. Drag a Button object from the Standard category in the Object Library palette onto your form, as shown in Figure 9-2.

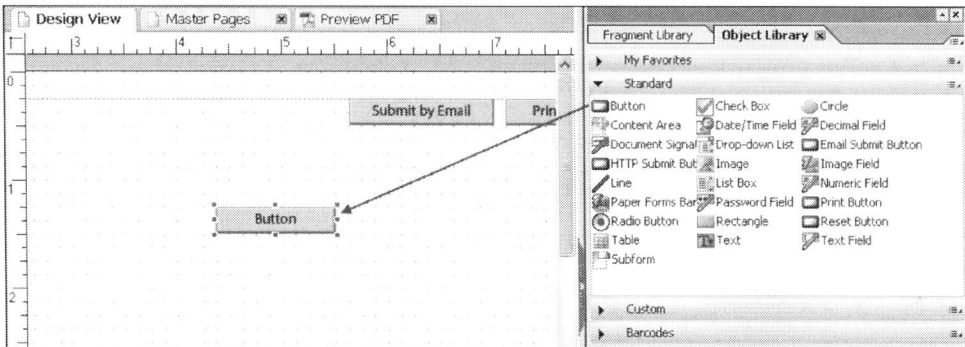

Figure 9-2. Dragging a generic button from the Standard category in the Object Library palette in preparation to change its data submission properties

3. Select the button on Design View to display the Object palette, as shown in Figure 9-3.

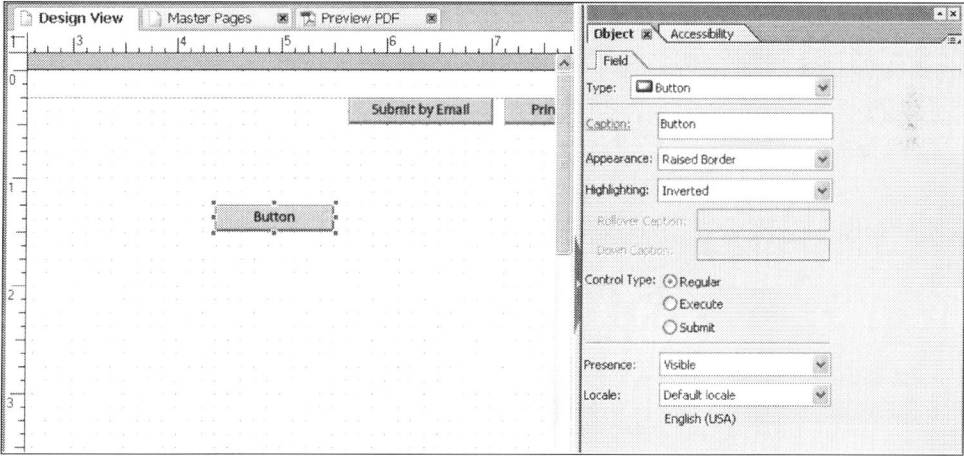

Figure 9-3. Selecting the button on Design View of your form causes the Button object's Object palette to appear.

The Object palette of the Button object contains the Control Type section. The Control Type section allows you to specify what action you want to apply to your button when the user clicks it in your form.

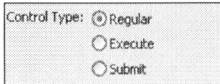

Figure 9-4. The Control Type section of the Object palette allows you to choose what kind of transaction you want applied to your button when it is clicked by a user.

As shown in Figure 9-4, the Control Type section of the Object palette offers three options for you to choose from: Regular, Execute, and Submit.

The Regular option of the Control Type section of the Object palette is used to run scripts and calculations, such as you saw in Chapter 6 when you applied a button to add cells to a table. You can also use it to add navigation, for example, to help a user switch between pages on a form with multiple pages or to play videos or music.

The Execute option of the Control Type section of the Object palette is used to call web services. You saw the effects of this in Chapter 7, when you created a form to call a web service to display geographical information.

The Submit option of the Control Type section of the Object palette is used to submit data or client requests to a server. It is the Submit option that you'll focus on here.

Click the submit button on your open form. You will notice the Submit tab appears in the Object palette, as shown in Figure 9-5.

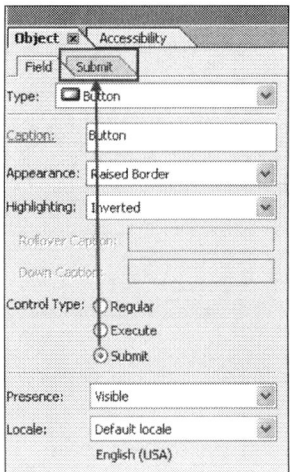

Figure 9-5. Choosing the Submit option in the Control Type section of the Button object's Object palette causes the Submit tab to appear.

So, just what is the Submit tab?

The Submit tab is where you manipulate the submission settings to specify the format and way you want the user to be able to send the data to you, as shown in Figure 9-6.

I'll now explain each section of the Submit tab.

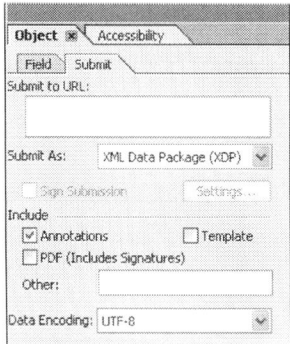

Figure 9-6. The Submit tab enables you to specify the format the data is going to be returned to you.

The Submit to URL field

The Submit to URL field (see Figure 9-7) sets the location of the web-hosted server to which you can send the form data. You can specify the HTTP, HTTPS, mailto, and FTP protocols.

Figure 9-7. The Submit to URL field allows you to specify the destination of your form data.

Submit As a drop-down list

The Submit As list, shown in Figure 9-8, sets the format of the data to submit. It offers four sections in the drop-down list: XML Data Package (XDP), PDF, XML Data (XML), and URL-encoded Data (HTTP Post). These options are explained in depth next.

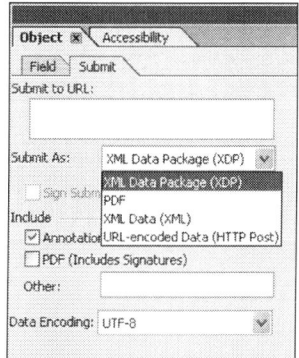

Figure 9-8. The Submit As list of the Submit tab enables you to specify the format in which the form user will send the data to you.

XML Data Package (XPD): Choosing this option submits a package in XPD format. As you learned in Chapter 1, the XPD format is the XML container that packages the PDF content and enables it to be transferred online via e-mail to a database or to other web services.

PDF: Choosing this option submits an embedded PDF file within a package. This is a good format to choose if the form and its data need to be submitted together or if there is a signature field contained within the form.

> *Don't choose the* PDF *option if there is any server-side processing initiated by the form or if you are initiating the form in conjunction with LiveCycle forms to render it in HTML.*

XML Data (XML): Choosing this option submits the XML data to your specified location.

URL-encoded Data (HTTP Post): Choosing this option uses the Post method to send a text stream to the specified URL, which is then parsed by a mail server, a web server, an FTP server, or a CGI script.

Email Submit Button objects

Email Submit Button objects in LiveCycle Designer make it easy for you to enable users to return their form data by e-mail because it is a standard button that has preset properties and a customized Object palette (see Figure 9-9).

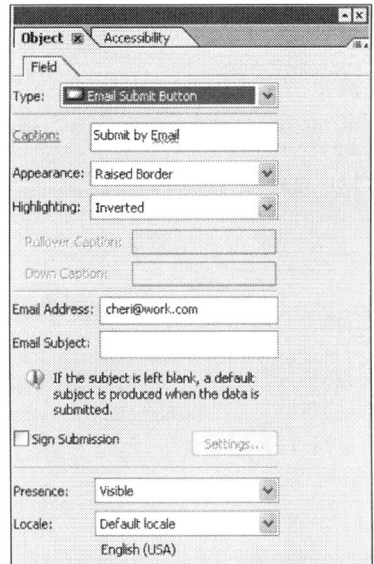

Figure 9-9. The Email Submit Button object comes customized with settings for returning PDF forms via e-mail.

> *Adobe Reader doesn't save changes to PDF files, so add an* Email Submit Button *object to expedite the user returning their data to you.*

Email Submit Button settings overview

The Email Submit Button object has a number of predefined settings applied to it in Adobe LiveCycle Designer.

Control Type set to Submit: This means the data the user returns to you is submitted in accordance with the settings that are preset on the Submit tab, as shown in Figure 9-10.

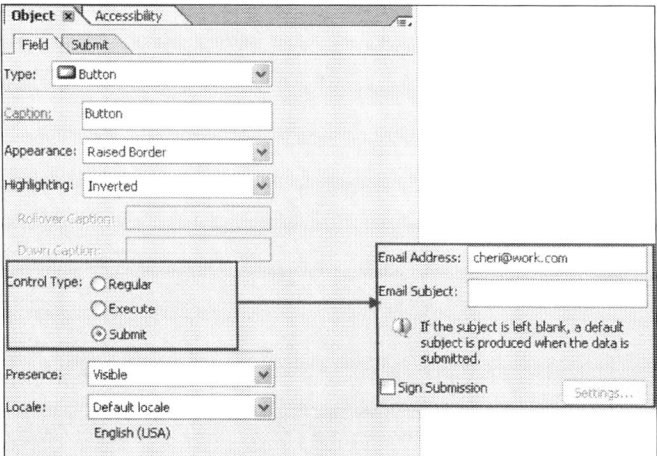

Figure 9-10. The Submit selection allows you to specify submission details.

Submit to URL set to use the HTTP protocol: This is invisible on predefined Email Submit Button objects.

Submit As set to URL-encoded Data (HTTP Post): This is also invisible on predefined Email Submit Button objects.

Data Encoding set to UTF-8: This is set by default by the Email Submit Button object. It means that when the form sends the data after the button is clicked, the data is sent with UTF-8 coding. UTF-8 coding is a variable-length character encoding for Unicode.

> *If you need your data to be submitted via the secure HTTPS protocol, you will need to customize a standard Button object. This is addressed later in this chapter.*

When you create a new form using the New Form Assistant in LiveCycle Designer, an Email Submit Button object and a Print Button object are automatically added to your new form. If you have created a form without the Email Submit Button object or have deleted it from your form design, you can add one to your form by following the next exercise.

Associate your e-mail address with a submit button

1. Drag and drop the Email Submit Button object from the My Favorites category of the Object Library palette onto your form, as shown in Figure 9-11.

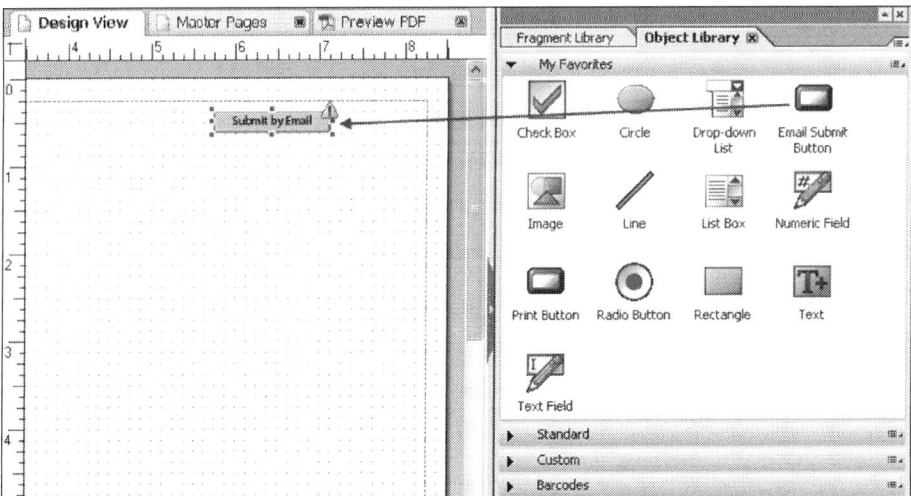

Figure 9-11. The Email Submit Button object is found in the My Favorites category of the Object Library palette.

You will notice that there is a warning sign on the button. This is because there hasn't been an e-mail address associated with the button yet. You will do that now.

2. Select the Email Submit Button object on the form. The Email Submit Button object's Object palette will appear (see Figure 9-12).

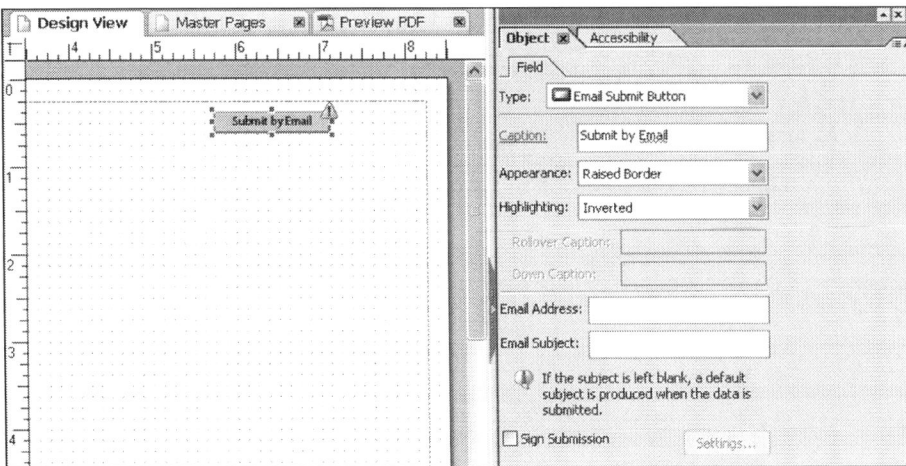

Figure 9-12. The Email Submit Button object displays a warning if an e-mail address hasn't been associated to it.

3. Enter your e-mail address in the Email Address field, as shown in Figure 9-13.

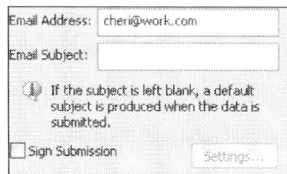

Figure 9-13. Entering an e-mail address into the Email Address field specifies where the data is going to be sent to.

There is also the option to add an e-mail subject that will be sent to your inbox along with the form data. If you choose not to add one, a default subject line will be sent along with the form data from the user. The default subject line reflects the automatic name assigned to the XML data file that is emailed to the form creator.

Using the HTTP Submit Button object

The HTTP Submit Button object is another predefined button that is included in the Adobe LiveCycle Designer ES installation. It is a standard button that has properties already defined and an Object palette customized to enable users to submit their data via HTTP.

Understanding the HTTP Submit Button object's settings

The HTTP Submit Button object has a number of predefined settings similar to the Email Submit Button object.

Control Type set to Submit: This means the data the user will return to you is submitted in accordance with the settings that are preset on the Submit tab.

Submit As set to URL-encoded Data (HTTP Post): Setting this option sends a stream of text using the HTTP Post method to the defined URL. This is then parsed by a mail, web, or FTP server or, alternatively, a script that parses HTML forms such as a CGI script.

> *When* Submit As *is set to* URL-encoded Data (HTTP Post), *the form must be opened by the user in a web browser such as Internet Explorer or Mozilla Firefox or in a PDF reader such as Adobe Reader 6.0 or newer.*

Submit As set to use the HTTP protocol: This setting enables the user to post the data to a URL.

Put an HTTP button on your form

You will now place an HTTP submit button on a form:

1. Open a new blank form in LiveCycle Designer.

2. From the Standard category of the Object Library palette, drag an HTTP Submit Button object onto your form, as shown in Figure 9-14.

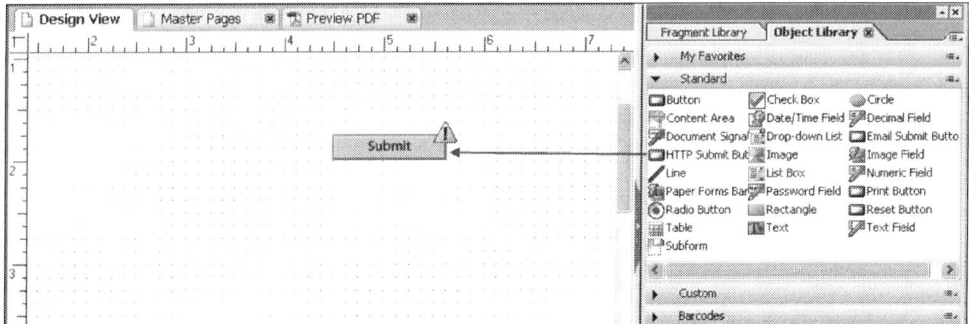

Figure 9-14. You can find the HTTP Submit Button object in the My Favorites category of the Object Library palette.

3. Click the HTTP Submit Button object on Design View to select it.

You will see in the HTTP Submit Button object's Object palette the ways you can manipulate the formatting of it (see Figure 9-15). I'll now discuss the different options.

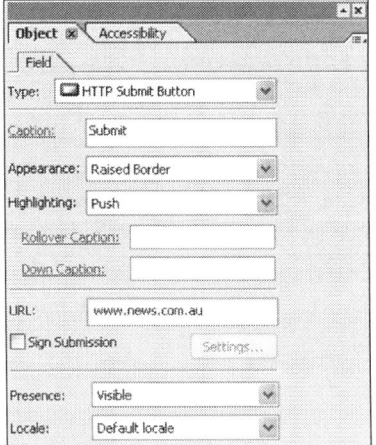

Figure 9-15. The Object palette for the HTTP Submit Button object allows you to manipulate its settings.

Caption: You are already familiar with the Caption field. It enables you to change the label on the button (see Figure 9-16).

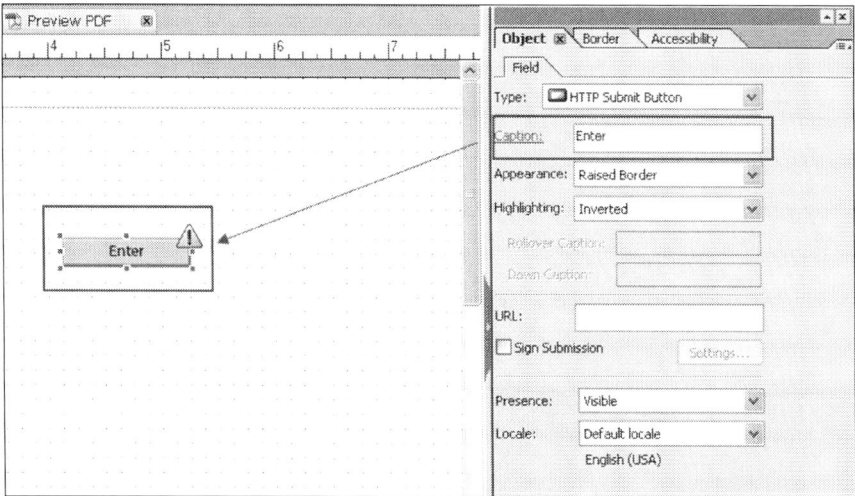

Figure 9-16. Caption fields on Object palettes enable you to change the label on the button.

Appearance: This drop-down offers you four options: No Border, Solid Border, Raised Border, and Custom. The Custom option allows you to create a custom appearance for your button via the Custom Appearance dialog box, as shown in Figure 9-17.

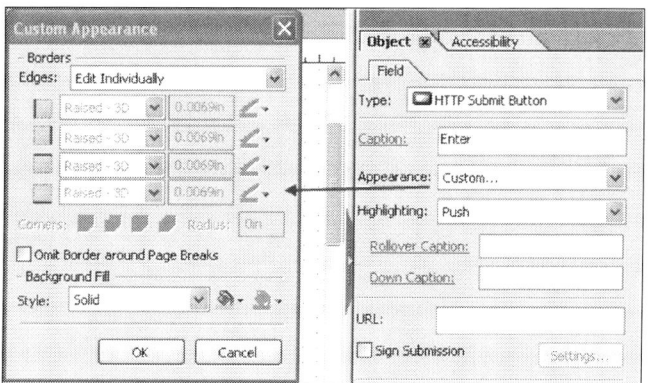

Figure 9-17. The Custom setting in the Appearance list allows you to customize the appearance of your button.

Highlighting: The Highlighting drop-down list offers you highlighting options for when the button is clicked. The options offered are Inverted, which displays the button as inverted when it is clicked; Push, which creates a shadow around the button giving it the appearance of being depressed; Outline, which causes a line to appear around the button after it has been clicked; and None, which cancels all highlighting on the button.

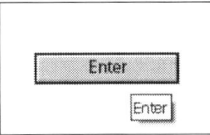

Figure 9-18. Setting rollover captions enables you to see the accessible text of an image. As you learned in Chapter 2, accessibility in this instance means creating your form so that people with disabilities can read and comprehend your form. Adding accessible text to a button means that a screen reader will be able to interpret it.

Rollover Caption: Using this option when the button highlight is set to Push means a label will appear when you mouse over the button object (see Figure 9-18).

Down Caption: Using this option when the button highlight is set to Push means a caption will appear when you click on the button.

URL: This field on the Object palette must be filled in to be able to submit data via the HTTP button. It is the URL to which the data will be sent.

Sign Submission: Selecting this check box will apply a data signature to the data that is being submitted. This is a great security measure because it ensures data integrity during the data transmission period. Clicking this box will pop up the Sign and Submit Setting dialog box, which is where you can specify digital signature properties.

Presence: This option controls where and whether an object is displayed in your form or whether it is displayed when users print the form.

Implementing types of submission buttons

You have now examined the precustomized submit buttons, HTTP and e-mail, as well as the Submit tab. In the next exercise, you'll create buttons for your forms that will enable your form users to submit data to you.

Buttons that send e-mail with XML

You will now insert a button that will send the data via an XML stream using the Chapter9a.pdf file:

1. Open the Chapter9a.pdf form you downloaded from the friends of ED website.

2. Drag a Button object from the Library palette's Standard category onto the form, as shown in Figure 9-19.

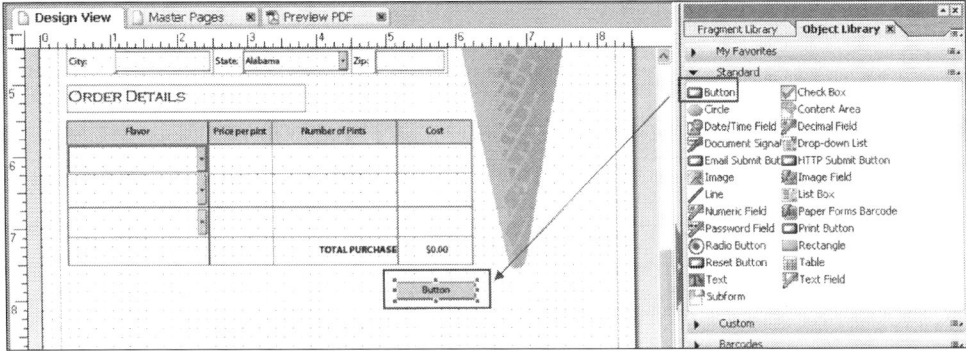

Figure 9-19. Dragging a button onto your form to set it up for data submission

3. Click the button on Design View to select it and display the Object palette.

4. In the Caption field of the Field tab, delete Button, and enter **Submit Data**.

5. Select the Submit radio button for the Control Type setting. You will see the Submit tab appear (see Figure 9-20).

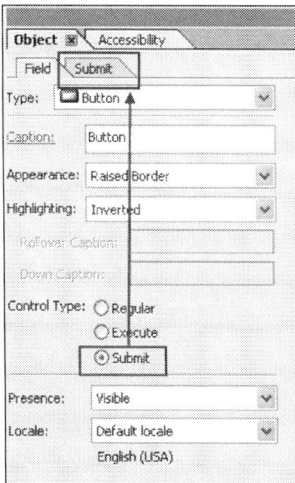

Figure 9-20. Choosing the Submit option for Control Type causes the Submit tab to appear.

6. Click the Submit tab.

7. Type the mailto protocol in the Submit to URL box, as shown in Figure 9-21.

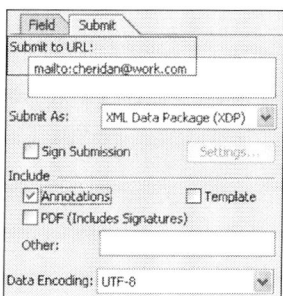

Figure 9-21. Enter a destination into the Submit to URL box

The mailto protocol is the e-mail URL that is used in websites extensively to launch the user's e-mail client. The mailto protocol is in this format: `mailto:username@email.com`. *For example, my e-mail address is* `cheri@work.com`; *therefore, to set up the mailto protocol that will send data to my address, I would enter* `mailto:cheri@work.com` *in the* Submit to URL *box.*

237

8. From the Submit As list, select XML Data (XDP), also shown in Figure 9-21.

9. Click the Preview PDF tab to test your form.

10. Fill out the form with data (see Figure 9-22).

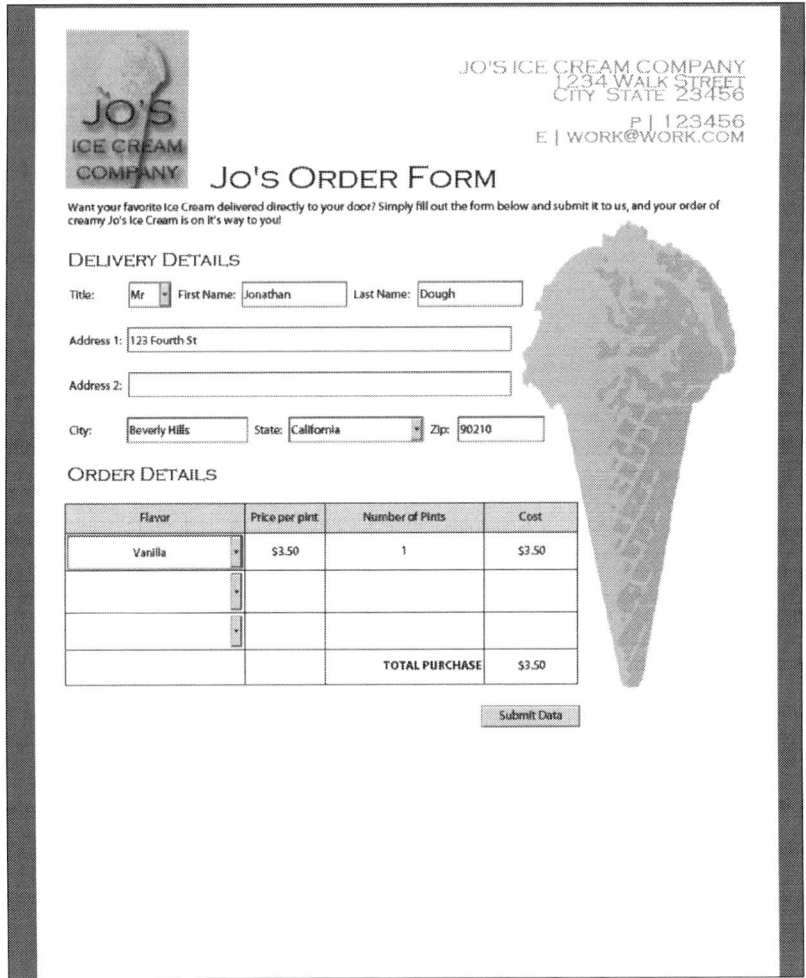

Figure 9-22. Filling out your form to submit the data

11. Click the Submit Data button.

When you click the Submit Data button, Adobe LiveCycle Designer ES will launch your e-mail client on your computer and automatically compose a message that consists of the destination e-mail address (as specified on the Submit tab) and a default subject line. It will also attach the XPD package, which contains the data you have entered into the form, as shown in Figure 9-23. To submit the data, simply click Send.

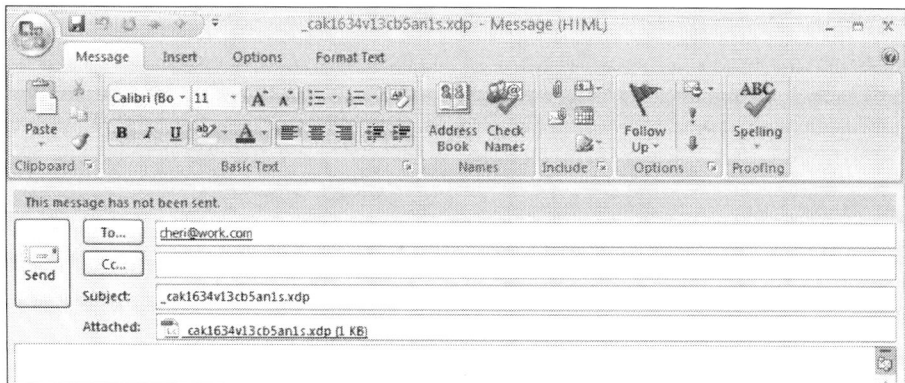

Figure 9-23. Upon hitting Send, your e-mail client sends the data.

Retrieving the data package from your e-mail client and opening it in LiveCycle Designer will allow you to view the XPD data package. You can see that the information you entered into your form has been rendered into an XML form upon opening the attachment to your e-mail, as shown in Figure 9-24.

```
<?xml version="1.0" encoding="UTF-8"?>
<?xfa generator="XFA2_4" APIVersion="2.6.7120.0"?>
<xdp:xdp xmlns:xdp="http://ns.adobe.com/xdp/">
<xfa:datasets xmlns:xfa="http://www.xfa.org/schema/xfa-data/1.0/"
><xfa:data
><IceCreamOrder
><mainsubform
><Title
>Mr</Title
><firstName
>Jonathan</firstName
><lastName
>Dough</lastName
><address1
>123 Fourth St</address1
><address2
/><city
>Beverly Hills</city
><State
>CA</State
><zip
>90210.00000000</zip
><Table1
><HeaderRow xfa:dataNode="dataGroup"
/><Row1
><Flavor1Set
>1</Flavor1Set
><Pint1
>3.50</Pint1
><Number1
>1.00000000</Number1
><Cost1
>3.50</Cost1
></Row1
><Row2
><Flavor2
/><Pint2
/><Number2
/><Cost2
```

Figure 9-24. The XML package of submitted data

239

Buttons that send information to a server

In Chapter 8, you created an order form that guided the user through selecting a product and selecting a payment option. One of these options was submitting credit card details. You as a form builder want this information from the customer as soon as they have filled out the form so that you can fulfil it! You will now add a button to the form you've been working with to send information directly to a server.

Add a server to send information to a server

For the following exercise, you can choose to either download the Chapter9.pdf form from the friends of ED website or complete the exercises in Chapter 8 to create the order form yourself. For the purposes of this exercise, we will refer to the form as Chapter9.pdf.

1. Open Chapter9.pdf in Adobe LiveCycle Designer ES. Drag a Button object from the Standard category of the Library palette to your form, as shown in Figure 9-25.

   When you place the button on the form, ensure that you place it within the cc subform.

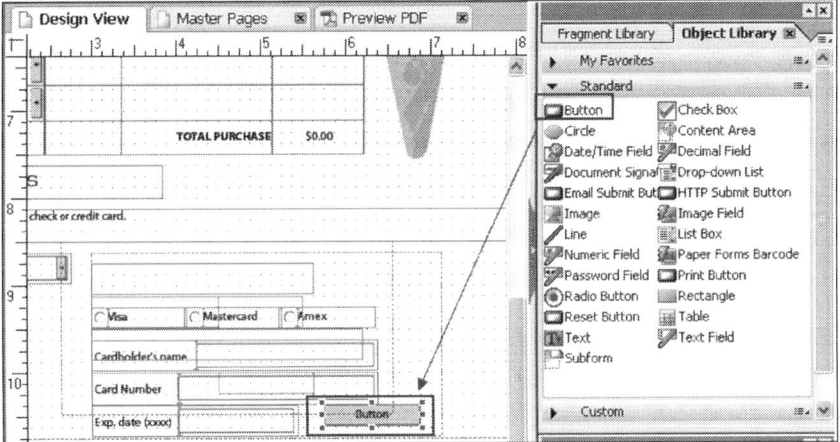

Figure 9-25. Dragging a button from the Object palette into the cc subform of the form

2. Click the button on Design View to display the Object palette.

3. Rename this button to be **Submit my Order** in the Caption field of the Object palette, as shown in Figure 9-26.

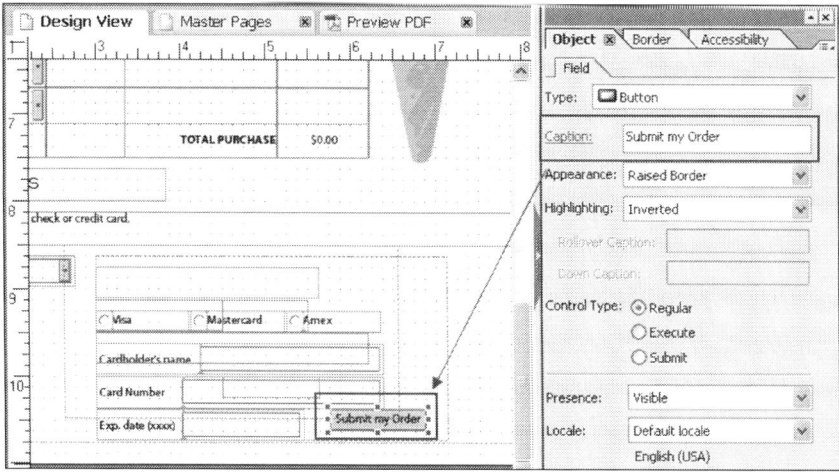

Figure 9-26. A button's labels should reflect its intent.

You can also rename a button's label by double-clicking it and, when the cursor appears, typing the new name.

4. Select the Submit radio button in the Control Type area of the Object palette. As before, the Submit tab will appear.

5. In the Submit to URL box, type **ftp://ftp.DriveHQ.com/** to send your form data via FTP directly to a server, as shown in Figure 9-27.

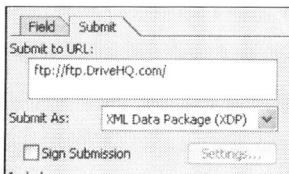

Figure 9-27. Typing the form's FTP address into the Submit to URL box directs the form where to send the data.

6. From the Submit As drop-down list, choose XML Data Package (XDP).

7. Select File ➤ Save As, and save your form as an Adobe dynamic XML document (*.pdf).

8. Open your form in Adobe Reader.

You will now see the form interact with the FTP address.

9. Fill out your form, and click the Send button.

As shown in Figure 9-28, Adobe Reader will notify you that your form is trying to contact the Internet via a Security Warning dialog box. To transmit the form data, click Allow in the dialog box. Your data has now been submitted to the FTP server.

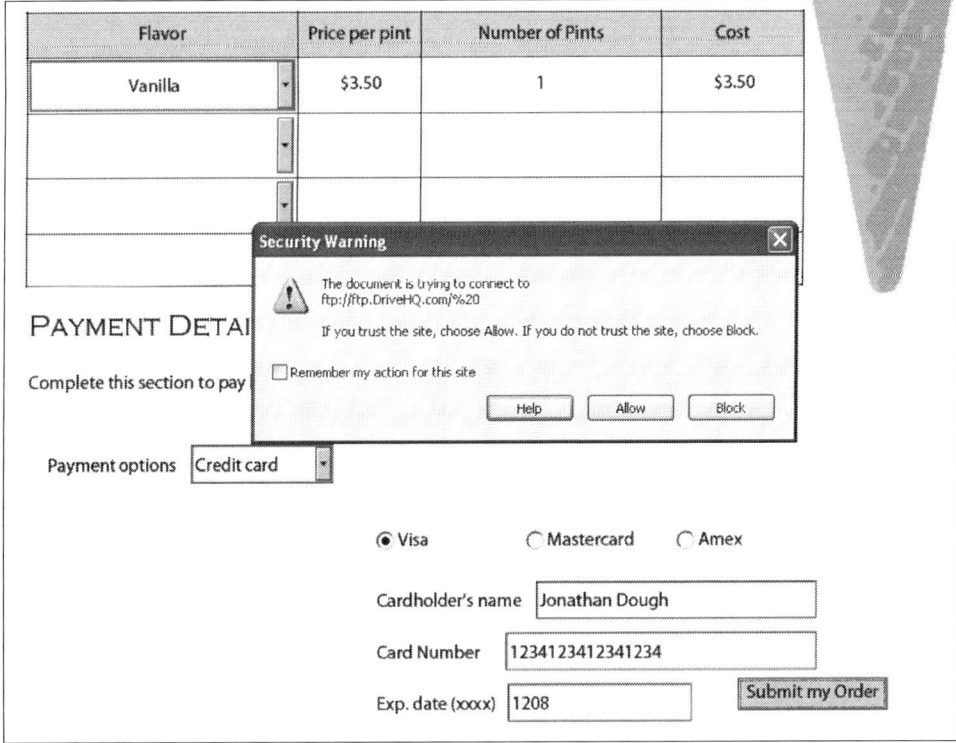

Figure 9-28. Security warnings from Adobe Reader alert the user that the form is attempting to contact the FTP site.

Sending data via the FTP protocol is one of three methods you can choose to submit your data. Each of these methods has their own HTTP protocol, as detailed in Table 9-1.

Table 9-1. The Standard Internet Protocols That Allow You to Specify Your Data Destination

Enter This in the Use This URL Field on the Submit Tab	Result After Clicking Send
http://myserver/cgi-bin	This action submits the PDF package to a web server.
https://myserver/cgi-bin	This action submits the PDF package to a secure web server.
ftp://ftp.myserver.com	This action submits the PDF package to an FTP server, as shown in the previous exercise.

When you are setting up your form to submit data to a URL, it's suggested that you use an **absolute URL** as opposed to a relative URL, because this means that as long as the computer that the form is saved on has Internet access, it will always be able to send data to the correct destination. An absolute URL is the complete Internet address of a page, for example, http://www.mywebsite.com/about.

Buttons that add a digital signature

The ability to add a digital signature to a submit button on the Button object's Submit tab is a useful feature that helps to ensure data security. It works like this: when a form user fills out their form and clicks the button to submit the form data, a digital signature certifies the security and protects the data and any attachments associated with the form submission. It's an electronic signature that is used to authenticate not only where the data has come from but that it is intact when it is received at the data destination.

This is incredibly valuable on many levels to everyone who comes into contact with the form, from the form user who can rest assured that his payment and credit card information is secure to the form owner who wants to ensure that all information that comes from his users is not only accurate but also secure.

Add a digital signature to a form

You will now apply a digital signature to the Chapter9.pdf form:

1. Open the Chapter9.pdf form as saved in the previous exercise, and click the Send button to select it.
2. Click the Submit tab to bring it to the front of the Object palette.
3. Click the Sign Submission checkbox, as shown in Figure 9-29.

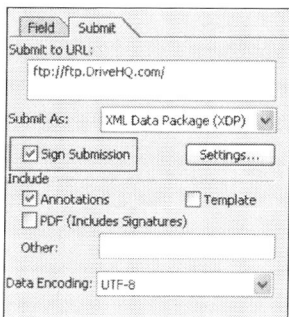

Figure 9-29. Selecting the Sign Submission check box allows you to add a signature to your form.

Clicking the Sign Submission button launches the Sign Data and Submit Settings dialog box, as shown in Figure 9-30.

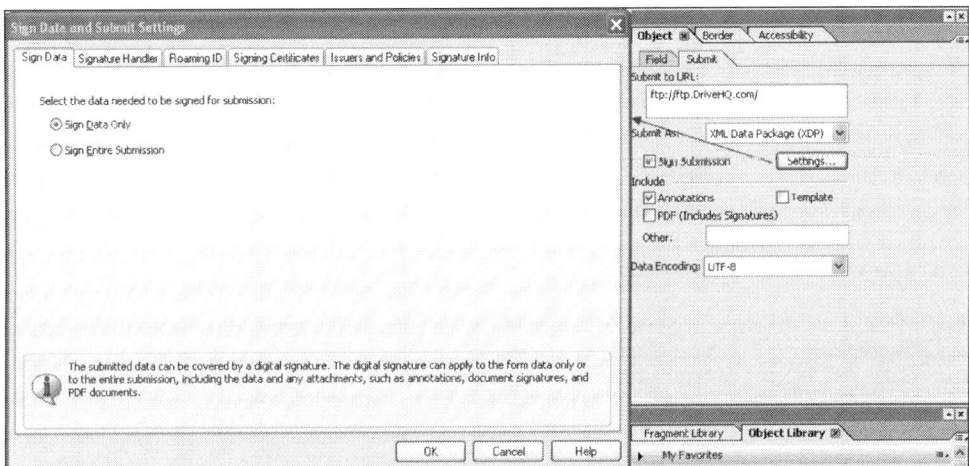

Figure 9-30. Clicking the Sign Submission button launches the Sign Data and Submit Settings dialog box.

The Sign Data and Submit Settings dialog box is where you specify the security settings for your form. The tabs are as follows.

The Sign Data tab specifies which part of the form is guaranteed by the digital signature. You can select for which part of your form's data you want to guarantee integrity via a digital signature—the form's data or any attachments that are also attached to the form (see Figure 9-31).

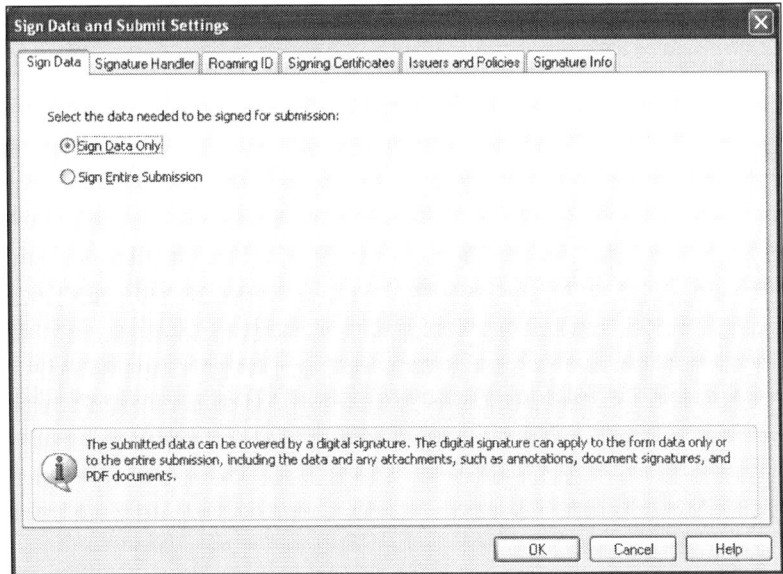

Figure 9-31. The Sign Data tab allows you to specify for which part of your form's data you want to guarantee integrity via a digital signature.

The Signature Handler tab enables you to implement a signature handler for your button that submits data over the Internet.

The Roaming ID tab contains the web server specifications that are utilized when signing your form upon clicking the button. It points to a web service that contains the digital information that is used to sign your form by a user. By clicking the Restrict to Specified URL Server check box, you can also instruct Acrobat to look for the authorization on the server that you have specified. If you do not select this check box, Adobe looks for this authorization on other web servers.

The Signing Certificate tab enables you to specify who is authorized to submit the form data.

The Issuers and Policies tab enables you allow only those form users who have been certified by specific issuers named by the form builder to submit data to you.

The Signature Info tab allows you to specify that form users with Online Certificate Status Protocol (OCSP) or the Certificate Revocation List (CRL) are screened upon attempting to submit the data.

Summary

In this chapter, you learned how to implement submit buttons in your form. Submit buttons in an interactive form enable the user to instantly send their form data to the form builder. You now know that you can use multiple protocols to fulfill data submission.

This final chapter brings this book to a close. I hope I have been able to open up a wonderful world of interactive and dynamic forms that will allow you to expand your business processes to greater efficiency and success.

INDEX

1-59059-543-2 $39.99 [US]

1-59059-518-1 $39.99 [US]

1-59059-542-4 $36.99 [US]

1-59059-517-3 $39.99 [US]

Flash 8 Video

1-59059-651-X $44.99 [

EXPERIENCE THE DESIGNER TO DESIGNER™ DIFFERENCE

1-59059-558-0 $49.99 [US]

1-59059-314-6 $59.99 [US]

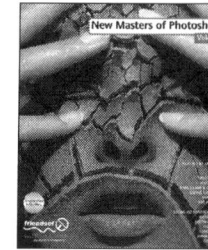

1-59059-315-4 $59.99 [U

1-59059-619-6 $44.99 [US]

1-59059-304-9 $49.99 [US]

1-59059-355-3 $24.99 [US]

1-59059-409-6 $39.99 [US]

1-59059-748-6 $49.99 [U

1-59059-593-9 $49.99 [US]

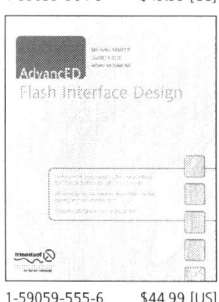

1-59059-555-6 $44.99 [US]

1-59059-533-5 $34.99 [US]

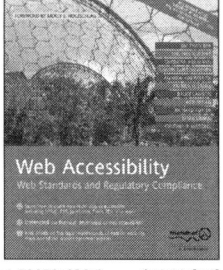

1-59059-638-2 $49.99 [US]

1-59059-765-6 $34.99 [U

1-59059-581-5 $39.99 [US]

1-59059-614-5 $34.99 [US]

1-59059-594-7 $39.99 [US]

1-59059-381-2 $34.99 [US]

1-59059-554-8 $24.99 [

30997865R00161

Made in the USA
Middletown, DE
14 April 2016